The Hajj Today

The Hajj Today

A Survey of the Contemporary Makkah Pilgrimage

DAVID EDWIN LONG

State University of New York Press Albany, 1979

in Cooperation with The Middle East Institute

The Hajj Today

First Printing 1979

Published jointly by
State University of New York Press
Albany, New York 12246
and
The Middle East Institute
Washington, D.C.
in cooperation with the
Georgetown University Center
for Contemporary Arab Studies
Washington, D.C.

Library of Congress Cataloging in Publication Data

Long, David E
The Hajj today.

Bibliography: p.
1. Muslim pilgrims and pilgrimages—Saudi Arabia—Mecca. I. Title.
BP187.3.L66 297'.38 78-7473
ISBN 0-87395-382-7

Contents

Tables

Preface

Over 1,500,000 people annually attend the Hajj, or Great Pilgrimage to Makkah, making it one of the largest exercises in public administration in the world. Nearly every agency of the Saudi government becomes involved, either in regulating the privately operated Hajj service industry, or in providing direct administrative services. Such a task would tax the most sophisticated government bureaucracy; and yet Saudi Arabia, where public administration is still in a developing stage, manages to get the job done each year. Moreover, since non-Muslims are not allowed in Makkah, it is done with almost no administrative assistance from more developed countries.

I first became interested in the Hajj during three years' residence in Jiddah, Saudi Arabia, from 1967 through 1969. Jiddah is western Saudi Arabia's principal sea and air terminus and the gateway to Makkah for most *Hajjis* (Hajj pilgrims). Although non-Muslims are not allowed in Makkah, living and working in Jiddah was sufficient for me to realize how large and complex the task of administering the Hajj is, and under what adverse conditions it is accomplished.

Hajjis come from every corner of the Muslim world and from all classes of society. They bring with them many different customs and habits, speak many different languages, and are often not literate in any. Adding to the problems of administration, most of the Hajj rites are conducted in the open air, where the desert heat sometimes exceeds 126 degrees F. Hajjis must be supplied with sufficient food, water, shelter, health and sanitation facilities, and transportation for a period of several weeks or more. Many of these services are supplied by the Hajj service industry; others are supplied by the Saudi government.

Given the size and scope of the modern Hajj, it is surprising that there is virtually no scholarly research on the current administration of the Hajj or on the impact of the Hajj on the host country, Saudi Arabia. Bernard Lewis has stated the case, "The effect of the pilgrimage on communications and commerce, on ideas and institutions, has not been adequately explored: it may never be, since much of it will, in the nature of things, have gone unrecorded."[1]

This study is an attempt to fill that gap, at least partially. It is divided into three parts. The first part, consisting of two chapters, introduces the general subject of the Hajj, briefly outlining its religious aspects. Chapter 1 discusses the origins of the Hajj, and Chapter 2 presents its specific rites.

Part Two analyzes the administrative aspects of the Hajj and consists of three chapters. The first examines the Hajj service industry, which is organized for the most part into highly specialized guilds. These guilds have been meeting the physical as well as spiritual needs of the Hajjis for centuries. Prior to the consolidation of the Hijaz into modern Saudi Arabia, the guilds were largely self-regulated and were notorious for their commercial exploitation of the Hajjis. Since first taking over the administration of the Hajj, the Saudi government has attempted to end this exploitation by strictly regulating the Hajj service industry.

The second chapter in Part Two examines the public administration of the Hajj by the Saudi government itself. The highest coordinating body in the government is the Supreme Hajj Committee, chaired by the amir (governor) of the Makkah area. It includes representatives from the ministries most involved in Hajj administration and from the Hajj service industry. The day-to-day administration of the Hajj, however, is primarily under the supervision of the Ministry of Hajj and Waqfs (a *waqf* [plural: *awqāf*] is an Islamic religious endowment). The Hajj Ministry, as it is called, coordinates the activities of the other ministries and independent agencies which have their own separate responsibilities. Because the health aspects of the Hajj developed separately from other administrative responsibilities—they were under international control until 1957—a separate chapter is devoted to them.

The final part of the study looks at the implications of the Hajj for Saudi Arabia. It is divided into two chapters. The first examines the social, economic, and political impact of the Hajj on the host country. The second, a concluding chapter, looks at the Hajj as it developed to the present and discusses what the prospects are for the future. The Hajj has made Hijazi society one of the most cosmopolitan to be found anywhere in the Muslim world. Over the centuries peoples from all over the Muslim world have been assimilated into the local population. Economically the Hajj, once the backbone of the Hijazi economy, has been overshadowed by the vast oil revenues of modern Saudi Arabia. It remains, however, a major commercial event and one of the country's major employers, for either full- or part-time workers. The Saudis have attempted to ban secular politics from the Hajj, but in recent years they have allowed it to be used as a forum for speaking out against Zionism and Marxist-socialist doctrines. Both are viewed by the Saudis, however, not so much as secular political problems but as threats to the Islamic way of life which Saudi Arabia strives to preserve.

The study concludes that the Hajj is synthesis: of the religious and the secular, and of the old and the new. It is also a synthesis of constancy and change. Despite the tremendous changes over the last fifty years, the Hajj as a focal point for the entire Muslim world, at least religiously, remains one of the few constants in the rapidly changing Middle East.

Because there is virtually no research on the modern administration of the Hajj, locating source material for this study has been a major problem. Primary sources are uneven, being rather complete for some portions of the study, such as the health aspects, and almost nonexistent for others, such as the impact of the Hajj on Saudi Arabia. Statistics are also uneven and, particularly the pre-World War II figures, tend to be unreliable. For that reason an analysis of the statistics was placed in a special appendix rather than being included in the body of the study. *Umm al-Qurá*, the official Saudi gazette, is an invaluable source, but it is not indexed and at times either fails to record an official decree or pronouncement or does not include the text. In some cases texts are available from the Saudi press. Research in Saudi Arabian documents is in general rendered difficult by the absence of any index or guide to the Saudi archives.

Secondary sources are also uneven. Studies for some of the historic portions of the subject are quite good. However most of what has been written in recent times, by western and Islamic scholars alike, has generally dealt with the religious aspects of the Hajj. There have been several handbooks published for Muslims about to make the Hajj, but they also concentrate more on the religious than the secular aspects of the undertaking. Even most books discussing the government and politics of Saudi Arabia devote little or no attention to the administration of the Hajj.

Because of the paucity of sources, I had to rely heavily on private papers and personal interviews. The papers of Ambassador Hermann Fr. Eilts and of Dr. Herbert J. Liebesny were particularly valuable, containing documents, references, and notes over a period of the last twenty-five years or more which might have been otherwise impossible to find. I also relied heavily on the papers and notes which I have collected since 1967.

Mr. Ibrahim Mosly of the Saudi Arabian Embassy in Washington and Dr. Muhammad Madani, formerly of the embassy, and Mr. Mahmoud Sieny of the Arabic Language Center in al-Riyāḍ also assisted me in obtaining documents and other information. On the health aspects of the Hajj, Rose Belmont of the Office of International Health of the Department of Health, Education and Welfare, Edith Blair of the National Library of Medicine, and Dr. Robert Oseasohn of the Department of Epidemiology and Community Medicine of the University of New Mexico rendered invaluable assistance.

During the time I was in Jiddah, I interviewed many Saudi officials, members of the Hajj service industry, Saudi businessmen, and Hajjis. Particularly in the first three categories, most of the interviews were given in confidence and I have withheld the names.

It was surprising to me that so few Saudis were familiar with how the Hajj was administered, outside the Hajj guild members themselves and those officials and businessmen who worked closely with them. Because there were so many facets to the administration of the Hajj and its impact on Saudi Arabia, and because so many of the individuals I interviewed were specialists in only one or two facets, putting together this study was like trying to fit together pieces of a mosaic. If I have left out pieces which others would wish to see put in, I can only hope that this study will encourage more research on a subject which has, in my view, been too long neglected.

In addition to those mentioned above, I should like to thank Dr. George Rentz and also my many Foreign Service colleagues who gave me their help and encouragement, particularly Philip Stoddard, Harold Glidden, David Newton, Arthur Houghton, and Sandra Shaw, and Jean Floyd, who typed much of the early drafts. My thanks also go to Lilli Mellenberg who typed the final draft. Finally I should like to thank Dr. Roderic Davison and Dr. Bernard Reich for their always valuable criticisms and encouragement through the writing of this study.

And proclaim unto mankind the Hajj. They will come to thee on foot and on every lean camel; they will come from every deep ravine, that they may witness things that are of benefit to them, and mention the name of Allah on appointed days over the sacrificial animal He hath bestowed on them. Then eat thereof and feed therewith the poor unfortunate. Let them make an end of their unkemptness and pay their vows and go around the ancient House. That [is the command]. And whoso magnifieth the sacred things of Allah, it will be well for him in the sight of his Lord. . . .

Qur'ān 22:28–31

PART ONE

The Religious Aspects of the Hajj

1. *The Origins of the Hajj*

The Hajj or Great Pilgrimage to Makkah is the only one of many pilgrimages in Islam which is *wājib* or obligatory.[1] It is the fifth of the five fundamental duties or so-called "Pillars of Islam."[2] Each adult Muslim who is able to do so must make the Hajj once in his or her lifetime. Sūrah (chapter) 3:90–91 of the Qur'ān stipulates:

> The first House of Worship founded for mankind was in Bakka [Makkah]. Blessed and guidance to mankind. In it are evident signs, even the Standing Place of Abraham [Maqām Ibrāhīm]; and whoever enters it is safe. And the pilgrimage to the temple [Hajj] is an obligation due to God from those who are able to journey there. . . .[3]

Each year, roughly 1,500,000 Hajjis[4] heed that injunction, many for the second time or more. In performing the Hajj, they are continuing a tradition that actually predates Islam.

THE PRE-ISLAMIC ORIGINS OF THE HAJJ

The many and complicated rites of the Hajj will be described in greater detail in the following chapter. Basically, they consist of a ritual purification or *iḥrām* prior to entering Makkah, marked by wearing special garments; the *ṭawāf*, or sevenfold circumambulation of the *Ka'bah* (literally "cube," it is the stone structure in the center of the Haram Mosque in Makkah); the *sa'y* or sevenfold transversing between al-Ṣafā and al-Marwah, two elevated spots near the Haram Mosque; a vigil, *wuqūf* (literally "standing"), which takes place at the plain of 'Arafāt near Makkah on the afternoon of the ninth day of the Muslim month of Dhū al-Ḥijjah[5] (known as Standing Day or Yawm al-Wuqūf) and continues until sunset; the *nafrah* or *ifaḍah*, the "rushing" to Muzdalifah, a town between 'Arafāt and Makkah, after sunset on Standing Day; ritual lapidations or stone throwing at three pillars (*jamrahs*) representing *shaytāns* (satans or devils), located in the town of Miná between Muzdalifah and Makkah; the 'Īd al-Aḍḥá or Feast of the Sacrifice, held at Miná (now often pronounced "Muná") but celebrated all over the Muslim world on the tenth through the thirteenth days of Dhū al-Ḥijjah; and finally various desacrilization rituals, including trimming hair and nails and a final ṭawāf.

Many of these Hajj rites were adopted by Muhammad from pre-Islamic religious practices known to have been common in Makkah. Muslim scholars tend to ignore pre-Islamic history which they term *al-jāhilīyah*, the "age of ignorance." Nevertheless, through the writings of a few Muslim scholars of pre-Islamic history, we have some idea of these practices.

One of the most important writers, Hishām Muḥammad al-Kalbī (d. A.H. 206–A.D. 821/822), writes in his *Kitāb al-Aṣnām* ("The Book of Idols") of stone cult worship practiced by the Quraysh, the tribe of Muhammad, and other Arabian tribes as well. Stone idols were located in or near the Ka'bah and were the object of pilgrimages and sacrifices. Ibn al-Kalbī, as he is better known, also writes of the practice of circumambulating the stone idols.[6] He also mentions vigils at 'Arafāt and Muzdalifah, but does not mention Miná.[7]

'Arafāt, Miná, and Muzdalifah were outside the sanctified area (*ḥaram*) of Makkah, which existed even in pre-Islamic times and had apparently no connection with the rites performed in Makkah.[8] On the other hand, a number of Arab tribes apparently made pilgrimages to 'Arafāt which culminated in the month of Dhū al-Ḥijjah; these were made possible by an annual truce when tribal feuds were at rest and weapons laid aside in the sacred precincts.[9]

There is evidence that the pagan ceremonies at Makkah included periodic feasts or fairs, which had taken on a decided commercial cast.[10] After all, Makkah was primarily a major stop on the spice trade route from south Arabia north to the Levant and beyond.

The word *ḥajj* itself is related to the Hebrew word *ḥag*, which refers to cyclical festivals involving pilgrimage and possibly also to circumambulation.[11] Arab lexicographers generally give the origin of *ḥajj* as meaning "to betake oneself to," more directly in line with the act of pilgrimage.[12]

The ritual lapidations, or throwing of stones at the three jamrahs, also appear to be a pre-Islamic custom. The French scholar Gaudefroy-Demombynes wrote that before Islam three stones were thrown at seven idols, whereas in Islamic practice seven stones are thrown at three jamrahs.[13] The lapidations were probably a form of ritual purification—i.e., casting away the profane. The ritual of hair and nail trimming at Miná, which for Muslims is a partial desacralization from the state of iḥrām, is also an ancient practice, and the wearing of special iḥrām garments appears to go back to pagan Arab and early Jewish customs.

In sum, although there are very few reliable sources (the Muslim scholars themselves must be assumed to be biased by their predominantly religious point of view), there appears to be sufficient evidence to conclude that the principal rites of the Hajj—ritual purifications, circumambulation, vigil, feast, and sacrifice—all had their origins in pagan cults practiced in Makkah from very early times and that some of them go back to ancient Semitic practice.

THE ISLAMIZATION OF THE HAJJ

It was during his years in al-Madīnah that Muhammad apparently first became interested in the Makkah pilgrimage as an Islamic rite. It was also during this period that the Ka'bah became incorporated into the Muslim cult as the center of worship and that Islam was "historized" by tracing the Ka'bah back to Ibrāhīm (Abraham). As a child and young man in Makkah, Muhammad undoubtedly participated in pre-Islamic pilgrimage rites. During the first years of his "revelation" of Islam, however, he appears to have paid little attention to the ceremonies. The earliest sūrahs of the Qur'ān, written in Makkah before he removed to al-Madīnah, do not even mention the pre-Islamic rites, and no evidence has been found that he had even formed an opinion about their religious significance at the time.[14]

In tracing Islam back to Ibrāhīm, Muhammad appears to have been influenced by the large Jewish population in al-Madīnah.[15] Not only did he learn from them of the Jewish traditions concerning Ibrāhīm, but while he was still seeking to gain their recognition of himself as a prophet, Muhammad utilized the commonly accepted tradition that Ibrāhīm was the physical father of both the Arabs and the Jews. When the Muslims finally broke with the Madinan Jews, the use of Ibrāhīm as a father figure was still appropriate since he predated both Christianity and the Jewish Torah. He was thus in a real sense neither Christian nor Jewish—the other two religions which together with Islam form what Muslims recognize as the "People of the Book." Linking Ibrāhīm with Islam was, moreover, an Islamic innovation and not an adaptation of pre-Islamic Makkan tradition.[16]

In those sūrahs which Muhammad wrote in al-Madīnah, there are many references to Ibrāhīm and his son Isma'īl (Ishmael). From them a whole body of Islamic legends have grown up. Although they are at times conflicting, they all follow the general pattern of

Islamic legends in that, as Von Grunebaum noted, "No detail must be allowed to go unexplained or unnamed and the action as a whole must be tied in with the sequence of history."[17]

One body of legend surrounds the Qur'ānic verse ascribing the building of the Ka'bah to Ibrāhīm and Isma'īl: "And remember when Ibrāhīm and Isma'īl raised the foundation of the House."[18] According to some accounts Ibrāhīm's Ka'bah was actually the second to be built on the site, the first having been built by Adam, who had gone to Makkah after being expelled from Paradise. This first structure, so the story goes, was washed away during the Flood.[19]

Ibrāhīm and Isma'īl were given supernatural assistance when they built (or rebuilt) the Ka'bah. According to one version God guided Ibrāhīm to the site of the first Ka'bah by a cloud, which stopped over the site and commanded Ibrāhīm to build an edifice over the shadow which it cast. Ibrāhīm began building, using stones brought to him by Isma'īl.[20] In another version the stones were quarried in three mountains: one overlooking Makkah, one Jerusalem (the Mount of Olives), and one Lebanon (Mount Hermon).[21] When the building rose above Ibrāhīm's reach, he stood on a large stone, the Maqām Ibrāhīm mentioned in Sūrah 3:90–91 (see p. 2), which still bears the imprint of his feet.

Built into the eastern corner of the Ka'bah is the famous Black Stone. According to legend it was brought forth to Ibrāhīm by the angel Jibrīl (Gabriel) from Jabal Abū Qubays (a mountain near Makkah), where it had reposed since the Flood, having been a part of the original Ka'bah. The stone was originally white but was turned black by being in contact with the sins of man. On Judgment Day the Stone will speak out in witness against mankind.[22]

Finally, when Ibrāhīm at last completed the construction of the Ka'bah, he again mounted the Maqām Ibrāhīm, which at that time towered above all the surrounding mountains, and proclaimed the obligation of all men to make the Hajj.[23]

Another set of legends linking Ibrāhīm with Islam and the Hajj deal with the holy Zamzam well located inside the Haram Mosque and the sa'y, or sevenfold transversing between al-Ṣafā and al-Marwah. There is no direct mention in the Qur'ān of the Zamzam well. Of al-Ṣafā and al-Marwah Sūrah 2:153 states:

> Verily! al-Ṣafā and al-Marwah are among the symbols of God. So if those who make Pilgrimage to the House [Hajj] or make 'Umrah, go around them both, it is allowed to them. And if

anyone obeyeth his own impulse to good—God is grateful, all knowing.

The legends concerning Zamzam and the saʿy vary, but the general story concerns Ḥajar (Hagar) and her son Ismaʿīl abandoned in the desert by Ibrāhīm. According to one version,[24] Ibrāhīm and his wife Sarah, having left Chaldea, had journeyed to Egypt. While there, the pharoah, Salatis, tried three times to seduce Sarah, but was miraculously disabled so that he could not. Releasing her to her husband, he gave her as a remembrance a beautiful slave girl, Ḥajar. At first things went well; Ibrāhīm sired a son, Ismaʿīl, by Ḥajar. But then Sarah began to grow jealous and demanded that Ibrāhīm abandon the two in the desert. Reluctantly he did so, leaving them in the Valley of Thirst (Wādī al-ʿAtash), the site of present-day Makkah. Ibrāhīm divined, however, that it was the site of the first Kaʿbah and that no ill would befall Ḥajar or Ismaʿīl. After he had departed, Ḥajar ran towards a mirage of water until she reached the top of al-Ṣafā; then turning back, she chased the mirage until she reached the top of al-Marwah. After running back and forth several times, she returned to her child only to discover water coming from where he lay. This was the water of Zamzam. In some accounts Ismaʿīl accidentally uncovered the water; in others Jibrīl struck the earth and caused it to come forth; while in still others it was the rediscovery of water originally provided for Adam and Eve when they were driven out of Eden.[25] At any rate the saʿy has come to commemorate Ḥajar running back and forth in search of water.

The sacrifice (ʿĪd al-Aḍḥá) and the lapidations at Miná are also connected to the Ibrāhīm legend. Near Makkah there is a cave where Ibrāhīm and Ḥajar lived together, as the story goes. Nearby is a large stone upon which Ibrāhīm had prepared to sacrifice Ismaʿīl. At the moment of sacrifice Ibrāhīm's knife was forced from his hand by divine intervention. As it fell, it partially split open another large rock also still located close by.[26] Ibrāhīm then sacrificed an animal in place of Ismaʿīl, which according to legend was the origin of the ʿĪd al-Aḍḥá.

The lapidations are also linked to Ibrāhīm's sacrifice. According to one version Ibrāhīm was ordered by God in a dream to sacrifice his son Ismaʿīl. The following day he told his son that they would go out to find firewood, but as they were walking, Ibrāhīm broke down and confessed to Ismaʿīl what God had instructed him to do. Ismaʿīl accepted his fate and set off behind his father to the place for the sacrifice which Ibrāhīm had seen in his dream—a bluff overlooking the third jamrah at Miná. On the way Satan appeared to Isma'īl three times— once at each of the jamrahs—and warned him of what his father intended to do. On each occasion Isma'īl cast stones at Satan. When Isma'īl was bound and placed face downward for the sacrifice, Ibrāhīm placed a knife at his throat, but the knife refused to enter the flesh. After a third try the angel Jibrīl appeared with a ram. He told Ibrāhīm that God had received his sacrifice and did not require the soul of Isma'īl, and to offer the ram in sacrifice instead.[27]

In view of the central role of 'Arafāt in the Hajj, it is surprising that no attempt seems to have been made to link it to the legends of Ibrāhīm. Dr. Partin, whose study concentrates on the religious aspects of the Hajj, noted this but stated that he was not able to find a satisfactory explanation.[28] There also does not appear to be an attempt to link Ibrāhīm with Muzdalifah, the first stopover after Standing Day (Yawm al-Wuqūf) at 'Arafāt. In the broader Adam and Eve tradition there is mention of 'Arafāt as the site "where banished from Paradise, lost in the wilderness and wastes of a strange world, Adam and Eve found one another after two centuries separation."[29]

Even though the Ibrāhīm, and to a lesser extent the Adam legends are highly developed in Islam, it should not be construed that Muhammad believed that he needed detailed explanations provided by the legends to justify the validity of the new faith. One of the most salient features of Islam is the portrayal of God as all powerful. The Hajj, seen from a Muslim perspective, is a duty not because of tradition beginning with Ibrāhīm or Adam before him, but because God willed it. Muhammad was less interested in history and legend than in revelation—the revelation of what God wills.

THE FAREWELL HAJJ

When Muhammad conquered Makkah in A.H. 9 (A.D. 630), he did not immediately make the Hajj. Some students of Islam have asked why, if the Hajj were so important to Islam, Muhammad did not make the hajj for the first time as master of the city. The explanation appears to be that he was not ready until the Hajj had been purged of pagan worshippers. In the A.H. 9 Hajj, the last in which non-Muslims could take part, Muhammad sent his father-in-law,

Abū Bakr (who would succeed him as political leader and first caliph) to represent him. He also entrusted his son-in-law, ʿAlī, who was to become the fourth caliph, to deliver for him a revelation concerning the Hajj:

> Disavowal by God and His Apostle (Muhammad) of all the polytheists with whom you have contracted alliances . . . .
>
> And a proclamation from God and His Messenger to the people (assembled) on the day of the Greatest Pilgrimage (Ḥajj al-Akbar) that God has nothing to do with the polytheists (nor does) His Apostle . . . .
>
> It is not for polytheists to visit the mosques of God while they witness against unbelief; the works of such are of no avail and in the Fire they dwell forever.
>
> The Mosques of God shall be visited only by those who believe in God and the Last Day, who perform the prayer, who render alms and who fear none save God. It is they who might be among those who are rightly guided.[30]

The above Qurʾanic references have been used to justify the exclusion of not only pagans, but even People of the Book (Christians and Jews) both from participating in the Hajj and from visiting the environs of Makkah and al-Madīnah as well. When Muhammad did lead the Hajj the following year, it was a purely Muslim Hajj.

The Hajj of A.H. 10 (A.D. 652) is called the "Farewell Hajj" (Ḥajj al-Wadāʿ). The Prophet died in al-Madīnah less than three months after its conclusion (A.D. 8 June 632), and he seemed to have realized that it would be his last. The Farewell Hajj is generally considered, therefore, to have been the culmination of Muhammad's life's work. Guidance for performance of the Hajj rites comes not from the Qurʾān but from Muhammad's own observances, particularly at the Farewell Hajj. Those observances were recorded in detail in the *ḥadīths,* or traditions of the Prophet. Although the Hajj ceremonies did not evolve into their definitive form until the late eighth century A.D., and while some of the practices attributed to Muhammad in the ḥadīths were apparently later modifications,[31] Muhammad's observances at the Farewell Hajj are still considered by Muslims to be the basis of the present-day ceremonies.

According to Muslim tradition Muhammad spoke to the Hajjis assembled at Arafat at the conclusion of the Farewell Hajj, exhorting them to follow the teachings of Islam, his words repeated sentence by sentence for all to hear by a black man with a "powerful and melodious voice."[32] At that time, so the story goes, Muhammad's final revelation from God was delivered with such force that the camel on which he sat sank to its knees. Then Muhammad delivered his final revelation, Sūrah 5:5, to the people:

> This day I have perfected your religion for you, completed my favor upon you, and I am well pleased that you have chosen Islam as your religion.

2. *The Rites of the Hajj*

It took between one to two centuries after Muhammad's death for the Hajj rites to evolve into a definitive form. From then on they have remained fairly constant. Minor variations are present, however, in each of the four *madhāhib* (singular: *madhhab*), or orthodox schools of Islamic jurisprudence.[1] These mainly concern whether a specific observance is obligatory or merely recommended and the precise manner in which it is to be done. All the madhāhib agree on four rites being obligatory (*wājib*), the so-called Pillars of the Hajj: the iḥrām, the wuqūf, the ṭawāf al-ifāḍah, and the sa ʿy.[2]

Hajjis are free to observe any rite according to the interpretation of any madhhab. Since nearly all Hajjis, especially if it is their first Hajj, are anxious to do all of the customary rites, obligatory or not, the distinctions of obligation are in fact not very important.

ELIGIBILITY FOR THE HAJJ

The Qur ʾānic injunction to make the Hajj states simply that it is obligatory for "those who are able to journey thither."[3] Islamic scholars have given much attention to what conditions constitute the ability to make the journey, thereby obligating the individual to go. As the science of Islamic law (*fiqh*) developed, conditions for deferring the obligation became more specific. In general a Muslim must be of sound mind, a free citizen, and have attained the age of puberty in order to be obligated to make the Hajj.[4] Those meeting the above qualifications may still defer the Hajj if they are physically unable to travel or have insufficient funds, either for the trip or, in the case of heads of households, to provide for families left at home. Women may defer the Hajj if they are unable to travel with their husbands or suitable members of their families. Political or other conditions making traveling too hazardous are also sufficient grounds to postpone the trip.[5] Despite the attention which has been given in the books of Islamic jurisprudence to conditions enabling a Muslim to make the Hajj, however, the decision of whether or not he meets those conditions is left almost entirely to the individual.

THE DEPARTURE

Before departing from his home, the Hajji is enjoined to put his affairs in order and acquire a proper spiritual attitude. He should pay his outstanding debts and provide for the welfare of those of his family he is leaving behind. Spiritually he should repent of and make the appropriate restitutions for his sins. He should also provide himself with sufficient travel funds from an untainted source, and, where possible, choose a virtuous and dependable companion or companions.[6]

By tradition it is preferable to depart on a Monday, Thursday, or Saturday,[7] having taken leave of family and friends with solemnity befitting the occasion. Upon departure each Hajji should say a prayer of two *rakʿahs*,[8] recite some verses from the Qurʾān, and implore God to protect his family, to bless and protect him and his companions on the Hajj, and to give them a safe return. An example of an appropriate invocation is given by al-Ghazālī:

> O Lord who art my companion in this voyage and my replacement with my wife, goods, children, and friends, keep me and keep them from every misfortune and evil. Grant me virtue and faith for this journey. Allow me to do those things which are agreeable to You. Cause the earth to pass painlessly under my feet; make this voyage easy for me. Grant security to my body, my faith, and my fortune. Allow me to accomplish the pilgrimage to Your House and the Visit to the tomb of Your prophet, Muhammad. O Lord, it is in Thee that I seek refuge from the hardships of the way and from the uneasy thoughts which will come to me concerning my wife, my fortune, my children, and my friends. O Lord, keep us all under Thy protection; do not withhold Thy favor from me nor from them; take not from us the happiness that is in each of us.[9]

Throughout the journey the Hajji must strictly adhere to religious duties, especially the ritual prayers (*ṣalawāt*; singular: *ṣalāh*). If the exigencies of the trip require, however, he may shorten prayers of over two rakʿahs to two, and other prayers may be combined.[10] At all events he must always remain on his best behavior.

IḤRĀM: THE RITE OF CONSECRATION

Iḥrām refers to the state of consecration or ritual purification. It must be assumed before entering Makkah to perform the rites of the hajj or of the Lesser Pilgrimage, the ʿUmrah.

There are special stations, or *mīqāts*, which have been designated for performing the rites of entering into the state of iḥrām and donning the special traditional garments. Hajjis approaching Makkah overland from the north perform the rite at Abyār ʿAlī, called Dhū al-Ḥulayfah in Muhammad's time. Those coming from the north by sea perform it when the ship is opposite Rābigh. For Hajjis traveling from the south, the iḥrām mīqāt is Yulamlam, or if coming by sea, a point in the Red Sea adjacent that town. There are two iḥrām stations for Hajjis coming from the east—at Qarn al-Manāzil, between al-Ṭāʾif and Makkah, and Dhāt-ʿIrq, on the route north of al-Ṭāʾif through the Wādī Fāṭimah. Since the Saudi Arabian government has constructed a paved highway from the Persian Gulf to the Red Sea via the al-Ṭāʾif-Qarn-Makkah route, the mīqāt at Dhāt-ʿIrq is no longer much used.

The establishment of these iḥrām stations did not take into account modern air travel, now the most widely used means of transportation to the Hajj. Most Hajjis traveling by air enter iḥrām either at the last stop before Jiddah, the air and sea port for Makkah, or else at Jiddah itself.[11] The inhabitants of Makkah perform the iḥrām rites at a spot just outside of Makkah at a place called al-Tanʾim.

The madhāhib differ on the precise order and degree of obligation of the rites of iḥrām, but they generally agree on the necessity of six acts: the *nīyah*, or statement of intention; the *ghusl*, or ritual bathing; cutting of the hair and nails; donning the iḥrām garments; ritual prayers; and pronouncing the *talbīyah*, a special statement to be repeated during the rest of the Hajj ceremonies.

The Nīyah

Many Islamic rites are preceded by a declaration of intention which serves to make their observance less mechanical. In the iḥrām nīyah, the Hajji is required to state whether he intends to perform the Hajj (or the ʿUmrah) alone (*ifrād*) or perform the Hajj jointly with the ʿUmrah (*qirān*).[12] The ʿUmrah, which includes the rites of ṭawāf and saʿy, can be performed at any time during the year. Muslim dignitaries visiting Saudi Arabia, for example, often perform the ʿUmrah during their stay. If it is performed in conjunction with the Hajj, it must be performed during the Hajj season. This consists of the last three months of the Muslim year—Shawwal, Dhū al-Qaʿdah, and up to the tenth of Dhū al-Ḥijjah.[13]

The Hajji must remain in iḥrām until the end of the Hajj unless he states his intention in the nīyah to enjoy normal life in the interim between the initial ʿUmrah rites and Hajj proper begining with the Standing Day ceremonies. This procedure, called *tamattuʿ* (enjoyment) entails a deconsecration consisting of cutting off locks of one's hair and laying aside one's iḥrām garments. For that privilege the mutamattiʿ (one enjoying tamattuʿ) should present a blood sacrifice, or if he cannot afford one, fast three days during the Hajj and another seven days after its completion.[14] The mutamattiʿ must again enter into iḥrām on the night of 7 Dhū al-Ḥijjah, generally traveling to al-Tanʿim for that purpose. Tamattuʿ is mainly for those Hajjis who come early to Makkah and do not wish to stay in iḥrām for an extended period of time prior to completing the Hajj.

The words of the nīyah are the same for all forms, excepting the mention of the type of pilgrimage intended:

> O God, I intend to take . . . [ʿUmrah, Hajj, etc.] and I am taking Ihram for it.
> Make it easy for me—and receive it from me.[15]

The Ghusl and Cutting of Hair and Nails

The ghusl, or bathing, is an obvious act of ritual cleansing. It is preferable to bathe all of one's body, but if there is a lack of water, time, or a suitable place (e.g., if thousands of Hajjis converge on a mīqāt at the same time), it is permissible to do a small ablution, (*wuḍūʿ*). Similar to the ablutions for Muslim prayers in general, the wuḍūʿ consists of washing one's hands, mouth, nostrils, face, arms, head, neck, and feet. Similarly, if no water at all is available, it is permissible to perform a "dry ablution," or *tayammum*, by passing one's hands on the sand or ground and placing them on the parts of the body to be cleansed by the ghusl. Certain verses are said during the ghusl, which begin:

> In the name of God the Compassionate, the Merciful. Praise unto God, who sent down water for purification and made Islam to be a light. . . .[16]

After the ablutions the Hajji is considered legally in a state of purity (*taharah*) and may enter iḥrām. The state of taharah is completed by cutting off or shaving the hair and trimming the nails.

Men usually shave their heads. Women generally cut only three locks and shampoo their hair. Underarm and pubic hair are also generally shaved. It is not permissible to cut hair or nails again while one remains in iḥrām.

The Iḥrām Garments

When ritually purified, the *muḥrim* (one who has entered iḥrām) dons special garments. They consist of two seamless, preferably white, strips of sheeting or toweling: the *izār*, which reaches from the navel to the knees, and the *ridā*ʾ, which is wrapped around the body covering the left shoulder but leaving at least part of the right arm free. The head must remain uncovered, although it is permissible to use umbrellas to ward off the harsh rays of the Hijazi sun. The instep must also remain uncovered, but sandals may be worn. Any cloth will do except silks and ornamental fabrics. For women no particular dress is required, but the usual costume is a long white gown reminiscent of a nun's habit. The face must be unveiled. Given the harsh desert sun, ihrām garb is not the most comfortable. As Von Grunebaum noted:

> When it is considered that this array is the only covering worn for many a day and, strictly speaking, also at night, the extremely uncomfortable character of the hajj period will be realized.[17]

This lack of comfort is compounded by some of the more strict Hajjis. For example, many Shīʿites, in observing the stricture against covering one's head, refuse to ride in covered buses. Special topless buses have been imported to carry them about.

Prayers and Talbīyah

After donning the iḥrām garments, each Hajji should say a prayer of two rakʿahs. Throughout the iḥrām rites and thereafter he is enjoined to repeat the most commonly expressed ritual prayer of the Hajj, the talbīyah:

> Labbayka-Allahumma, Labbayk!
> La Sharīka laka, Labbayk!
> Inna al-ḥamda wal-niʿamata laka wal-mulk!
> La Sharīka laka, Labbayk![18]

The talbīyah may be said in any language but is generally said in Arabic. Little can capture the excitement of expectation during the

Hajj, especially on Standing Day, as much as hearing hundreds of Hajjis chanting the talbīyah in unison.[19]

After completing the iḥrām, one is spiritually ready to perform the Hajj. For the period that he is in iḥrām, the muḥrim must abstain from wearing sewn clothes, covering the head (or for women, the face), bathing and bodily care, sexual activity, marriage,[20] using perfumes, personal combat and shedding blood, hunting wild game, and uprooting plants. Making a sacrifice or fasting can atone for any violation except sexual intercourse, which voids the entire Hajj.

THE ARRIVAL ṬAWAF

The arrival ṭawāf (*ṭawāf al-qudūm*) is to be done either as a part of the ʿUmrah or as part of the Hajj proper if it is performed alone (ifrād). Basically it consists of walking seven times around the Kaʿbah.

The Kaʿbah, located in the center of the Haram Mosque, is the spiritual and geographical center of Islam. It is toward the Kaʿbah that all Muslims face when praying. The stone structure is about fifty feet high, forty feet long, and thirty-three feet wide, although none of its sides are exactly the same length.[21] It has a single door, on the northeast wall, which is six or seven feet above the ground. Inside gold and silver lamps hang from the ceiling. The three wooden beams which hold up the ceiling have recently been replaced.[22] Imbedded in the eastern corner is the Black Stone, which Rutter described as actually being "of a dark red-brown colour approaching in places to blackness."[23] It is encased in a silver band and is in fact composed of about a dozen stones cemented together: according to Muslim historians it was originally a single stone, but was fragmented in a fire.[24]

Prior to each Hajj the *kiswah*—the thick black and gold embroidered cloth which covers the Kaʿbah—is replaced by a white covering somewhat analogous to the iḥrām garment. Then on 8 Dhū al-Ḥijjah, known as *Yawm al-Tarwīyah*, this covering is removed for the ceremonial washing of the Kaʿbah, led by Saudi Arabia's king and other distinguished Hajjis. Afterwards a new kiswah, made in a factory in Makkah, is placed on it.[25]

The arrival ṭawāf is the first religious act to be performed in Makkah. The Hajji enters the great Haram Mosque, right foot first, through the northernmost door on the northeast side, called the Bāb al-Salām. He then goes through a stone arch, the Portal of the

Banī Shaybah, to the Black Stone. There he repeats a nīyah, or declaration of intention, to perform the ṭawāf and begins his circumambulation in a counterclockwise direction. It is traditional (*sunnah*), but not required, to touch the large stone in the southern or Yemeni corner of the Ka'bah as one passes by.[26] Each succeeding circuit is begun by kissing, or at least touching, the Black Stone. At the height of the Hajj season, it may be impossible to get near it, however, and in that case it is permissible to simulate touching the stone.[27]

The first three circuits are made at a quick pace, almost a jog, known as *ramal*, the term for an Arabic poetic meter. The final four are made at a normal walking pace.

During each circuit special prayers are said. The main themes are praise of and refuge in God and asking his forgiveness and acceptance of the Hajj. Since most Hajjis are not familiar with the words, they generally repeat them after their *muṭawwif* (Hajj guide) or one of his staff, whose job it is to see that the Hajjis' physical as well as spiritual needs are met. In his Hajj guidebook Ahmad Kamal added a practical suggestion:

> Any pilgrim who cannot follow the pilgrim guide's words, unable to hear because of the tumult or separated from him by the crowding, and who is not able to recall the lines. . . , may in perfect confidence substitute any prayer and praise God in whatever language. There are many races of men and many languages—and One God, and the contents of all hearts and the meanings of all languages are known unto Him.[28]

For the aged and infirm the press of the Hajj crowds is so great that many are carried on the ṭawāf on litters.

After completing all the circuits, the Hajji may desire to acquire special grace, though it is not mandatory, by pressing himself to a part of the Ka'bah wall called the *Multazim*, or "the place where one pressses," located between the Black Stone and the door.

Next he goes to the rear by the Maqām Ibrāhīm, says a prayer of two rak'ahs, and from there to the Zamzam water. Then, unless he desires to pray at the *Ḥijr*, an enclosed area adjacent the Ka'bah where are said to be located the tombs of Ḥajar and Isma'īl, the first rites are over. After touching the Black Stone a final time in farewell, the Hajji leaves the Great Mosque by the Bāb al-Ṣafā (al-Ṣafā Gate), on the southeast side, left foot first.

THE SAʿY

The saʿy consists of seven one-way trips between al-Ṣafā and al-Marwah, the two small hills some 400 yards apart near the Haram Mosque between which Ḥajar was said to have run in search of water. The concourse between al-Ṣafā and al-Marwah is called the Masʿá (literally: "the place of running"; saʿy itself means running) and is located just beyond Bāb al-Ṣafā. If the Hajji is performing the ʿUmrah, he must perform the saʿy immediately after having completed the arrival ṭawāf. If he is performing the Hajj rites only, he may defer the saʿy until after the ṭawāf al-ifāḍah, at the end of the Ḥajj.

The saʿy begins at al-Ṣafā. Men are required to climb the steps to the top of both elevations, but women, especially when the Masʿá is crowded with Hajjis, may do the rite below. After facing the Kaʿbah (obstructed from view by the walls of the Haram Mosque) and repeating a prayer of intention, the Hajji begins his seven trips. At each elevation he repeats a small prayer with hands outstretched toward the Kaʿbah. During each trip male Hajjis must jog (ramal, sometimes also called *harwal*) between two markers about 250 feet apart. This is after the example of Muhammad. Ironically, although the saʿy is said to commemorate Hajar's running in search for water, women need not run.[29]

The final trip ends at al-Marwah. Those who have completed both ṭawāf and saʿy (i.e., the ʿUmrah) are called *muʿtamirīn* (singular: *muʿtamir*). Nearby are barbers for those who intend to reenter iḥrām for the Hajj; the haircut (*taḥallul*) is generally token clipping of three hairs.

THE HAJJ RITES

The Hajj rites are the culmination of the entire pilgrimage and alone meet the requirement of the Fifth Pillar of Islam. They encompass all the ceremonies held between the eighth and twelfth days of Dhū al-Ḥijjah (though, of course, not all of these ceremonies are mandatory, i.e., wājib). To be eligible to participate in the Hajj rites, each Hajji must have completed the arrival ṭawāf (ṭawāf al-qudūm) and be in a state of iḥrām.

On the previous day, 7 Dhū al-Ḥijjah, it is customary (*sunnah*) after noon prayers in the Haram Mosque to hear a sermon (*khutbah*) in preparation for the ceremonies to come.[30] This is the first of several khutbahs (sermons) traditionally delivered during the

Hajj. It is also the day for those who have not done so or have left it to enter into the state of iḥrām.

The eighth day of Dhū al-Ḥijjah is called Yawm al-Tarwīyah (the Day of Washing). In addition to the washing down of the Ka'bah, described above, it is the traditional day for departing for 'Arafāt—a wide, barren, gravelly plain some twelve miles east of Makkah.[31] Rising up from the plain on its eastern side is a low hill or rock outcropping about 150 to 200 feet high. Called Jabal al-Raḥmah (the Mount of Mercy), or sometimes Jabal 'Arafāt (Mount 'Arafāt), it is the holiest spot on the plain. At the crest is a stone column about twenty feet high rising from a stone-paved platform. Nearby, to the southwest, is the Nimrah Mosque (also called Namīrah).

Most Hajjis would like to emulate Muhammad, who on his Farewell Hajj left Makkah before noon of the eighth on foot for Miná, a little over halfway to 'Arafāt. The following morning he continued his march to 'Arafāt. Because of the hundreds of thousands who now make the Hajj, however, the trip has had to be highly organized to get everyone there, and many Hajjis are transported by bus or auto directly to 'Arafāt.[32]

The Wuqūf

The ninth day of Dhū al-Ḥijjah is the grand climax of the entire Hajj. On this day, Standing Day (Yawm al-Wuqūf), each Hajji must be in attendance at sunset on the plain of 'Arafāt or the whole Hajj is forfeited. In the morning, if possible, each Hajji says morning prayers at the Nimrah Mosque. Then, as noon approaches, the thousands of Hajjis gather at Jabal al-Raḥmah, or as close to it as they can get, to begin their vigil. The wuqūf proper lasts from noon through sunset. During that period two khutbahs are delivered from the platform atop Jabal al-Raḥmah. They traditionally contain instructions to the Hajjis on performing the rites and on their obligations.

During the wuqūf the air is filled with excitement. Everywhere is heard the talbīyah, chanted by hundreds of voices. In the cryptic phrase of tradition, the wuqūf *is* the Hajj—the supreme hours. Kamal has attempted to capture the extreme spiritual fervor of the ceremony.

> The soul-shaken pilgrim entering the Sanctuary of Makkah and for the first time beholding the Holy Ka'bah and the Black Stone knows a humility and an exaltation which are but a prologue for 'Arafāt. Here by the mountain, the pilgrim will pass

> what should be, spiritually and intellectually, the noblest hours of life. The tents of the faithful will cover the undulating valley as far as the eye can see. This immense congregation with the sacred mountain at its center is the heart of Islam. This is the day of true brotherhood, the day when God is revealed to his servants.[33]

The Nafrah or Ifāḍah

Sunset on Standing Day is followed by the nafrah (literally: "rushing"; it is also called the ifāḍah or "pouring forth") to Muzdalifah, a small town about four miles from ʿArafāt. With thousands of Hajjis, most of them in motor vehicles, rushing headlong for Muzdalifah, the potential is there for one of the world's largest traffic jams, and indeed the nafrah of 1968 took up to twenty hours to untangle.[34] At Muzdalifah each Hajji should say sunset and evening prayers. Afterwards he hunts around in the darkness for seventy stones (or forty-nine if he plans to cut the Hajj short by a day) for the lapidations at Miná the following day. There is special grace for praying at the roofless mosque in Muzdalifah called al-Mashʿar al-Ḥarām (the Sacred Grove). During the night there is another wuqūf and khutbah at Muzdalifah.[35]

Lapidations: Stoning the Jamrahs

On the morning of the tenth Dhū al-Ḥijjah the Hajjis leave Muzdalifah (it may be any time after midnight) for Miná, about three or four miles west towards Makkah. Proceeding through the town to the western end, one finds the first of the three pillars or jamrahs to be stoned, the Jamrat al-ʿAqabah. Seven stones are thrown at this jamrah. Generally after each stone the Hajji repeats the "Takbīr" (i.e., "Bismi Allah; Allāhu Akbar," or "in the name of God; God is most great").[36]

No stones are thrown that day at the other jamrahs—al-Jamrah al-Waṣtá in the middle of Miná and al-Jamrah al-ʿUlá at the eastern end. On the following two days, however, all three jamrahs are stoned, each day with seven stones.

The lapidations are considered a desacralization process.[37] For example, after stoning the Jamrat al-ʿAqabah on the first day, the talbīyah, first repeated in the iḥrām ceremonies, is no longer said.[38] Those too old or infirm to throw the stones (or as it often turns out, unable to fight the crowds to get into a position to throw them) can delegate another to throw for them.

The ʿĪd al-Aḍḥá

The tenth, eleventh, twelfth, and thirteenth of Dhū al-Ḥijjah comprise the ʿĪd al-Aḍḥá, or the Feast of the Sacrifice.[39] Unlike the other rites, the ʿĪd al-Aḍḥá is celebrated not only by those performing the Hajj, but throughout the Muslim world, where it is a happy occasion generally accompanied with visits to family, friends, and colleagues, giving and receiving gifts, and special prayers at the mosque.

The rite is simple, merely slaughtering an unblemished sacrificial animal—generally a sheep or a goat but sometimes a camel. The animal is faced toward the Kaʿbah and as its throat is cut, the sacrificer says the Takbīr. Even small animals such as fowl are permitted to those unable to afford larger animals, but Hajjis, after all the expense of the Hajj, generally spurn such animals.

The ʿĪd al-ʿAḍḥá is supposed to be the act of giving up something one cherishes, rather than a blood sacrifice, and even money may be given to charity in lieu of a sacrifice. In slaughtering an animal the charitable act is in giving to the poor some of the meat that is not immediately eaten. Unfortunately, with so many at the Hajj, and the host country having so much oil money, there is more meat than there are poor people, and disposing of it has become a great problem. Another problem is that the Hajjis generally want to slaughter an animal on the first day, even though it is permissible to do it during any of the four days.[40]

THE CLOSING CEREMONIES

After the sacrifice the next step of desacralization is taken. First is a ritual haircut (taḥallul). Again, three hairs will do, but many men get a full haircut or head shaving at this time. After completing taḥallul, the Hajji is free from all iḥrām restraints save sexual intercourse. He then goes to Makkah to perform the *ṭawāf al-ifāḍah*, which should be performed as quickly as possible after the stoning and sacrifice on 10 Dhū al-Ḥijjah. The procedure is roughly the same as the ṭawāf al-qudūm. If the Hajji did not perform the saʿy after the ṭawāf al-qudūm, he must do so after the ṭawāf al-ifāḍah. Otherwise it is not required. After the ṭawāf al-ifāḍah many not only drink of Zamzam water, but if possible bathe in it.[41]

Following the ṭawāf al-ifāḍah, the Hajji is free from all iḥrām restrictions. He returns to Miná until the thirteenth, completing the stonings. The eleventh, twelfth, and thirteenth days are called *ayyām al-tashrīq* ("flesh-drying days," presumably after the former practice of drying sacrificed meat for the homeward trip; or possibly referring simply to the carcasses drying in the sun). According to ritual law a Hajji may leave on the twelfth if absolutely necessary.[42]

The final rite of the Hajj is the *ṭawāf al-wadāʿ* or "farewell ṭawāf." It is to be performed just before the Hajji leaves Makkah. After entering iḥrām at al-Tanʿim, the Hajji performs the farewell ṭawāf much as the two previous ṭawāfs, completing it with a final draught of Zamzam water, and then departing the Haram Mosque from the Bāb al-Wadāʿ (Farewell Gate). The Hajj is now over, and if he has not performed a Hajj already, the pilgrim is now qualified to use the title "Ḥājj" (or, in the Persian form, *Ḥājjī*) before his name.

THE VISIT TO AL-MADĪNAH

Although not strictly a part of the Hajj, Muslims who have not already done so are encouraged to visit al-Madīnah sometime during their journey. The central site of importance in al-Madīnah is the Mosque of the Prophet (Masjid al-Nabī), which ranks with the Haram Mosque of Makkah and the al-Aqṣá Mosque in Jerusalem as the three most holy shrines in orthodox (Sunnī) Islam.

For the *Ziyarah* or "Visit" to the Prophet's Mosque, one generally enters through the Bāb al-Salām (Gate of Peace) at the southern end of the western side of the mosque.[43] Upon entering, he repeats the Takbīr and other verses. It is then customary to go first to the *Rawdah* ("Garden," sometimes called the "Garden of Paradise"), originally an open space adjacent Muhammad's house where he led his followers in prayer. There one says a prayer of two rakʿahs.[44] After that he visits the Prophet's tomb and the tombs of the caliphs Abū Bakr and ʿUmar bin Khaṭṭāb and then repeats more prayers. Nearby is the tomb of Muhammad's daughter Fāṭimah.

Other places of interest in al-Madīnah are the al-Baqīyah cemetery, where relations of Muhammad and some of his early followers (companions) are buried; the Qabah Mosque, one of the earliest founded by Muhammad; and the Mosque of the Two Qiblahs. (A *qiblah* is a recess in a mosque pointing the direction of Makkah, toward which Muslims turn while praying. This mosque also has a recess facing Jerusalem, toward which Muhammad and his followers faced for a brief period in the early days.) The nearby Jabal Uḥud battlefield, where Muhammad lost an early engagement, is another site frequently visited. The recommended stay in al-Madīnah is eight days, in order to be present for forty prayers.

This, in summary, is the basic procedure of the Hajj. Since the earliest days of Islam, it has been performed in much the same way. Despite the divergence among the four madhāhib, or orthodox schools of Islamic jurisprudence, over which rites are mandatory, most Hajjis perform all of the rites, particularly if it is their first Hajj. In recent times, with the huge numbers making the Hajj each year, administrative rather than theological considerations are having an increasing role in how the rites are performed.

PART TWO

The Administrative Aspects of the Hajj

3. *The Hajj Service Industry*

From laissez faire to government regulation

The inhabitants of Makkah, al-Madīnah, and to a lesser extent Jiddah have for centuries gained a considerable part of their livelihood serving pilgrims. In the case of Makkah, of course, this even predates Islam. Not only do the pilgrims require assistance for their physical needs, but they also require assistance in performing the precise but complicated Hajj rites. Eldon Rutter, a British Muslim who made the Hajj in 1924–25, stated:

> . . . few newcomers can possibly be so familiar with Mekka by hearsay or reading, as to be capable of performing the rites correctly by themselves, without making certain enquiries. Even learned Muhammadeans employ mutawwifs [guides] on their very first visit to the Holy City.[1]

Snouck Hurgronje, writing thirty-seven years earlier, was even more emphatic:

> No matter how exactly the stranger may have studied the ceremonies of the great and small pilgrimage (and most do not so study them) he can in no case dispense with the help of a man familiar with the local conditions; and the same thing must be said of the voluntary visits to the holy spots. Immediately on his arrival on Arabian soil, that is generally in Jeddah, he needs a guide, to take charge of him at the outset, . . . and later to hire for him camels and drivers for the journey to Mekka. If the pilgrim is not an Arab, the guide must also serve him as interpreter; and also, in Mekka, in househiring, making ordinary purchases and so forth, he would meet the greatest difficulties if he attempted to make his way without the official go-between. At least during the first weeks of his stay he can make no step, enter into no relations with others, have recourse to no official, without the help of his [guide] . . . .[2]

Although nearly all the citizens of the Hijaz appear to be involved in one way or another with the Hajj, the primary responsibility for guiding the Hajjis through the prescribed rites, supplying food, shelter, and water, and generally providing for their welfare during their stay in the Hijaz rests with a group of highly specialized individuals whose families have been providing these services for centuries. Over time they and their descendants have become organized into four tightly knit guilds: the *muṭawwifīn*, the *wukalāʾ*, the *adillāʾ*, and the *zamāzimah*.

The muṭawwifīn (singular: *muṭawwif*)[3] comprise the most important guild (an alternate term for the mutawwif is shaykh al-Ḥajj). Members of the muṭawwifīn have primary responsibility for the Hajjis during their stay in Makkah and environs. In recent years the other guilds have become more or less subordinate to them. The wukalāʾ (singular: *wakīl*),[4] who are generally based in Jiddah, serve as agents for the muṭawwifīn. They meet incoming Hajjis, help them chose a muṭawwīf if they have not already done so, and are responsible for them until they depart for Makkah and again when they return to Jiddah en route to home. The adillāʾ (singular: *dalīl*)[5] care for Hajjis who visit al-Madīnah; and the zamāzimah (singular: *zamzamī*) provide Hajjis while in Makkah, ʿArafāt, and environs with daily supplies of water from the holy Zamzam well.

THE HAJJ SERVICE INDUSTRY BEFORE 1924

The Hajj service industry, based primarily on these four guilds, reached a zenith of unbridled laissez faire capitalism around the turn of the century. In succeeding years, particularly after the Saudi takeover of the Hijaz in 1924/25, the guild system became increasingly subject to government supervision, until it could now more properly be called a "public utility" industry. Before tracing the development of government regulation over the Hajj service industry, it would be well to describe the guilds as they existed before modern effective controls were introduced.

The Muṭawwifīn

The muṭawwif of fifty to a hundred years ago was a far more colorful figure than the "all-expense tour guide" of today. According to Eldon Rutter:

> Before each band [of Hajjis] marched a Mutawwif. Some of these were bearded shaykhs, while others were mere youths. With their heads swathed in large yellow turbans, their waists girt with broad sashes of scarlet, of green, or of yellow; their gaudy jackets and fantastic sandals, they presented a dashing, even gallant sight. Striding past with their heads held high, and throwing vivid glances of their dark eyes over either shoulder, in order to see that the drove of bare headed white-clad hajjis

> heard and repeated their words, they intoned the ritual in a loud voice and beautiful enunciation. . . . Many of them, however, mutilate their language when "guiding" the non-Arabic-speaking pilgrims. This they do to make the repetition of the prayers more easy to the hajjis.[6]

In fact, however, even then a large percentage of muṭawwifīn delegated most of their responsibilities to a large coterie of helpers. According to Snouck Hurgronje, those who worked in the service of others were called *dalīls* (not to be confused with the al-Madīnah adillāʾ) or, if they were new to the work, *ṣabīs* (apprentices).[7] Apprentices often began to work guiding Hajjis while quite young. Rutter observed:

> . . . a small boy of perhaps nine years "guiding" a mob of Bokharans. One of the brawny hajjis carried the youngster round the Kaaba on his shoulder, while the little fellow boldly cried out the words of the ritual—the bearded hajjis repeating them after him.[8]

Muṭawwifīn did rent out their own properties and directly provide for the welfare of some of the Hajjis, particularly the more prosperous. But they also served as brokers, referring their clients to chosen associates. Apparently nearly all Makkans (and probably most al-Madīnans) were engaged in supplying these services. Snouck Hurgronje noted in 1888:

> Mekka has no hotels, but, on the other hand, in the last months of every [lunar] year, every Meccan becomes an hotel keeper whether he has a whole house, or only one storey or half a storey. . . .[19]

He added, however:

> As all the sheikhs [muṭawwifīn] *cum suis* at once from the moment of his arrival lead the stranger by the nose, they have great influence in the choice of lodging: all Mekkans therefore are interested in getting on good terms with several sheikhs, as on the other hand the latter set great store on extensive connections among the public.[10]

The muṭawwifīn, like the other guilds, were traditionally divided according to the countries of origin of the Hajjis they guided. The reasons for specialization are obvious: with Hajjis coming from such diverse areas, speaking a babel of languages and dialects, and possessing a myriad of different habits, customs, and characteristics, the man who learned their ways and language would have a great advantage in being chosen to serve as their guide. Moreover his name would be remembered when the Hajjis returned home, and given to the next year's Hajjis.

As a result of this specialization, the muṭawwifīn for a specific area formed tightly knit subguilds, whose ranks were closed even to other bona fide muṭawwifīn. Each subgroup was called a *ṭāʾifah* (plural: *ṭawāʾif*).[11] Over each ṭāʾifah there was appointed a shaykh al-mashāʾikh (shaykh of shaykhs). At the head of the entire guild was the shaykh al-muṭawwifīn. In late Ottoman and Hashimite times he had the dual responsibility of representing the muṭawwifīn's interests with the authorities, and, as a quasi-government official, of helping implement governmental regulations over the muṭawwifīn. The shaykh al-muṭawwifīn was invested in office by the civil authorities. As a sign of office he would receive a mantle (*jubbah*) and his appointment denoted by the word *labis* ("he who wears," i.e., who wears the government mantle).[12]

Since the guild system was based on tradition, there were no formal rules for joining, and theoretically anyone could become a muṭawwif. In case of an interloper, however, the muṭawwifīn would rise to a man to prevent him from becoming established. The few outsiders who persisted were called *jarrars* (those who drag someone along) and dealt primarily with Hajjis too poor to hire the services of a bona fide muṭawwif.

New members were periodically admitted to the guild, particularly if they or members of their families had served as helpers. In this way many whose families had originally come from the land of the Hajjis they served eventually became muṭawwifīn in their own right. In fact membership in the guild could be considered as much by family as by individual—the latter, in other words, representing his extended family.

The responsibility to decide who could join rested with the shaykh al-muṭawwifīn. At the time of admission a small party called a *muʿallimīyah*[13] would be held by the candidate to which other muṭawwifīn, generally of the same ṭāʾifah, would be invited. Before the group, he would say, "I ask our shaykh [al-mashāʾikh] for leave to practice the profession which is allowed by God." The muṭawwifīn would reply, "Who is our shaykh?" After the appropriate answer and the promise to obey him and be a worthy guild brother to his "sons," all would repeat the *Fātiḥah* (the first chapter of the Qurʾān), and the candidate would be welcomed into the brotherhood. This was then followed by a meal or coffee and sweetmeats.[14]

Even within this closely knit group, there were great variations in the scope of operations of the muṭawwifīn. Some had large networks including numbers of agents who traveled abroad each year to recruit Hajjis from the countries in which the muṭawwif specialized. Others participated on a much smaller scale, occasionally on just a part-time basis.

There are no available statistics on the number of the muṭawwifīn in this period. If we take Nallino's estimate in 1938 that there was one muṭawwif for about every 200 Hajjis[15] and apply it to a figure of roughly 100,000 non-Hijazi Hajjis per year,[16] we arrive at 500 muṭawwifīn. If all the helpers and apprentices were added, the number would probably be several thousand.

The Wukalāʾ

Each muṭawwif generally had a deputy or wakīl, based in Jiddah, although a wakīl could work for more than one muṭawwif. The wukalāʾ were responsible for the Hajjis from their arrival until their departure to Makkah. This included meeting the Hajjis on their arrival, guiding them through customs, finding adequate housing, food, and water for their stay in Jiddah, and hiring transportation for their journey to Makkah.[17] Occasionally for very distinguished Hajjis the muṭawwif would journey to Jiddah in person to meet them, but generally he would leave these details to his wakīl. As steam navigation displaced sailing ships and an increasing proportion of Hajjis came by sea, the role of the wakīl in Jiddah increased in importance.

The guild of wukalāʾ, like that of the muṭawwifīn, was divided into subgroups according to the nationality of the Hajjis they served, as it was also headed by a government-appointed guild master. Appointment of a guild master or shaykh al-wukalāʾ appears to have been done in the same manner as in the other guilds.

Because the wukalāʾ worked for muṭawwifīn, the working relationship between these two guilds was more formal than those between the muṭawwifīn and other guilds. When the Hajj service industry subsequently came under more stringent government regulations, all of the guilds came into closer formal working relationships with each other.

The Adillāʾ and Muzawwirīn

The evolution of a fraternity of guides in al-Madīnah in many ways paralleled that of the muṭawwifīn in Makkah. There were, however, some notable differences. Whereas the muṭawwif was responsible for both the spiritual and physical needs of the Hajjis he served, his al-Madīnah counterpart did not necessarily meet both kinds of needs.

One who guides the visitor (there is no set time for such a visit and, since it is not an absolute requirement of the Hajj, not all of the visitors are necessarily Hajjis) to the holy shrines of al-Madīnah—particularly the tomb of Muhammad—is called a *muzawwir*, or "one who conducts a visit." Burton, who visited al-Madīnah in 1853, wrote:

> The visitor, who approaches the Sepulchre [i.e. Muhammad's tomb] as a matter of religious ceremony is called a "Zaʾir," his conductor, "Muzawwir,". . .[18]

Burton further stated that "all the citizens of al-Madīnah who have not some official charge about the temple qualify themselves to act as muzawwirīn."[19]

In Burton's day the muzawwirīn do not appear to have been so tightly organized as the muṭawwifīn (although Burton may simply have failed to inquire into the organizational structure of their guild). He stated:

> They [the muzawwirīn] begin as boys to learn the formula of prayer, and the conducting of visitors; and partly by begging, partly by boldness, they pick up a tolerable livelihood at an early age. The Muzawwir will often receive strangers into his house, as was done to me, and direct their devotions during the whole time of their stay.[20]

In more recent times a separate guild developed for meeting the physical needs of the visitors: the adillāʾ. The guild of adillāʾ was organized very similarly to that of the muṭawwifīn, with subguilds divided by nationality and a government-appointed shaykh al-adillāʾ as guild master. Members of the adillāʾ were generally muzawwirīn, but not all muzawwirīn were adillāʾ.[21] This is where the system differed from Makkah. There those who made a livelihood from guiding Hajjis through the religious rites, if not muṭawwifīn in their own right, were either apprentices or helpers of muṭawwifīn. In al-Madīnah all who were qualified to guide visitors were muzawwirīn, whether working for a dalīl or working on their own.

Two other factors contributed to making the service industry in al-Madīnah differ from that in Makkah. Since the visit to al-Madīnah was not absolutely vital to performing the Hajj, not all

Hajjis made the trip,[22] and those who did were not obliged to arrive at the same time to perform a particular rite on a particular day as had to be done at ʿArafāt. Secondly, the Hajjis traveling from the north[23] could visit al-Madīnah either before or after the Hajj. These two factors obviously helped to diffuse the number of visitors to al-Madīnah at one time and to reduce the scope of the logistical problems facing the adillāʾ. During the latter part of the nineteenth century, sea travel, because it was cheaper and safer, began to rival overland travel as the most popular means of transportation to the Hajj. During the brief period that the Hijaz Railroad ran all the way to al-Madīnah (1908–1918), overland travel greatly increased.[24] But with the closure of the railroad in the Hijaz, overland travel again declined until the large-scale introduction of motor travel.

The Zamāzimah

The zamāzimah comprise what is probably the oldest of the Hajj service guilds. As Rutter stated, "The office of 'waterer' to the Hajjis is pre-Islamic, and is hereditary."[25] The zamāzimah's function is basically to distribute water to all who wish it from the sacred Zamzam well located inside the Haram Mosque. Although distribution of Zamzam water is especially required during the Hajj, specifically during the ṭawāf rites, the zamāzimah, like the muzawwarīn, perform their services throughout the year. For example, Snouck Hurgronje described in detail how the zamāzimah set up their trade in the Haram Mosque at the evening breaking of the fast during the month of Ramaḍan:

> Soon the Zemzemis began to bestir themselves: from their *Khelwas* (the low dark rooms which surround the colonnades of the mosque on the ground floor) they drag out their mats and carpets and spread them on the usual seats of their clients; over the gravel of these long stretches of carpet they put earthen jars (*doraq*'s) of cooled Zemzem water, about one for every five persons: before the places of distinguished customers they place moreover one or two drinking vessels of sweet water, rainwater, or water from the aqueduct, according to the taste of their patrons.[26]

Nevertheless the Hajjis provided the zamāzimah with by far the greater part of their revenues, both by their use of the water and their desire to take containers of it home with them. Supplying the latter was also a very profitable enterprise.

Theoretically there was nothing to prevent anyone from drawing water from the well for himself. It was, however, clearly more convenient, especially for Hajjis, to have this service performed for them. Moreover since the water coming straight from the well was quite warm, it became more palatable after it had cooled in the porous jars of the zamāzimah. It was also the practice to have Zamzam water delivered, often twice a day, to the lodgings of more prosperous Hajjis. Those who could afford the luxury would not only drink it but pour it on themselves.

The zamāzimah were organized similarly to the other guilds, with their own guild shaykh. Individual zamāzimah, particularly if they had a large operation, likewise employed ṣabīs (youths or apprentices) to do the actual distribution. There was also specialization by nationality. According to Snouck Hurgronje, "One of the accomplishments acquired in view of competition is the speaking of several foreign languages whereby the Zemzemis inspire confidence in their customers."[28] The zamāzimah, though independent, frequently had working arrangements even during this period with muṭawwifīn, especially those of a ṭāʾifah specializing in the same geographical areas.

Remuneration: The Gratuity System

Few of the writers of this and preceding periods who have described the temporal aspects of the Hajj have had many good words for the Hajj service industry. Their most common observation was that those who served Hajjis charged extortionate rates. These complaints extend far back in the history of Islam. Islamic jurists of the period of Ibn Jubayr (thirteenth century A.D.), for example, considered the obligation to make the Hajj to be void, "given the incredible vexations to which the pilgrims were submitted at the hands of the inhabitants of the Hijaz."[29]

Snouck Hurgronje, discussing the Makkans' practices in changing money for the Hajjis, wrote, "These usurious practices should make the Mekkans daily expect the Judgment."[30] Rutter, also discussing the Hijazis' exploitation of Hajjis, opined that they "never miss an opportunity of picking up unearned increment, and are eternally trying to evolve new ways of doing it."[31] Even a contemporary writer, Ahmad Kamal, writing a sort of Hajj tour guidebook, *The Sacred Journey*, said:

> All pilgrim guides belong to closed Makkan guilds, each guild organized to cater only to pilgrims of a particular nation or area whose languages or dialects the guild members speak

> and with whose peculiarities they are familiar—knowledge which is a two edge blade, bleeding the unwary as often as it protects them. . . . Dwelling in close proximity to the Holy Ka-ʿbah has not transformed them into angels.[32]

Kamal further warns his readers who plan to make the Hajj to "enquire into the character of a Shaykh al-Hajj [muṭawwif] by consulting those who made the journey under his guidance in past seasons."[33]

Despite obvious abuses and exploitation of Hajjis, however, the unqualified indictment that all those plying the Hajj service trade during this period were totally rapacious is somewhat unfair. After all, they were offering Hajj services as a means of livelihood, not as a nonprofit charitable endeavor. Second, it was certainly consistent with the Middle Eastern business ethic of that day (and this as well) to charge what the traffic would bear. It was the system more than the individuals which lent itself to so much abuse of the Hajjis.

One of the Hajj service industry's more glaring weaknesses was the absence of set fees for their services, since theoretically guidance through the Hajj rites was free. Rutter wrote of the purveyors of Zamzam water:

> Nobody is ever forbidden to drink from the jugs but their owner naturally expects a gratuity from those who can afford to give it. . . . The gratuity is usually given after the completion of the Hajj.[34]

Of muṭawwifīn he observed:

> If he [a Hajji] be so destitute as to be unable to pay for guidance [in performing his Hajj rites in the Haram mosque], then a mutawwif will conduct him in the tawaf and "running" [saʿy] without reward.[35]

He continued, however:

> Such an act is rarely done out of kindness. It is done in order to sustain the delusion that rites performed without the guidance of a mutawwif are valueless in the sight of Allah—for such is the impious connection advanced by the fraternity of guides for their own financial advantage.[36]

On the other side of the coin, the gratuity system did not always benefit the purveyors of Hajj services either. "Only ask most of the Mutawwifs' assistants," wrote Snouck Hurgronje, "how [hard they work] . . . to earn a piece of bread; how long they waited upon their pilgrims for no other reward than some gifts of doubtful value."[37] Thus making a living by offering services to Hajjis for a gratuity was not entirely without risk, and such abuses as existed were largely a matter of degree.

The Ottoman and Hashimite Role

A dual system of government existed in the Hijaz for much of the Ottoman period. Ruling authority was shared by the grand sharif, a local figure and member of the Makkah *ashrāf*, or descendants of the Prophet, and the Ottoman *vali*, or governor. They coexisted in harmony or conflict, depending on the season, until 1916. At that time the incumbent grand sharif, Sharif Husayn, rebelled with British assistance against Turkish authority and established the Kingdom of the Hijaz. Husayn reigned in the Hijaz until October 1924, when he was forced into exile. His son ʿAlī "reigned" in Jiddah for about a year longer, until he too was forced into exile by ʿAbd al-ʿAzīz Āl Saʿūd, amir of Najd and creator of the Kingdom of Saudi Arabia.

Under the Ottoman and Hashimite regimes the Hajjis were by all standards greatly exploited. In addition to the weaknesses of the guild system, this exploitation was caused to a great extent by the system of governmental administration of the Hajj. The authorities, although they did make some efforts to control the Hajj service industry more effectively, did so with largely the same motives as the guildsmen—the financial exploitation of the Hajj. While desire for personal gain was no doubt a strong element of this motivation, it should also be noted that the Hajj was the only major source of revenue in this otherwise largely barren land; and except for a subsidy from the Ottoman treasury (and later a British subsidy to the Kingdom of the Hijaz), the public sector as well as the private sector had to depend on the Hajj to remain solvent. This situation continued, in fact, until after World War II, when oil production surpassed the Hajj as Saudi Arabia's leading source of revenue.

The grand sharif and the vali sat at the pinnacle of what amounted to a great "shakedown system." The Hajj guildsmen shook down the Hajjis; their guild masters, while protecting their interests, were also shaking the guildsmen down; and the government authorities shook down the Hajjis, guildsmen, and guild masters alike. Snouck Hurgronje described how it worked:

> Failing regular taxes, the Prince (i.e., the Grand Sharif) and the Resident (i.e., the Turkish Wali) can only in indirect ways get for themselves a part of that which the Mekkans and especially the sheikhs [mutawwifīn] earn.[38]

He then gave several examples. One was the requirement for non-Turkish Hajjis to buy a Turkish government pass to travel from Jiddah to Makkah, which pass was "quite useless to them, the cost of it forming a concealed tax."[39] Another was to request "free contributions" from the Hajjis for some ostensible project; and Hajj shaykhs "who seemingly let too many pilgrims pass as unable to pay . . . [could] be easily replaced by more skillful sheikhs."[40]

The government's primary tool in shaking down the guilds was in the issuance of licenses. The only means of securing protection from the government was to obtain a license (*taqrīr*) from the grand sharif. It seems that at an earlier time each guildsman, once admitted, obtained a license which was good for life unless he forfeited it by misconduct. By the late nineteenth century, however, forfeiture had become a capricious weapon in the hands of the government. Not only did the new member have to pay for a license, but once in office he had continually to pay to keep himself there. Moreover if business appeared too prosperous the government would "suggest" to the guild master (who for fear of losing his own job could hardly resist) that all those serving Hajjis of a particular area have their licenses revalidated according to some new ordinance. For example, Grand Sharif ʿAwn al-Rafīq (in office 1882–1905) decided to sell to the muṭawwifīn the right to serve Hajjis from a particular geographical area—that which they were already serving in most cases.[41] This tended to eliminate "Hajji stealing," which had been a problem, but the Hajji was now confronted with an even more monopolistic situation, since no muṭawwif other than one from among those responsible for his area would offer his services.

FROM LAISSEZ FAIRE TO GOVERNMENT REGULATION

Since one expressed purpose ʿAbd al-ʿAzīz Āl Saʿūd had for conquering the Hijaz was to protect Hajjis from the abuses of the Hashimite Hajj administration, it is not surprising that regulating the Hajj service industry was one of his first priorities. In November 1926 the Hijaz government, headed by ʿAbd al-ʿAzīz's son

Prince Fayṣal as viceroy, issued a decree (*niẓām*) setting forth the first comprehensive regulations for the Hajj service industry. Consisting of forty articles, the decree defined the functions of the muṭawwifīn, the zamāzimah, the wukalāʾ, and the *mukharrijīn* (camel-brokers who provided in-country transportation in the pre-automobile era).[42] The adillāʾ-muzawwirīn were not at this time considered an integrated part of the Hajj service industry.

Article I of the decree defined the muṭawwifīn as "persons of the population of Makkah nominated by His Majesty the King from among people of religion and trustworthiness, to provide for all those who come for the Hajj, and to each of them will be assigned a group of Pilgrims."[43] Thus the Saudi government of the Hijaz quickly confirmed its right to license and regulate the Hajj guilds.

Government regulation of the Hajj service industry was administered through boards or committees representing each muṭawwif, wakīl, and zamzamī of a particular ṭāʾifah. This ṭāʾifah board system is still in effect.[44]

In time the process of bringing the Hajj guild system under government control, which was begun with the 1926 decree, was successful; and today the regulations governing the Hajj service industry are quite stringent and comprehensive.

One abuse ʿAbd al-ʿAzīz early tried to curb was the exorbitant fees the guildsmen charged. Rates were set for the entire service industry and schedules were published and distributed informing the Hajjis.[45] In 1948 the fee for the combined services of a muṭawwif, wakīl, and zamzamī was 74½ Saudi riyals (SR), out of a total fee (including Saudi government taxes and payments for certain religious endowments) of SR 401½ (or 35½ pounds sterling).[46] The breakdown for the service fees according to the English text of the tariff schedule was:

SR	51	Mutawwif (Moallim)
	3½	Zamzami
	7–	The agent in Jeddah
	2–	The house rent in Jeddah for two nights
	4–	Rates for porters who carry the luggage on arrival and return
	–½	A servant rate
	4½	Chief of Mutawwif and his committee
	–½	Poor Mutawwifs
	1–	A chief agent in Jeddah (Nakieb)
	–½	A chief agent in Mecca (Nakieb)[47]

The following year the overall fee was reduced from 35½ pounds sterling to 28 pounds sterling.[48]

These fees, however, were not all-inclusive, since the dalīl's services in al-Madīnah and housing during the Hajj after leaving Jiddah were not included (except for certain Asian Hajjis who paid a fixed fee for shelter). According to the 1948 tariff schedule:

> The rent of houses in Mecca, tents in Arafat and tents or houses in Mina—besides Java and Malaya pilgrims—fees of the guide in Medina, the rent of the house at Medina and porters' rents in Mecca, all these are not fixed in the tariff but must be arranged by the pilgrims with the owners of due—the pilgrim is free to choose the way which fits him.[49]

It was only in the late 1930s, when the number of foreign Hajjis greatly increased (see Appendix A) and internal transportation became so vastly improved that the trip to al-Madīnah could be made in a few hours, that the adillāʾ guild came more directly under the Saudi regulations for the Hajj service industry as a whole. A royal decree was issued in 1938 which, for the first time, regulated the activities of the adillāʾ as the 1926 decree regulated the other guilds.[50]

CONTEMPORARY REGULATORY PROCEDURES

The current procedures for regulating the Hajj are based on a series of decrees beginning with the 1938 decree on the adillāʾ and culminating with a single statute regulating the entire Hajj service industry. It was issued in 1965 and continues with amendments to be in force today. In September 1946 a new decree had been issued further regulating the wukalāʾ and also setting out in detail the special services which were rendered to Indonesian (Jawah) and Malayan Hajjis.[51] Two years later another decree further regulated the muṭawwifīn;[52] and in May 1964 a ministerial decree (*qarār*) was issued defining the role of the ṭawāʾif in the Hajj operation.[53]

In 1965 all of the regulations stipulated in these decrees were brought together into a single act—Royal Decree (*Marsūm*) No. M/12 dated 9 Jumādá I A.H. 1385 (5 September 1965).[54] The decree set out in detail the responsibilities of the Hajj service industry, the responsibilities of their members, a schedule of fees, and travel instructions for arrival, departure, and in-country travel for the Hajjis.[55]

Hajj Fees and Services

According to Article IX of the Royal Decree of 1965, the fee for services by a muṭawwif, wakīl, zamzamī, and their helpers was set at SR 74 ($16.44); and the fees for the dalīl in al-Madīnah was SR 10 ($2.22).[56] The fee for the traditional special accommodations offered to Indonesians and Malaysians, and additionally to Thais and Filipinos, was SR 200 ($44.44). The article stipulated, however, that this service was entirely optional. These fees have not been altered since they were first put into effect and are published each year in the Hajj Ministry's annual "Statement of Hajj Instructions," which is distributed throughout the Muslim world.[57]

The Hajj fees are collected by the wukalā' and deposited with the Saudi Arabian Monetary Agency. The Saudi government then pays the muṭawwifīn and the others based on official records of payments received.[58] Moreover it is specifically forbidden for those serving Hajjis to accept any additional payments for their services beyond what is stipulated in the regulations.[59]

The services to be rendered in return for these fees were also specified in the 1965 Royal Decree and are published yearly in the Hajj Instructions. Those of the muṭawwifīn are:

(a) Receiving the Hajjis when they arrive in Makkah. Formerly the muṭawwif or one of his staff would be the first to meet his Hajjis when they arrived in Makkah. Eldon Rutter observed that they "often go out on the Jiddah road . . . to meet the pilgrim caravans. On these occasions they usually take a jar of Zamzam water, from which they offer a drink to any of their own Hajjis who may be in the caravan."[60] In recent years, with thousands of Hajjis arriving by bus and auto, the procedure has been vastly streamlined. Hajjis, upon their arrival in Makkah, are sent to official reception centers operated by the Hajj Ministry, where they are processed and then introduced to their muṭawwif or a member of his staff.

(b) Assisting Hajjis to find suitable lodgings and helping them to move in. Although lodgings in Makkah (and al-Madīnah) are still provided by the private sector, the government has instituted strict rent controls. According to Statement No. 4 of the 1972 Hajj Instructions:

> . . . expenses [for accommodation in Makkah, 'Arafāt, Miná, and al-Madīnah] are to be paid amicably by the Hajjis to the owners of the house and tents.
>
> The following is the approximate rental value:

Riyals	
100	Rent of a house in Makkah
30	Rent for a tent in ʿArafāt and Miná
20	Rent of a house in al-Madīnah[61]

The muṭawwif is enjoined from arranging lodgings at a rate more than a Hajji can afford. On the other hand he is also prohibited from allowing a Hajji "to dwell in unhealthy places because they are cheaper or in the streets so that he may not pay any rent at all."[62] In order to regulate housing procurement, a Hajjis Accommodation Control Committee has been established by the Saudi government to oversee all housing procurement and investigate possible violations.

In addition to assisting the Hajji to find lodgings, the muṭawwif must also assist with other physical needs, such as helping the Hajji obtain fair prices when he shops, and so forth. Foodstuffs and other consumer goods are all provided by the private sector in the open market. Water for the Hajjis (excluding Zamzam water) is provided by the Ministry of Hajj and Waqfs.

(c) Guiding the Hajjis through the prescribed religious rites. The manner of performing this duty, which refers primarily to the ṭawāf and saʿy, has changed little over the years. According to the 1972 Hajj Instructions, the muṭawwifīn are instructed to "guide the Hajjis on religious matters, assist them in the ṭawāf and in the performing of the Hajj and the ʿUmrah."[63]

(d) Supervising the stay at ʿArafāt and Miná and the return. Explicit instructions have been set up for supervising the transportation and stay of the Hajjis at ʿArafāt and Miná. As soon as the Hajji has been received and has found lodgings in Makkah, the muṭawwif or member of his staff must take from him his passport and issue in its stead a special card stating his name, nationality, Makkah address, the name of his muṭawwif, the date fixed for his departure from Makkah, and the means of transportation.[64] This card is the Hajji's travel document and identification while he is in the Makkah area.

At a specified time each muṭawwif must arrange transportation for his Hajjis from Makkah to ʿArafat and provide for accommodations in the huge tent city which is set up yearly on the surrounding plain. Prior to the Standing Day rituals each Hajji is issued a second card showing the site of his tent in ʿArafāt and also his tent in Miná. "Cards shall include the number of the plot, square and street."[65] In addition the muṭawwif must erect signs giving the same information "so that the Hajjis may see clearly their places in ʿArafāt and Miná."[66] Assistance must further be given for the Hajj rites at ʿArafāt, for the nafrah to Muzdalifah, for the ceremonies there and in Miná, for the accommodations in Miná mentioned above, and for transportation back to Makkah.

(e) Assisting in onward travel to al-Madīnah or Jiddah. Three days before the Hajji is to leave Makkah, his name is submitted to the Hajj Ministry for inclusion on a departure list and for checking reservations and tickets either for the visit to al-Madīnah or directly home. Passports, tickets, and reservations are then returned to the Hajji and he is directed to the bus or auto contracted to carry him on the next stage of his journey.

Each wakīl, in addition to collecting Hajj fees, is required to render the following services to the Hajjis assigned to his muṭawwif:

(a) Meeting and assisting Hajjis from their arrival in Saudi Arabia until their departure for Makkah or al-Madīnah. As with the muṭawwifīn, the wakīl is no longer the first to meet Hajjis entering the kingdom. The Hajji is first processed through customs and quarantine; only after his muṭawwif is determined is he introduced to the muṭawwif's wakīl or one of his staff. The wakīl then shows him to his quarters. In contrast to the situation of Makkah and al-Madīnah, there are government-operated "Hajj villages" in Jiddah port and airport and at Yanbuʿ to provide lodgings for Hajjis. Of course a Hajji may also seek private accommodations if he wishes. Until his departure for Makkah or al-Madīnah the wakīl also assists him in his other physical needs.

(b) Processing Hajjis' travel and other documents. The wakīl is responsible for completing an official form which states the name of each Hajji, his nationality, passport and visa numbers, the number of persons accompanying him, the name of his muṭawwif and wakīl, and other required information.[67] A copy of this form is distributed to the Passport Office, and another copy, together with the passport and information on internal travel arrangements is forwarded to the Hajj Ministry.[68]

(c) Assisting in onward travel to Makkah and al-Madīnah. The wakīl must arrange transportation according to the desires and financial means of the Hajji. Transportation rates are set by the government. Regularly the wakīl notifies his muṭawwif (or muṭawwifīn if he is working for more than one) of those Hajjis processed and their expected time of arrival in Makkah. Manifests of each Hajji traveling on a particular bus or auto are prepared and given to the driver, who in turn surrenders it at the Makkah reception center where he delivers his Hajjis. This aids the reception officials in getting the Hajjis to the correct muṭawwif. Finally, when the time to leave for Makkah or al-Madīnah arrives, the wakīl or a member of his staff must insure that the Hajji is present and aboard the correct carrier.

(d) Receiving Hajjis on their return from Makkah or al-Madīnah, attending to their physical needs, and assisting in their final departure. At the end of the Hajj, the wakīl is again responsible for the Hajjis, much as on their arrival. He must see to their lodgings and other physical needs, obtain exit visas and complete other travel formalities, and insure that they are present in order to board the ship, bus, car, or aircraft to take them home.

A dalīl may either work independently or in cooperation with a muṭawwif. In either case, whether the Hajjis choose him of their own will or are assigned to him, his responsibilities are the same:

(a) Receiving Hajjis when they arrive in al-Madīnah. The process for receiving Hajjis from the reception centers is much the same as in Makkah.

(b) Assisting Hajjis to find suitable lodgings and helping them to move in. The dalīl's duties in this regard are also the same as those of the muṭawwif in Makkah.

(c) Guiding the Hajjis to the principal religious shrines in al-Madīnah and assisting them in the appropriate devotions during the visits. According to the 1972 Hajj Instructions this duty entails, "Accompanying and guiding the Hajji during his visit to the Prophet's Mosque [al-Ḥaram al-Nabawī al-Sharīf], during his visit to the Baqīʿ [cemetery], and in visiting other [shrines] . . . ."[69]

(d) Assisting in onward travel to Makkah, Jiddah, or Yanbuʿ. In most cases transportation arrangements have already been made by the wakīl or muṭawwif prior to the Hajji's departure for al-Madīnah. If not, the dalīl assists him in arranging transportation. In any case he must insure that each Hajji boards his scheduled carrier at the completion of his trip.

The zamzamī has two main responsibilities:

(a) Supplying Hajjis with Zamzam water. The zamzamī must supply the Hajjis with water from the Zamzam well while they are within the Haram Mosque and at their lodgings "at least twice a day."[70] He is responsible for the cleanliness of the containers and of those working for him who actually distribute the water.

(b) Attending to the Hajjis' needs during prayers. This refers primarily to supplying water for ablutions prior to prayer and prayer mats on which to pray.

The service guilds also have several general responsibilities. These include procedures in case a Hajji gets lost; procedures for notifying health officials of suspected quarantinable diseases and generally being responsible for the health of the Hajjis; and procedures in case of death. The general responsibilities also include the stipulation that each zamzamī and wakīl must submit to the Hajj Ministry by Jumādá II (the sixth lunar month) the names of the muṭawwif (or muṭawwifīn) whose Hajjis they have agreed to serve for the coming Hajj. The agreement is binding and signed by both the wakīl or zamzamī and the contracting muṭawwif.

Efforts to Eliminate Abuses

In addition to stipulating fees and specific services to be rendered, the Saudi government has attempted to eliminate abuses connected with the solicitation of Hajjis by the muṭawwifīn. One of King ʿAbd al-ʿAzīz's earliest moves after taking the Hijaz was to abolish the monopolistic practice whereby a Hajji was more or less obliged to choose the muṭawwif serving his area. But the vested interests of the muṭawwifīn were initially too powerful even for the great Ibn Saʿūd, and his first efforts failed.[71] Subsequently each Hajji was given the right to choose, but in most cases muṭawwifīn whose ṭāʾifah serves the Hajji's area had already solicited his business before he ever departed from his homeland.

At each Saudi port of entry there is an Interrogation Board (Suʾāl) which asks each Hajji the name of his muṭawwif. If he has no preference, the board assigns him one. The boards are composed of wukalāʾ and Hajj Ministry officials. The largest, at Jiddah, is headed by the guild master of the Jiddah wukalāʾ.[72]

Up to 1967 assignment of those with no preference was made to a muṭawwif whose ṭāʾifah served the Hajji's homeland. In that year, however, the regulations were changed to allow assignment to any muṭawwif, a move aimed at reducing the inequities of a situation in which the muṭawwifīn who catered to countries with a large number of Hajjis each year were getting the lion's share of the Hajjis. In order to discourage a muṭawwif from taking on an inordinately large number of Hajjis, the fee he is permitted to collect is reduced for all Hajjis above a specified maximum number.[73]

These regulations, however, still did not prevent the muṭawwifīn, or their "brokers," from engaging in all sorts of tactics to induce Hajjis to commit themselves prior to their arrival in Jiddah. In an attempt to end this "traffic" in Hajjis, the Hajj Ministry announced at the conclusion of the 1967 Hajj yet a new set of regulations.[74]

According to the 1967 regulations each active muṭawwif must fill out a special form supplied by the Ministry. It is stipulated that "only persons from families authorized as muṭawwifīn can fill out the form."[75] On the form he must designate the area of specialization he wishes. These have also been delineated:

Hajjis of Arab countries
Hajjis of Turkey, Iran, and Muslims of Europe [presumably including the entire Soviet Union] and the United States [and presumably the whole of the Western Hemisphere]
Hajjis of Africa excluding Egypt, Sudan, Morocco, Libya, Tunisia, and Algeria
Hajjis of Pakistan, India, Afghanistan, and Ceylon
Hajjis of Indonesia, Philippines, Malaysia, Burma, Thailand, and Muslims of China and Japan[76]

Failure to fill out and sign the form will cause the muṭawwif to forfeit his position, and the "elders of his family" will have to choose another.

The muṭawwif is required to submit the form for approval to the appropriate ṭāʾifah board. The first three categories fall in the Arab Ṭāʾifah, the fourth in the Indian Ṭāʾifah, and the fifth in the Jawah (Java) Ṭāʾifah. The muṭawwif is no longer allowed to solicit Hajjis outside his approved area, and Hajjis with no preference must choose from among the muṭawwifīn assigned to their area. Finally, the regulations impose further government restrictions on the annual "solicitation trips" made by the muṭawwifīn or agents working in their names. Thus while still affording the Hajji the freedom to choose a muṭawwif, his choice has been limited to curtail the unhealthy competition which had arisen. There are, however, sufficient government controls to counter abuses from a monopolistic system. In cases of disputes among muṭawwifīn, the regulations dictate that "seniority within the profession will rule."[77]

The Saudi government has also attempted to control the quality of helpers employed in the Hajj service industry. The 1965 Royal Decree states that each employee must be of good conduct, physically fit, of suitable age to perform his required services, and competent and licensed for that service. It further stipulates that:

> The muṭawwif, wakīl, dalīl, and zamzamī, for their part must take the necessary steps to supervise the said persons during their work and guarantee good performance. Each is to

> be supplied with a card containing all the [required] information including the name of his employer.[78]

THE INTERNAL HAJJ TRANSPORTATION INDUSTRY[79]

The Hajj transportation industry of today is relatively new, having come into existence with the introduction of modern mechanized travel in the Hijaz. For a while the auto and the camel coexisted side by side, but gradually the latter, together with the traditional transportation system built around it, was displaced. As a result of mechanized travel, the administration of the Hajj has probably changed more in the last fifty years than in all its previous history.

The Internal Hajj Transportation Industry Prior to 1924

Internal transportation prior to 1924 was almost exclusively by camel caravan. The caravans were as much for safety as convenience, since the deserts between Jiddah and Makkah, and between Makkah and al-Madīnah were inhabited by fierce *badu* (Bedouin) tribes, notably the Ḥarb and, on the fringe of Najd, the ʿUtaybah. These tribes gained a considerable part of their livelihood by extorting payment from travelers passing through their lands or else by raiding them.[80] In fact much of the Ottoman and British subsidies was allocated to the tribes in return for keeping the overland routes open, especially during the Hajj.

Hiring a camel was done through a mukharrij (from the Arabic root, kh-r-j: to go forth), a camel broker, "without whose help no townsman could make an agreement with the badu for camel transport."[81] According to Burton:

> He brings the Badawin with him; talks them over to fair terms; sees the "Arbun," or earnest-money, delivered to them; and is answerable for their not failing in their agreement.[82]

The mukharrijīn were also organized into guilds similar to those of the muṭawwifīn and others described above. So important were the mukharrijīn to the conduct of the Hajj that they came under the Saudi Hajj regulations of 1926.[83]

By then, however, the caravans' days were numbered. Firmin Duguet, writing in 1932, observed Hajjis motoring through Syria:

> Today, outside the Hijaz, the caravan is disappearing. The automobile is master, which traverses the deserts of Persia, Iraq and Syria.[84]

Still, camel travel did not immediately die out. Possibly one reason was the association of the camel with the Prophet as his means of transportation. In the Hajj tariff for 1949 camel fares were still listed:

	[Pounds sterling]	[Indian rupees]
3. Camel Transport Fares:		
Jiddah-al-Madīnah and return	£5	RS 67
Makkah-ʿArafāt-Miná and return	1½	20
Jiddah-Makkah and return	1	13

4. Fare for camel does not include the shuqdhūf[85] as this will have to be rented separately with the following rates for each person:

	[Saudi riyals]
Jiddah-Makkah	4
Makkah-Jeddah	4
Makkah-ʿArafāt-Miná and return	6
Jiddah or Makkah to al-Madīnah and return	15[86]

The Evolution of Modern Hajj Transport

Internal travel in the Hijaz was a dangerous undertaking during the last Ottoman period and under the Hashimite regime became even more precarious. Badu tribesmen, who intimidated travelers as a time-honored way of life, refused to recognize the authority of Sharif (later King) Ḥusayn, particularly after he reduced their subsidies. In 1922 they actually captured his son ʿAlī between Makkah and al-Madīnah and held him ransom for 5,000 Egyptian pounds.[87] It took ʿAbd al-ʿAzīz and his fierce Najdi warriors finally to subdue the Hijazi badu and to make travel safe for Hajjis when he conquered the Hijaz in 1924–25.

Thereafter mechanized travel quickly spread. A new automobile route had already been opened from Tehran, through Baghdad, Damascus, and Amman, to the Hijaz in 1924, the year ʿAbd al-ʿAzīz took the Hijaz.[88] It shortened overland travel to five days; and, of course, the automobiles, trucks and buses entering the Hijaz were used for internal travel during the Hajj as well. A feature of the 1928 Hajj was "the busy motor traffic between Jiddah, Mecca and Medina, which was said to be supervised by a Scottish engineer."[89] In 1929, according to Duguet, automobile traffic in the Hijaz had greatly intensified, and of those who made the trip from Makkah to al-Madīnah, "only half of them went by caravan."[90]

He estimated that out of 66,000 Hajjis to visit al-Madīnah that year (40,000 before the Hajj and 16,000 afterwards), 25,000 came by auto.[91] By 1929 the first private transportation companies had already appeared in the Hijaz. Because of high government taxes and unbridled competition, however, most of the early companies went out of business. According to a report in *Near East and India* in 1930:

> The twenty or more motor transport companies which have been competing for the favour of the pilgrims have, during the past year, been engaged in a disastrous throat-cutting competition, with the not surprising result that practically every company has shown a loss on the year's working. They have only themselves to blame, but the effects of their general failure are too widespread to be any longer ignored by the Government. And it is anticipated that the Government will reimpose the control, experimentally imposed the previous year and wrongly withdrawn at the request of the companies themselves, in the matter of the fair distribution of pilgrims among the cars available from time to time. Some of the weaker companies could be eliminated without loss to anyone, and then the fair distribution of passengers should do much to eliminate the worse elements of the existing competition.[92]

There were also early efforts at air transportation for the Hajj. In January 1936 the Saudi government contracted with Misr Airlines of Egypt to transport Hajjis from Jiddah to al-Madīnah. During the 1937 Hajj season a Misr airliner made two flights a day with up to five passengers a flight for a total of 105 passengers. The cost was 30½ Egyptian pounds, half of which was government tax.[93] In the following year the aircraft developed engine trouble after three flights, and further service was discontinued.[94]

The Modern Hajj Transportation System

Two external factors severely impeded the full development of mechanized Hajj travel—the Great Depression and World War II. Both greatly reduced the number of Hajjis on which the budding Hajj transportation companies would have to depend. The modern Hajj transportation system, therefore, essentially began after World War II.

In 1946 ʿAbdallah al-Sulaymān, the legendary finance minister and confidant of King ʿAbd al-ʿAzīz, established the Arabian Transport Company for the primary purpose of transporting Hajjis. The company carried a major portion of the Hajjis in the 1947 Hajj. In 1948 the Bakhashab Transport Company was first established. After a slow start the latter company was relaunched and has since become a major Hajj carrier. The impact of these two companies on the Hajj transportation industry was so strong that by 1950 the camel had virtually disappeared as a Hajj carrier.[95]

In the 1948 tariff schedule transportation fees were listed:

Transportation Rates for Every Pilgrim:

The trip to al-Madīnah and return	From Makkah to Miná and ʿArafāt and return	From Jiddah to Makkah and return
£	£	£
24	9	6 First class (car)
12	4½	3 Second class (autobus)
8	3	2 Third class (new truck)[96]

As it became apparent that overland motor transport would care for virtually the entire internal transportation needs of the Hajj,[97] the Saudi government created the Niqabat al-Ṣayyarāt (Motorcar Syndicate) to have exclusive right to carry foreign Hajjis to and from the Holy Places. The syndicate is administered by the Transportation Department of the Hajj Ministry and can be joined by any private company that is able to supply a minimum of 100 buses and 20 sedans, all of which have passed government inspection.[98] In 1970 there were five companies: the Arabian Transport Company, the Tawḥīd Transport Company (formerly Bakhashab), the Tawfīq Transport Company, the Muḥammad al-Maghribīyah Transport Company, and the ʿAbd al-ʿAzīz Kaʿkī Transport Company.

The schedule of fares for 1972 was:

SR	32.00	[$ 7.11]	Fare for one person from Jiddah to Makkah by sedan.
SR	22.50	[$ 5.00]	Fare for one person from Jiddah to Makkah by autobus.
SR	67.50	[$15.00]	Fare for one person from Makkah to ʿArafāt, to Miná, and back to Makkah by sedan.

SR	35.00	[$ 7.78]	Fare for one person from Makkah to ʿArafāt, to Miná and back to Makkah by autobus.
SR	90.00	[$20.00]	Fare for one person from Jiddah or Yanbuʿ to al-Madīnah and back to Jiddah or Yanbuʿ by autobus.
SR	144.00	[$32.00]	Fare for one person from Jiddah or Yanbuʿ to al-Madīnah and back to Jiddah by sedan.
SR	160.00	[$35.65]	Fare for one person from Jiddah or Yanbuʿ to al-Madīnah and from there to Makkah by sedan.
SR	101.25	[$22.50]	Fare for one person from Makkah to al-Madīnah and from there to Jiddah or Yanbuʿ by autobus.[99]

Each Hajji may choose the mode of travel and of course whether he wishes to visit al-Madīnah. Nevertheless the basic bus fare from Jiddah or Yanbuʿ to Makkah and return must be paid by all Hajjis. This is justified on the grounds that the buses are used only during the Hajj and are kept in storage for the rest of the year by government order—a high capital intensive investment for only about two months of work. In addition the companies maintain that they must provide sufficient capacity for all the foreign Hajjis, whether it is used or not.

COMPLAINTS PROCEDURES

Under best of circumstances the regulatory system for the Hajj service industry is bound to have lapses and abuses. Despite fixed rates, for example, there have in recent years been numerous complaints of latecomers having to pay as much as $100 a night for a room, or of six or ten Hajjis having been packed into a single room. Private taxis have been known to charge exorbitant prices to Hajjis hurrying to get to ʿArafāt by sunset on Standing Day.

Presumably the circumstances under which abuses to Hajjis can occur are infinite. In recognition of this the government has created procedures whereby Hajjis may lodge complaints. Each year the Hajj Ministry establishes offices at key locations in the Makkah, Jiddah, and al-Madīnah areas to hear complaints.

The complaints are then investigated by either the Primary Ṭawā'if Committee or the Higher Ṭawā'if Committee to which the muṭawwif, wakīl, dalīl, or zamzamī in question belongs and which are under the auspices and supervision of the deputy minister for Hajj affairs. In investigating complaints the committees may hear testimony from the complainants, the defendants, and witnesses for both sides as well. The results of the investigation and the recommended punishment are referred to the deputy minister for implementation. The deputy minister also has the right to suspend temporarily the defendant's Hajj receipts until the investigation is completed.

Prior to 1972 the complaints procedures were governed by Hajj Ministry regulations, "until such time as a decision governing the proceedings and penalties of disciplinary courts in respect to the ṭawā'if is issued."[100] Beginning with the 1972 Hajj these procedures were specified in detail in Ministerial Decree No. 102/Q/M of 12 Rabī' II A.H. 1391 (7 June 1971). This decree set up administrative procedures for hearing complaints and carrying out investigations and prosecuting alleged offenders. It also lists the penalties to be applied for the various infractions of the government's regulations. Thus, although great progress has been made, the Saudi government is still endeavoring to make the Hajj more equitable and more efficient.

4. The Public Administration of the Hajj

Under the late Ottoman and Sharifian regimes the administration of the Hajj was left almost entirely to the Hajj service industry. The previous chapter describes how the Saudi Government preserved this system while attempting to regulate it to meet present-day needs. The rapid expansion in the number of Hajjis in recent years and their increasing demands for more services, as standards of acceptable living and travel conditions have risen, have necessitated a commensurate expansion of direct administrative support for the Hajj by the Saudi government. In fact the scope of the task is so great that nearly every ministry and agency of the Saudi government is involved, if not totally absorbed, in the public administration of the Hajj for two or more months of each year.

THE DEVELOPMENT OF GOVERNMENTAL INSTITUTIONS

Driving today down Airport Road in the Saudi Arabian capital of al-Riyāḍ, past the vast, modern ministry buildings, it is hard to realize that just a few decades ago the Saudi regime had no formal governmental institutions at all. The development of such institutions, moreover, did not follow a rational, phased pattern which some colonial administration might have instituted—Saudi Arabia was never under colonial rule. Rather the evolution of governmental institutions in Saudi Arabia has followed a haphazard course, with each stage being created as the need arose.

As amir and later sultan of Najd, ʿAbd al-ʿAzīz had a personal patriarchal style of rule which was adequate for central Arabia of that day. Even after the creation of the Kingdom of Saudi Arabia in 1932, public administration in Najd lagged behind that of the more sophisticated Hijaz.

When ʿAbd al-ʿAzīz conquered the Hijaz in 1924–1925, he inherited a relatively structured bureaucracy. And since, initially, the Hijaz was linked to the rest of his dominions only through the person of a common ruler,[1] it was natural for the Hijazi government to continue to function as a separate entity, at least bureaucratically.

On 29 August 1926 ʿAbd al-ʿAzīz promulgated a new Hijazi constitution—the Organic Law for the Kingdom of the Hijaz ("al-Taʿ-

līmāt al-Asāsīyah lil-Mamlakah al-Ḥijāzīyah").[2] Administration of the Hijaz was entrusted to a viceroy (*nā'ib 'amm*). Prince Fayṣal bin 'Abd al-'Azīz Āl Sa'ūd, the second surviving son of 'Abd al-'Azīz (and subsequently king), was appointed to this position and held it throughout the remainder of his father's life.

By Royal Decree of 19 Sha'bān A.H. 1350 (30 December 1931), the Hijazi government was further streamlined by the creation of a Council of Ministers with three portfolios: Foreign Affairs, Interior, and Finance. Faysal, as president of the Council, directed all the ministries as well as the Consultative Council (Majlis al-Shūrá), judicial affairs, and military affairs for the Hijaz. Most of the Hijaz's public administrative machinery was under the Ministry of Interior, which included Departments of Public Health, Public Instruction, Posts and Telegraphs, Maritime Health and Quarantine, Public Security, Sharī'ah Courts, and Municipalities.[3]

On 22 September 1932 the Hijaz and Najd were formally united in the Kingdom of Saudi Arabia.[4] The decree, however, did not immediately transform public administration from regional to national institutions. The process took over twenty years. Not until October 1953 was the first Saudi Council of Ministers created. It was one of the last acts of King 'Abd al-'Azīz, who died a month later.[5]

One reason for the long delay was that at the outset most administrative requirements of the government were in fact limited to the Hijaz. Foremost among them was administration of the Hajj. Thus for many years most of the Saudi administrative structure continued to be located there.

Another reason was the highly personalized system of rule followed by King 'Abd al-'Azīz. Personalities rather than positions were the key to decision-making, and administrative lines of demarcation during this period were fuzzy. For example, Fayṣal had been made overall minister of foreign affairs on 16 December 1930, nearly two years before the unification of the Hijaz and Najd in the Saudi Arabian Kingdom.[6] Presumably the constitutional basis of Fayṣal's authority as foreign minister at that time was the foreign affairs section of the Hijazi Organic Law of 1926. Yet Fayṣal in fact represented his father on a full range of foreign affairs matters extending far beyond the parochial interests of the Hijaz. As a further example of how personalities counted far more than the formal administrative structure, many of Fayṣal's viceregal decrees were applied throughout the kingdom as if they were royal decrees, and not confined only to the Hijaz.[7]

Gradually much of the public administrative machinery for the entire kingdom came under the Saudi Ministry of Finance, much as it had previously been under the Hijazi Ministry of Interior, which was abolished in June 1934. The Saudi Finance Ministry, headed for years by ʿAbdallah al-Sulaymān, evolved from the Hijazi Ministry of Finance, first created as an agency general in 1928. Following the unification of the country into the Kingdom of Saudi Arabia in 1932, it was established as a national ministry and came to include most government services. In 1954 it merged with the previously created Ministry of National Economy (1953) to become the Ministry of Finance and National Economy. In 1944 a separate Ministry of Defense (later Defense and Aviation) was created. During the 1950s additional departments were raised to ministerial levels: Agriculture and Water Resources, Communications, Education, Interior, and Health. In the 1960s Ministries of Hajj and Waqfs, Petroleum and Mineral Resources, Labor and Social Affairs, Commerce, and Information were created. In 1970 the Ministry of Justice was established, and in 1975 Ministries of Posts, Telegraph and Telephones; Public Works and Housing; Planning; Municipal and Rural Affairs; Industry and Electricity; and Higher Education were added, rounding out the present number of Saudi Ministries at twenty. It is within this present structure that the Hajj is currently administered.

THE OVERALL SUPERVISION OF THE HAJJ

Early Saudi Hajj Supervision

From the very first days of Saudi rule over the Hijaz, King ʿAbd al-ʿAzīz took personal interest in the administration of the Hajj. Providing physical security to Hajjis traveling in the kingdom and protection from exploitation during the Hajj were two of his chief concerns when he first conquered the Hijaz. Moreover, no administrative detail was too small to escape his attention:

> . . . it is astonishing how wide is the range of his administrative activity—from quite petty concerns, such as the allocation of a camel or a motor-car to a pilgrim, to the highest affairs of state such as the signing of a treaty with a foreign power.[8]

On the operational level, however, the overall supervision of the Hajj was in the hands of the king's son, Fayṣal, viceroy and head of the Hijazi government. Fayṣal continued in his role until the death of his father and the succession to the throne of his brother, Sa'ūd bin 'Abd al-'Azīz Āl Sa'ūd, in 1953.

To assist Fayṣal in supervising the Hajj a special Hajj Committee was established under the Hijazi Organic Law of 1926. Of the six articles of the Organic Law dealing with "Internal Affairs," three dealt with this committee:

> Article 14
>
> The Pilgrimage Committee shall comprise all the chiefs of departments dealing with the pilgrimage and a number of qualified notables[9] who will be nominated under the direction of the Agent-General [viceroy].
>
> Article 15
>
> The Pilgrimage Committee is fully authorized to examine everything in connection with the pilgrimage and to carry on every form of investigation which they deem necessary in connection with the pilgrimage.
>
> Article 16
>
> All regulations made by the Pilgrimage Committee should be enforced by the Agent-General [viceroy] after they have been sanctioned by His Majesty the King.[10]

The Committee on the Administration of the Hajj, to give it its complete title (Lajnat Idārat al-Ḥajj), was designed both to give overall direction for the Hajj (under the supervision of the viceroy) and to regulate the Hajj service industry. On 5 October 1930 it was superceded by a new Committee on the Hajj and the Muṭawwafīn, which had much the same function.[11] The latter was composed of ten members, the chairman appointed by the government and the others elected from "four groups of Mutawwifs and Zamzamis."[12]

About the same time an Office of the Pilgrimage and Propaganda was created to disseminate information about the Hajj.[13] It published details on Hajj conditions and facilities available, costs, including set fees for transportation and other Hajj services and government taxes, and also on what important personages were making the Hajj. Such information was disseminated both to the press and through Saudi diplomatic and consular missions abroad. Publication of Hajj instructions and tariffs also apparently came under its purview.

Current Hajj Supervision

With the death of King ʿAbd al-ʿAzīz, the vice royalty of the Hijaz under Fayṣal was allowed to lapse. Through much of Saʿūd's reign, Fayṣal, in addition to remaining foreign minister, also served as president of the newly formed Council of Ministers; and in 1964 he succeeded his brother as king. Under the circumstances, with the weight of the entire government administration on him, Fayṣal no longer had the time to oversee the entire administration of the Hajj. Operational supervision, therefore, was delegated to the senior Saudi official in the Hijaz, the amir (governor) of Makkah.[14] This is not to say, however, that Fayṣal no longer took a keen personal interest in Hajj administration. He continued, on occasion, to give attention to minor details, much as his father had done before him.

In order to aid the amir of Makkah in supervising the administration of the Hajj, the Supreme Hajj Committee was established, beginning with the 1966 Hajj. Chaired by the amir, its members include the mayors of Jiddah and Makkah; the senior representatives in the Hijaz for the Ministries of Health, Interior, Hajj and Waqfs, and other interested ministries; and representatives from the local police, customs, quarantine, and other offices.[15]

The Committee convenes several months before the Hajj to plan strategy for coordinating the many administrative services to be provided, to discuss measures which need to be taken for the Hajj, and to make recommendations to the various ministries and agencies to carry them out. For example, at a meeting in February 1967, a month before the Hajj, the Committee passed recommendations concerning the regulation, inspection, routing, and parking of vehicles bearing Hajjis to Makkah. These recommendations were then submitted to the Ministry of Interior, which is responsible for directing traffic during the Hajj. Other recommendations for the 1967 Hajj concerned prohibitions against private use by government officials of government vehicles and lodgings during the Hajj. Subcommittees were created to serve as liaison with the various agencies and to check on how well the measures were being carried out.

After the Hajj the Committee again sits to evaluate the Hajj administration and make recommendations for the following year; for example, after the 1968 Hajj, during which there were serious traffic jams, the Committee recommended remedial action be initiated immediately to improve the transportation system.

In sum, the Supreme Hajj Committee serves as the principal

steering committee for the supervision of the Hajj under the amir of Makkah, much as the Committee on the Administration of the Hajj and its successor, the Committee on the Hajj and the Muṭawwifīn, served the then Viceroy Fayṣal in the early days of the Saudi regime.

SAUDI ADMINISTRATIVE SERVICES FOR THE HAJJ

Providing for the General Welfare of Hajjis

The Ministry of Hajj and Waqfs has the greatest range of administrative responsibilities of all Saudi governmental agencies providing for the general welfare of the Hajjis. The Ministry had its origins in the 1930s as the Directorate-General of Hajj Affairs under the Ministry of Finance. At that time the Hajj was the most important source of state revenue. In 1962 it was joined with the semi-autonomous Directorate-General for Waqfs, which had also been under the control of the minister of finance, and raised to ministry level.[16] The dual responsibilities of the Ministry are still reflected in its basic division into Directorates for Hajj Affairs and for Waqfs, each under a deputy minister.

The principal administrative task of the Hajj Affairs Directorate is the regulation of the Hajj service industry. Thus each Hajj guild and ṭawāʾif, as well as the Hajj transportation syndicate, comes under the Directorate's purview. Also under the Hajj Affairs Directorate are local Hajj departments for Makkah and al-Madīnah and the reception centers where Hajjis are first sent and processed upon their arrival in the two holy cities.

For the welfare of the Hajjis there are not only regulations covering the Hajj service industry, but regulations for the Hajjis to follow as well. These are published in the annual Hajj Instructions. They have to do mainly with arrival and departure procedures, but also enjoin Hajjis not to turn streets or mosques into sleeping places, nor defile them in any way. They also call on Hajjis to go to the nearest Hajj Ministry office to report "any complaint against anyone or if any of the duties included in this statement [of Hajj Instructions] is violated."[17]

In addition to its regulatory responsibilities the Hajj Ministry also provides lodging for incoming Hajjis. Special "Hajj villages" have been constructed in Jiddah and Yanbuʿ for this purpose. In addition to hostel-style rooms, they have their own markets, mosques, and even post offices, the last operated by the Directorate of Posts and Telecommunications of the Ministry of Communications. Traditionally the Hajj villages at Jiddah were operated by the Idarat ʿAyn al-ʿAzīzīyah—the Jiddah-Makkah water administration named for an historic spring near al-Tāʾif. The ʿAyn al-ʿAzīzīyah, which has been incorporated into the Ministry of Hajj and Waqfs as a waqf, provides water for the Hajjis in large cisterns located in Makkah, ʿArafāt, Muzdalifah, and Miná, for which it collects from the muṭawwifīn.

Administration of International Hajj Travel

With the advent of steam power and the opening of the Suez Canal in the nineteenth century, sea travel became the fastest growing means of transportation to the Hajj. Steam navigation, however, was a mixed blessing, for with it contagious diseases, particularly cholera, spread from Asia to Makkah and thence to North Africa, Europe, and beyond, making the Hajj an international health problem. Whereas contagion could more easily run its course during the slow pace of camel caravans and sailing ships, steam ships deposited infected Hajjis in the Hijaz before the disease could be adequately treated or even detected. Because of this, by the time ʿAbd al-ʿAzīz conquered the Hijaz, international Hajj travel, particularly sea travel, had come under strict international health controls[18].

By the late 1920s, however, overland travel to the Hijaz was also becoming a serious health threat, as the motorcar began to replace the camel. Thus in January 1929 the International Office of Public Hygiene in Paris (one of the precursors of the World Health Organization) convened a Conference on the Pilgrimage in Beirut. The governments of Egypt, Palestine, Transjordan, Lebanon, Syria, and Turkey sent delegates; and Iran and the Soviet Union adhered to its agenda but sent no delegates. Saudi Arabia, however, did not participate.[19]

The conference centered on overland travel to the Hajj. In Duguet's words:

> . . . The Conference on the Pilgrimage held at Beyrouth was preoccupied with regulating desert travel, and, in particular, with entrusting it to enterprises with a recognized warranty.[20]

The text of the official agenda read in part:

> 1. The provisions decided by the present Conference and which represent particular agreements (Article 57 of the Con-

vention of 1926)[21] will be executed beginning with 1929 by the states represented at the Conference. These provisions will be implemented within the limits of possibility of each Government, with the understanding that these provisions will be sent for ratification to the International Office of Public Hygiene.

2. Each of the interested states pledges to communicate to the Regional Office in Alexandria [the Egyptian Sanitary Board] two months before the beginning of the Pilgrimage the approximate number of pilgrims and in so far as is possible the itinerary chosen by the Pilgrims.

3. The obligatory vaccinations are smallpox and cholera (two injections), both to take place in the country of origin less than six months before the departure date.

The vaccination against plague is optional and shall be executed only if the existence of epidemics in the countries of origin or transit should prevail at the time . . . .

4. Pilgrimage passports [librettos] which are to be mandatory for all Pilgrims will be for the time being modeled after those extant today in the countries represented at the conference. They shall have a photograph and especially for women, thumb prints.

5. No Pilgrimage passports shall be issued without presentation of a roundtrip ticket and eventually, a deposit of warranty.

6. The country of origin of the Pilgrims will be responsible for the repatriation [of Pilgrims] from all countries of transit and will also be responsible for the expenses incurred by the Pilgrims as a result of illnesses, indigence, etc.

The country of origin will be considered the one whose authorities have issued the Pilgrimage passport. It will be the responsibility of such authorities to determine the requirements they deem best (deposits of guaranty, a warranty by the transportation agents, etc.)

7. The transit of Pilgrims overland shall take place, so far as possible, by means of guarded convoys which will be assembled as near as possible to the point of departure.

8. During the period of the Pilgrimage, all the Muslim travelers who hold an ordinary passport with a visa issued by the Consular Agents of the Hijaz Government are to be con-

> sidered Pilgrims and fall under the special regulations of the Pilgrimage.
>
> 9. The Pilgrims must follow one of the approved itineraries. Nevertheless, each Government reserves to itself the right to establish . . . [its own itinerary] on its own territory . . . .[22]

An agreement based on the Beirut Conference was deposited with the International Office of Public Hygiene in October 1930.[23] Although most Muslim states had long been regulating the travel of their Hajjis by sea, this was the first international agreement on overland travel. Moreover, although British and Dutch colonial governments had long had such requirements, it was the first international acceptance of the necessity for Hajjis to prove that they had the financial means to make the trip. In the nineteenth century the Ottoman government had steadfastly refused to accept any such restrictions, considering the Hajj a religious obligation with each Muslim having the right to decide for himself whether he was physically and financially able to go.[24]

The Beirut Conference placed primary responsibility for Hajjis traveling overland on the countries of origin, but transiting third countries overland was placed under international regulation, just as prior International Sanitary Conventions placed Hajj sea travel under international regulation. The Saudi government was not even a party to these agreements, but it did recognize the necessity for regulation of international Hajj travel. Current Saudi regulations reflect in large part the agreements reached at the Beirut Conference and previous International Sanitary Conferences, such as the one which drafted the 1926 Convention.

Saudi administrative responsibilities for international Hajj travel begin each year several months before the Hajj, when thousands of Hajjis or Hajj travel agents (the latter usually in the employ of muṭawwifīn)[25] apply to Saudi diplomatic and consular missions abroad for special Hajj visas.

Obtaining a regular visa to visit Saudi Arabia is fairly difficult; each applicant, for example, requiring a sponsor resident in Saudi Arabia. But most visa requirements are waived for Hajj visa applicants, with the exception of payment of fees for various services. In 1973 these fees, required whether or not the services were used, included SR 63 ($16.76 at the February 1973 rate) for general services; SR 12.60 ($3.35) for lodging at the seaports of Jiddah and Yanbuʿ or SR 40 ($10.64) for lodging at the airport Hajj villages (the principal one being at Jiddah); plus SR 4 ($1.06) for muṭawwifīn and adillāʾ services.[26] For air and sea Hajjis the fees are paid with the purchase of their round-trip tickets. Hajjis traveling overland can either pay at Saudi missions or consulates when they obtain their visas or else at the Saudi border. All fees collected abroad must be in hard currency. Payments are sent via diplomatic channels to the Saudi Foreign Ministry for delivery to the Saudi Arabian Monetary Agency, which in turn deposits them to the account of the Ministry of Hajj and Waqfs.[27]

In addition to round-trip transportation and payment of fees, the Hajji must also demonstrate to the Saudi visa officer that he has the money to cover food, internal travel, and lodging expenses during the Hajj.

With the influx of so many visa applicants to missions abroad, many small crises are likely to arise. Many West African Hajjis literally walk across the continent, working as they go and sometimes taking years to make the journey.[28] When they arrive, for example, at the Saudi Embassy at Khartoum, Sudan, many are without proper travel documents; and the flood of thousands of such visa applicants can at times almost overwhelm not only the Saudi Embassy in Khartoum, but the embassies of the Hajjis' home countries, where they attempt to obtain proper documentation.[29]

In 1967 a similar crisis arose when several thousand Turks traveling overland were told by their travel agents that Hajj visas were easy to obtain in Amman, Jordan. They so overwhelmed the Saudi Embassy there that a team of Saudi foreign service officers was dispatched to Amman to help take care of the load, but even this measure proved inadequate. Accordingly in order not to bar any of them from making the Hajj, the Saudi Government took the unusual step of allowing a large number of the Turkish Hajjis to obtain visas at Tabuk, well inside Saudi Arabia.[30]

There are also restrictions on international travel itineraries. All Hajjis are generally expected to return the same way they came. If a Hajji desires to return home by means or routes different from those used on his journey to the Hajj, he must apply through the Hajj Ministry, which will make the required arrangements, refund his unused ticket, if any, and notify the Passport Office and the transportation companies involved. Hajjis who did not arrive overland are generally not allowed to depart overland, and those who wish to do so, "the Hajj Affairs Directorate and the Passport Office shall consider emergency cases."[31]

Sea passengers from the north wishing to visit al-Madīnah before the Hajj are required to land at Yanbuʿ and depart from Jiddah. Those wishing to visit al-Madīnah after the Hajj reverse the process. Finally, the Hajj Instructions also include the overland routes which Hajjis are required to take and the final arrival and departure times for Hajjis at all ports of entry. For example, Hajjis from Baghdad are permitted to follow one of two routes—via Amman to al-Madīnah or via Kuwait to al-Riyāḍ to al-Madīnah (the first one is recommended).[32] All Saudi land borders are closed to Hajj traffic on 1 Dhū al-Ḥijjah; Jiddah Port is closed to Hajj traffic after 5 Dhū al-Ḥijjah and the Jiddah Airport after 6 Dhū al-Ḥijjah.[33] Each year, however, some ships and planes arrive late, often through no fault of the carriers, and the closing date for the ports and airports is seldom strictly adhered to. In 1967 a plane carrying four Hajjis landed on 9 Dhū al-Ḥijjah, Standing Day itself, before the Jiddah Airport was finally closed.

Part of the reason for such stringent travel restrictions is to avoid overloading the administrative facilities set up to handle the Hajjis. The Saudis also have been concerned in recent years that unless these measures are taken, thousands of Hajjis will remain in the kingdom (often by choice). Without regular visas or work permits, they will become wards of the state.

Two other ministries which play key roles in international Hajj traffic are the Ministry of Communications, which operates the seaports at Jiddah, Yanbuʿ, and Dammam (on the Persian Gulf), and the Civil Aviation Directorate of the Ministry of Defense and Aviation, which operates the airports. In recent years the latter has been aided by a team from the International Civil Aviation Organization. Hajj air traffic has reached such proportions—as many as 350 movements a day at the height of the Hajj season—that plans are well along for a new international airport at Jiddah.

Occasionally other Saudi governmental agencies also participate in international Hajj traffic on an emergency basis. In 1969 the Royal Saudi Air Force airlifted several thousand Yemeni Hajjis from Jīzān (Jāzān). The Yemenis had hoped to fly from there to Jiddah on Saudi Arabian Airlines only to find all the flights long since sold out.[35]

Administration of Internal Hajj Travel

The Saudi government has also adopted stringent regulations for internal Hajj travel. In the main these are administered by the Hajj Ministry through its regulation of the Hajj motorcar syndicate.

Saudi administrative support for internal Hajj traffic is also reflected in the ambitious nationwide road system. In 1950 there were only two paved roads in the country—Jiddah to Makkah and al-Khubar to Abqayq (Buqayq) in the Eastern Province. Subsequently a nationwide grid of paved highways was planned and construction is nearing completion. Hajj traffic was a major consideration. For example, the first major segment completed was the Jiddah-al-Madīnah road, the major overland Hajj route; it was graded and paved in 1958.[36] The Jiddah-Makkah road has been widened to four lanes, and a road from Makkah directly to al-Madīnah, by-passing Jiddah, has been constructed to alleviate traffic congestion during the Hajj season.

By the early 1970s paved roads extended across the peninsula from Jiddah to Kuwait, with a link directly from al-Riyāḍ to al-Madīnah, and northward from al-Madīnah to the Jordanian frontier, thus facilitating international as well as internal overland Hajj traffic. Road construction is also underway south of al-Ṭā'if toward the Yemeni border, and roads linking Saudi Arabia to the lower Persian Gulf states are likewise being constructed.

Another important road-building project has been the multilane highways from 'Arafāt to Makkah, planned to accommodate the mass movement of the roughly one and a half million Hajjis during the nafrah. Even in road building, however, crises can arise. Just prior to the 1968 Hajj unseasonably late and heavy rains (the area is in fact a desert with normally no more than a shower or two a year and sometimes not even that) turned 'Arafāt into a sea of mud and did extensive highway and other damage. (The Haram Mosque reportedly was under two meters of water after a January 1968 deluge.) Yet as the result of a major effort, supervised personally by the amir of Makkah and the minister of interior (both brothers of the king), the Hajj sites were probably in better condition that year than they might otherwise have been. In fact four new roads were built from 'Arafāt to Makkah, raising the total to twelve.[37]

Public Safety, Internal Security, and Law Enforcement

The Saudi Ministry of Interior is the principal agency responsible for public safety, internal security, and law enforcement in the kingdom. Its responsibilities are, of course, greatly increased during the Hajj season, with the influx of hundreds of thousands of people into a relatively small area. The Ministry was created in 1951 from the semiindependent Public Security Agency, which had been under the Minister of Finance.[38]

One of the most urgent public safety problems of the Hajj is directing traffic. The traffic buildup is greatest at 'Arafāt. The writer was told by a UN expert in Saudi Arabia in 1968 that between 90,000 and 120,000 vehicles were used to transport Hajjis to and from the Standing Day ceremonies.

In order to get some idea of the magnitude of the traffic problem at ʿArafāt during the nafrah, one might picture about twelve Rose Bowl football games all getting out at the same time, with all the fans heading for the same place; only, in the case of the Hajj, there is a multitude of different languages, types of vehicles, and many foreign drivers not familiar with the road system. In order to cope with this situation, special cadres of traffic police are trained for the Hajj and are given extra assistance by the Saudi army. In recent years such modern devices as closed circuit television have also been installed to help guide the traffic flow. Moreover Hajjis traveling overland are required to use designated routes on entering al-Madīnah, Makkah, Muzdalifah, and Miná; the vehicles must be parked in designated places until the Hajjis are scheduled to depart. While in these cities and at ʿArafāt the Hajjis must utilize Saudi transportation (for which they have paid anyway).[39]

Despite all these measures the traffic situation can still get out of hand. In 1968 a mammoth traffic jam developed during the nafrah, and some Hajjis were delayed as much as twenty hours trying to get from ʿArafāt to Muzdalifah.[40] Making matters worse, an exceptionally large number of Saudis attended the Hajj because of the special religious significance of Standing Day falling on Friday and because of the extension of the highway system throughout the kingdom. Not subject to the parking regulations for non-Saudi Hajjis, many took their private autos to ʿArafāt. In addition many Turkish buses, which had been allowed to drive to ʿArafāt because they contained sleeping and eating facilities, broke down during the long tie-ups, further contributing to the traffic jam. Sixteen new, black-and-white-checkered police cars especially marked for the purpose, were wrecked as they sought to cross lanes of moving or stalled traffic. In the post-Hajj evaluation by the Supreme Hajj Committee, traffic control was a major topic, and since then no such major tie-ups have been reported.[41]

The problems of internal security during the Hajj expand and contract with the general political climate in the Muslim, and particularly the Arab, world. In times of political tension extra precautions are taken against the possible use of the Hajj for political purposes—demonstrations, the handing out of propaganda, and so forth. During the turbulent intra-Arab political atmosphere preceding the 1967 Hajj—the Yemeni civil war was at its height, involving Saudi Arabia on the side of the royalists and Egypt on the side of the republicans—Saudi concern for the internal security of the Hajj was reflected in a meeting of the Consultative Military Council in al-Riyāḍ on 22 February. Attending the meeting, in which were discussed measures to be taken for the Hajj season, were the under secretary of interior, the chief of public security, the commander of the Coast Guard and Frontier Force, and the chief of Civil Defense.[42] Since 1967 the threat to internal security during the Hajj has diminished considerably as intra-Arab tensions have been overshadowed by the Arab-Israeli problem.

In law enforcement, in addition to the normal policing responsibilities, the Ministry of Interior cooperates with the Customs Department of the Ministry of Finance to combat smuggling. Customs officials, who meet the Hajjis at points of entry, check to see that commercial goods are not brought in without paying customs. Hajjis from Iran, Iraq, and other places, for example, have traditionally brought carpets with them as sort of commodity travelers' checks, selling them in Saudi Arabia for living expenses. Each Hajji is now allowed to bring in only one, presumably his prayer rug. Still there always seems to be a proliferation of carpets for sale in Jiddah and elsewhere during the Hajj. The Ministry of Commerce and Industry also works with customs officials in attempting to prevent illegal commercial transactions by Hajjis.[43]

Saudi officials must also be on the lookout for illegal items such as narcotics and drugs. Although this is not a major problem at a time of such high religious consciousness, particularly since drugs are prohibited in Saudi Arabia, there are those who do attempt to smuggle in "hashish" during the Hajj, either for sale or private use. A Saudi customs official told the writer in 1968 that "Congo pills"—a type of homemade dexadrine—were popular among many Central and West African Hajjis.

Liaison and Protocol

One of the most pervasive administrative responsibilities of the Saudi government is dealing with foreign officials and dignitaries during the Hajj. Many foreign embassies in Jiddah (the diplomatic community and Foreign Ministry are still located in Jiddah rather than al-Riyāḍ, the capital) have "Hajj affairs officers" whose chief function is ministering to the particular needs of Hajjis from their home countries. (For some states the Hajj is the major reason for having diplomatic representation in Saudi Arabia.) Many states send special administrative missions to aid the embassies during the Hajj.

Other types of special missions are also sent: official Hajj missions, as well as medical, religious, informational, and other types.[44] The most important are the official Hajj missions, usually headed by well-known religious figures. In the days immediately preceding and following the Hajj, the Foreign Ministry is almost completely preoccupied with the protocol aspects of receiving these delegations and all other foreign dignitaries making the Hajj. In addition to the normal courtesies, all ranking dignitaries generally attend a banquet in Makkah traditionally given by the king on the eve of Standing Day, and following the Hajj the king customarily grants audiences to all the official Hajj missions. He generally travels to Jiddah several weeks before the Hajj, in large part for reasons of protocol—e.g., to meet with heads of Hajj delegations and other distinguished Hajjis. Thus the Office of Royal Protocol also becomes deeply involved in Hajj administrative duties.

Other Administrative Services

Two major additional administrative services performed by the Saudi government are assuring that the Hajjis are all accounted for during their sojourn in the kingdom and providing health care. The former is performed by the General Directorate of Passports and Nationality of the Ministry of Interior. The Passport Office keeps a list with the name of each Hajji, his nationality, passport and visa numbers, and other pertinent information, which is submitted by the wukalāʾ who do the processing.[45] Thereafter the Office keeps track of the Hajjis until they depart the country. The Office also publishes an annual statistical review of each Hajj, giving numbers of Hajjis, countries of origin, mode of transportation, and other information. The review is in some ways a carryover from the *Rapports* prepared by the Egyptian Quarantine Board in the 1930s.[46]

Health services, one of the most important responsibilities of the Hajj, are administered by the Ministry of Health. Because of the unique development of Hajj health services, they are discussed separately in the following chapter.

The Ministry of Information has a heavy workload during the Hajj. Each year Saudi Radio and Television cover the highlights of the Hajj, including live broadcasts from ʿArafāt. Press releases and dissemination of Hajj information are also important Information Ministry responsibilities.

Finally, the Saudi government has the continuing task of maintaining the holy sites. In Snouck Hurgronje's day upkeep of the shrines was undertaken on a semicommercial basis by certain old families:

> . . . the exploitation of the Kaabah is the privilege of the old noble family of Sheybah; they do a trade in the used *Kiswah* (great holy covering of the Kaabah) of each year, selling small scraps of it as amulets, and on the days when the Kaabah is opened to the public, or on the rare days when a rich stranger pays a large sum for an extra opening the Sheybahs receive money presents from the rich and from nearly all strangers entering. A Mekkan says in joke, when he sees a Sheybah smiling: "It seems they have opened the Kaabah today."[47]

The Saudi government has subsequently taken over the maintenance of the holy shrines and in the 1950s undertook the largest-scale renovation of both the Prophet's Mosque in al-Madīnah and the Haram Mosque in Makkah ever attempted. The projects were originally conceived by King ʿAbd al-ʿAzīz, who on 8 June 1946 addressed a letter to Muslims throughout the world, informing them of his intention to renovate and enlarge the Prophet's Mosque.[48]

Work began on 9 July 1951. The first step was to acquire land surrounding the mosque, compensate the owners, and raze the buildings already on the land. All the debris had finally been removed by 20 September 1952, and on 20 November 1953 the foundation stone for the new construction was officially laid with thousands of Saudis and foreign Muslim dignitaries in attendance. Two years later, on 22 October 1955, the project was officially completed. Costing $11 million, it added 6,024 square meters to the mosque proper, making a total area of 16,326 square meters. The rest of the 22,955 square meters acquired was devoted to enlarging the grounds around the mosque and building parking lots.[49]

Plans to renovate the Haram Mosque were first announced on 22 September 1955 and were placed under the supervision of the late King (then Prince) Fayṣal. The foundation stone was officially laid on 5 April 1956. This project has enlarged the mosque from 29,127 square meters to a massive 160,168 square meters. The enlarged mosque can now accommodate 300,000 Hajjis at a single time, and when the entire project is completed, the parking lots around the thirty-meter wide road which surrounds the mosque will have a 4,000-car capacity. The cost of the project exceeds $155 million.[50]

The Saudi government is also engaged in smaller projects to improve the holy sites. In 1958 it was discovered that the roof and walls of the Kaʿbah needed repair. Work, begun on 7 February of that year, has since been completed.[51] In May 1972 the Directorate of Waqfs of the Ministry of Hajj and Waqfs invited bids for "covering the floor of the Holy Mosque in Makkah with carpets."[52]

Another Hajj-related responsibility of the Saudi government is to provide the kiswah, the black brocade and gold covering annually placed over the Ka'bah. The kiswah had traditionally been brought from Egypt with the annual Egyptian Hajj caravan. This practice was stopped in 1927 because of an Egyptian-Saudi disagreement over the entry of the Egyptian maḥmal (a procession of ceremonially equipped camels—see pp. 108–109).[53] The following year King 'Abd al-'Azīz had the kiswah made in India.[54] Subsequently a factory for making the kiswah was established in Makkah under the Directorate of Waqfs.

As could be expected in an undertaking of the magnitude of the Hajj, there are numerous minor and related administrative details such as foreign exchange transactions, processing Saudi commercial imports intended for resale during the Hajj, and so forth. Even the Ministry of Petroleum and Mineral Resources is involved. Its subsidiary Petromin, which supplies retail petroleum products within the kingdom, must maintain adequate petrol supplies for all the vehicles at the Hajj. In sum, almost every government agency becomes involved in one way or another in the administration of the Hajj.

5. The Health Aspects of the Hajj

Modern health procedures for the Hajj developed separately from other administrative procedures. They had their origin in international concern that the Hajj was serving as a conduit for the spread of contagious diseases—plague, cholera, yellow fever, smallpox, and typhus—from endemic areas in Asia. Hajjis from the Orient mingled with those from the Levant and North Africa, who in turn spread the diseases to Europe and even to America. In the world cholera epidemic of 1865 for example, which began at the Hajj, an estimated 15,000 of 90,000 Hajjis died; 60,000 in Egypt subsequently died; and by the time the disease had spread to Europe and on to New York six months later, over 200,000 had died in large cities alone.[1]

Efforts to halt these diseases from spreading by way of the Hajj date back to the first half of the nineteenth century. By 1892 direction of health and quarantine procedures for the Hajj was under international control, which continued until 1957. At that time, the World Health Organization (WHO) relinquished all responsibilities held by it and its predecessor organizations to the Saudi Arabian government.[2]

THE PERIOD OF INTERNATIONAL CONTROL

Early Efforts

Europe had long been aware of the threat of epidemic diseases, particularly plague, being introduced from the East. As early as 1348 a Sanitary Council was established in Venice for disease prevention. It was followed in 1423 by a quarantine station;[3] and in 1485 the Venetian government created a permanent Health Magistracy, which in 1504 was given powers of life and death. These measures were taken primarily to prevent the spread of plague from the Levant. By the end of the century nearly all major European states had adopted similar quarantine measures.[4]

Plague had largely disappeared from Europe by the nineteenth century, but a new disease, cholera, now struck fear in the hearts of the Western world. Cholera had long been known as a deadly disease in India, but beginning in about 1817 it began to spread westward, reaching England by the end of 1831 and the United States in the summer of 1832. The focal point for the spread of cholera was the Hajj. Makkah and al-Madīnah, "the Holy Places of Islam, habitual staging points of these deadly epidemics, have always been the axis around which, directly or indirectly, the anxious attention of watching Europe has revolved."[5]

In recognition of the threat of contagious diseases, especially cholera, Sultan Mahmud II established the Constantinople Superior Board of Health (Le Conseil Supérieur de Santé de Constantinople) in 1839. The Board was administered largely by the foreign consulates in Constantinople. Sultan Mahmud II and his successors had discovered that without the presence of representatives of the capitulatory states, the Board could not enforce the quarantine regulations it had promulgated in 1839. Nevertheless the Board was constantly hamstrung by political intrigue of its European members as well as Ottoman lethargy and obstructionism to what it felt was infringement by the European powers on its sovereignty.

The Board at one time maintained a sanitary service in the Red Sea, primarily because of the Hajj, as well as at the chief ports in the Black Sea and the eastern Mediterranean. It had a large staff with numerous Levantine medical officers and ample funds. The Board ceased to operate during World War I and was formally abolished by the Treaty of Lausanne in 1923, a process completed in 1927.[6]

Probably the earliest international health body, the Egyptian Quarantine Board was originally established in 1831 as L'Intendance Generale Sanitaire d'Egypte. As in the case of the Constantinople Board, it was administered primarily by foreign consuls, but with greater success. Later reconstituted as Le Conseil Sanitaire Maritime et Quarantenaire d'Alexandrie (later d'Egypte),[7] the Board played a major role in sanitary control in the Suez Canal and the Red Sea until its functions were transferred to the Egyptian government in 1938.[8]

Although proposals for an international conference to develop uniform quarantine regulations were first made as early as 1834, it was not until 1851 that twelve states sent two delegates each, a doctor and a diplomat, to Paris for the International Sanitary Conference.[9] Due to ignorance of the origin and mode of transmission of diseases such as cholera and plague (a British "Report on Quarantine" published in the mid-nineteenth century concluded that "the only real security against epidemic disease is an abundant supply of pure air. . . .")[10] and political infighting (". . . pressures of the non-maritime powers to bar the entrance of disease, at any cost [and of] . . . the great shipper, the United Kingdom . . . at any cost, to keep commerce moving."),[11] the conference took six months to draft a convention of 136 articles. Only France, Portugal, and Sardinia ratified the convention, and it lapsed altogether in 1865. Although the primary targets of the regulations, including the Hijaz and its Muslim Holy Places, came under Turkish jurisdiction, the Ottoman government refused to ratify the convention. Indeed the Ottoman Empire either refused to ratify any of the sanitary conventions or else did so with such stringent reservations as to render ratification a hollow act.[12]

A Second International Sanitary Conference, held in Paris in 1859, also came to naught over a lack of agreement on terms by the states involved.[13] In 1865, however, a new sense of urgency developed when Europe experienced its fourth pandemic of cholera, originally introduced into Makkah by Indian Hajjis. At the suggestion of the French, the Ottoman government invited seventeen states[14] to send delegates to the Third International Sanitary Conference which convened in Constantinople on 13 February 1866.

During the conference, which lasted seven months, reports of cholera outbreaks in the Hijaz prompted a proposal to cut off all communication with the Arabian coast of the Red Sea, but the Turks (with the support of Britain, Persia, and Russia) demurred, claiming they could not force the Hajjis to remain in the Hijaz against their will. The Turks did, however, promise to construct quarantine stations in Sinai and the Hijaz and to improve quarantine conditions.[15]

The conference divided into six groups to study: (1) origins and genesis of cholera; (2) its transmissibility and propagation; (3) preventive measures (a) hygienic measures, (b) quarantine and disinfection, (c) special measures for the Hajj area and various related regions; and (4) the route of spread of the 1856 pandemic. Goodman summarizes the conclusions including those relating to the Hajj:

> 1. Origins of Cholera.
>
> (a) Cholera is endemic in India, particularly in the Ganges Valley, and not elsewhere.
>
> (b) Its epidemic spread since 1817 marks a new era.
>
> (c) Conditions causing its epidemic spread are not known but it is always imported into the Hijaz (Britain dissenting) and pilgrimages are a major factor in its epidemic spread.
>
> . . . .

3. Prevention.

. . . .

(f) As regards the Mecca pilgrimages, the conference believed that the number of pilgrims should be restricted and their "quality" improved by the enforcement of a "means certificate" as was done in Netherlands East Indies and that embarkation should be stopped or regulated if cholera was epidemic in India. (The British opposed this as interfering with the free exercise of religion and pointed to the Native Passenger Act of 1858 which regulated the numbers, etc., of pilgrims per vessel. It was suggested in reply that this Act was not properly or universally enforced and hinted, as at later conferences, that profits of shipping companies lay behind the British religious scruples.) A Red Sea Sanitary Service was recommended with headquarters at Suez, assisted by an international commission there, and with two quarantine stations at El Tor [al-Ṭūr] and El Wesch [al-Wajh] and one in the Straits of Bab el Mandeb, the latter to be under international direction: five sanitary posts should be established for the service, three on the African coast and one at Jeddah and Yambo [Yanbuʿ], respectively. (The British opposed both the international direction of the quarantine station and the international commission.)[16]

The conclusions were adopted, with reservations by various states, in a Final Act, but no convention resulted. Nevertheless the exchange of views which came from the conference went far to define the type of actions which were needed and ultimately carried out.

THE FIRST EFFECTIVE REGULATIONS

Between 1866 and 1892 three more international conferences were held (Vienna, 1879; Washington, 1881; and Rome, 1885), during which there was much discussion but little accomplishment. It was not until 1892 that the first convention which dealt effectively with the sanitary control of the Hajj was concluded. The International Sanitary Convention of 1892, signed in Venice, focused on maritime traffic between Asia and Europe, particularly during the Hajj season. Articles dealing with the Hajj traffic formed the basis of nearly all subsequent sanitary and quarantine regulations for the Hajj, including regulation of pilgrim ships passing through the Suez Canal, which had been opened in 1869. Since the convention was limited to pilgrim ships ("navires à pèlerins qui transportent au Hedjaz ou qui ramenent des pèlerins musulmans"),[17] it received the approval of Great Britain as posing no threat to its maritime interests with the Orient.

The 1892 Convention required all northbound ships calling at cholera-infected ports in the Hijaz to call at the quarantine station to be established at al-Ṭūr on the Sinai Peninsula. Hajjis were to be put under observation for a period of fifteen days if the ship carried an unclean bill of health and for three to four days if the ship carried a clean bill of health. The ships transiting the Suez Canal from there were to be in quarantine. The Convention also recognized and accorded administrative powers, including administration of the al-Ṭūr station, to the Egyptian Quarantine Board, which had been reconstituted the "Conseil Sanitaire Maritime et Quarantinaire" by khedivial decree of Egypt of 3 January 1881.[18]

Following a Dresden Conference and Convention of 1893, largely prompted by a plague scare from India, the first Sanitary Conference on the Mecca Pilgrimage (the Ninth International Sanitary Conference) was convened in Paris in 1894. Considered a milestone in sanitary conferences, it produced a convention which greatly advanced the work done at Venice two years earlier. The 1894 Convention concentrated on checking cholera at the source (i.e., at the ports of embarcation for the Hajj). Each Hajji was required to undergo a medical examination at his home port and remain five days under observation before embarking for the Hajj from any port infested with cholera. Sanitary regulations for policing maritime Hajj traffic from the ports of embarcation and at sea were also expanded. The establishment of a quarantine station on Kamarān Island south of Jiddah in the Red Sea was stipulated for ships arriving in and departing from the Hijaz from the south, and another quarantine station was set up on the Shatt al-ʿArab at the northern end of the Persian Gulf. A graduate physician was required on ships carrying over 100 Hajjis, and two physicians were required for ships carrying over 1,000.[19] Penalties were set for infringements, the fine for failure to have the required number of doctors aboard being up to 300 Turkish pounds.[20] An effort was made to include a financial "means certificate," such as was approved in 1886, but the Ottoman delegate again remonstrated that no one could be arbitrarily prevented from making the Hajj.[21]

A second Convention of Venice was signed in Venice in 1897. It retained most of the same Hajj regulations, but focused on an outbreak of cholera which had occurred in India. In 1903 at the Eleventh Sanitary Conference, a general Convention combining the provisions of these four conventions was drafted by delegates of twenty-three states.[22]

In 1912 the Convention of 1903 was updated, *inter alia* extending the provisions to cover travel on the Hijaz railroad by Hajjis coming from the Levant. Thereafter only two additional international agreements dealing with Hajj sanitary regulations were signed—the International Sanitary Convention of 1926, drafted in Paris by the Thirteenth International Sanitary Conference (and amended in 1938 and 1944), and the International Sanitary Regulations of 1951, adopted by the Fourth World Health Assembly of the WHO.

The 1926 Convention incorporated most of the previous Hajj sanitary regulations. They were placed in a special section, Title III, "Provisions Specially Applicable to Pilgrimages," which included Articles 91 through 161.[23] These "Pilgrimage Clauses," as they came to be called, established a detailed and comprehensive set of health (including vaccination), sanitation, and quarantine measures governing the Hajj. Medical observation was required not only in the Hijaz but also at infected ports of embarcation and aboard pilgrim ships. As in previous conventions ships carrying over 100 Hajjis required a physician and those carrying over 1,000 required two (Article 106). Sanitary regulations for the voyage were enumerated, including, for example, two latrines for 100 Hajjis (Article 102). Ships arriving from the south were required to call at the quarantine station at Kamarān Island (Article 127)[24] and those from the north at al-Ṭūr station. Sanctions were again stipulated for failure to follow the regulations (Articles 152–161), including a fine of 7,500 gold francs for failure to have the required number of physicians aboard (Article 156).

In addition, Article 148 provided that:

> Whatever the sanitary conditions of the Hedjaz may be, pilgrims traveling by caravan must repair to one of the quarantine stations upon their route, there to undergo according to circumstances the measures . . . for [seaborne] pilgrims who have landed.[25]

For pilgrims coming by rail Article 150 established a much weaker requirement:

> The government of the countries through which the Hedjaz Railway passes shall make all necessary arrangements to or-

> ganize the sanitary supervision of pilgrims during their journey to the Holy Places, and the application of prophylactic measures in order to prevent the dissemination of infectious diseases presenting epidemic features, bearing in mind the principles of the present convention.[26]

The 1926 Convention also included a provision (Article 93) requiring pilgrims to have a round-trip ticket, "and, if circumstances permit, to prove that they have the means necessary for the accomplishment of the pilgrimage."[27]

The 1926 Convention made the Office International d'Hygiène Publique in Paris (the "Paris Office") responsible for coordinating the sanitary control of the Hajj.[28] For this purpose a standing Pilgrimage Commission was created, which met yearly to keep the health and sanitation of the Hajj under continuous review. The Paris Office also assumed some of the regulatory responsibilities which had earlier been carried out by the Contantinople Superior Board of Health.

The 1926 Convention also gave to the Egyptian Quarantine Board the responsibility for transmitting health information to the Paris Office, including an annual report "concerning the sanitary condition of the Hedjaz and countries through which the pilgrims pass."[29] The Board also ran the quarantine station at al-Ṭūr and administered international quarantine regulations for the Suez Canal and at Alexandria.

The *Rapports sur le Pèlerinage du Hedjaz*, published by the Board from 1927 to 1938, were well documented and gave an excellent account of health and other aspects of the Hajj for each of the years covered. Separate sections reported on Hajjis originating from and transiting Egypt; those traveling up the Red Sea from the south; health conditions before and during the Hajj; conditions at the al-Ṭūr and Kamarān quarantine stations; and Hajj measures taken by Algeria, French and Italian Somaliland, the French-mandated states of the Levant, Iraq, Morocco, Palestine, the Sudan, Tangier, Transjordan, and Tunisia. The *Rapports* gave detailed evidence that Hajj health regulations were being rigorously applied during the interwar period. For example, the 1930 Hajj sanitation inspectors at al-Ṭūr discovered a cholera carrier; subsequently all Hajjis en route to Egypt were kept in quarantine at al-Ṭūr eight days, and those bound for other states were kept five days.[30]

The 1951 Regulations and the End of International Control

After World War II there was general international consensus that all previous international sanitary agreements, no one of which had fully superseded all its predecessors, should be brought together in a single body of regulations under the newly organized World Health Organization. The question of consolidation was studied by the Technical Preparatory Committee of the International Health Conference in 1946 and again by the Conference itself in July of that year. The Conference thereupon included provisions in the WHO constitution granting authority to adopt and administer international sanitary regulations.[31]

Subsequently the Interim Commission of the WHO set up a special committee (Expert Subcommittee on the Revision of the Pilgrimage Clauses) to study the sanitary control of the Hajj and the question of revision of the "Pilgrim Clauses" in Title III of the 1926 Convention. Saudi Arabia, with the support of a number of other states, had long protested that the regulations as stated in Title III were an infringement of Saudi sovereignty. The Saudi position was reflected in a subsequent official Ministry of Health publication:

> Certain provisions in the 1926 Paris International Sanitary Agreement concerning the Mecca pilgrimage have always been acting as a source of irritation on the Saudi Arabian Government, who never ceased to submit their protests on many occasions to the proper authorities, requesting the deletion of these articles . . . and . . . the amendment of certain [other articles] as being incompatible with [the establishment of sanitation procedures]. . . .[32]

The committee of experts prepared a technical report which aimed at reducing the sanitary regulations for the Hajj to a minimum consistent with preventing the spread of communicable diseases. Their findings were in turn used by the WHO Expert Committee on International Epidemiology and Quarantine, which had been created in 1948 to draw up guidelines for the new sanitary regulations. The Expert Committee also visited Saudi Arabia to inspect the quarantine facilities there. It found that they were sufficient to meet the task of receiving Hajjis but recommended enlargement of the Jiddah quarantine facilities and improvements of Saudi health services for the Hajj generally.[33]

The precepts of the Expert Committee were accepted by the Second World Health Assembly in 1949. The Expert Committee then drew up a draft of the international sanitary regulations which was submitted for final revision to a Special Committee appointed by the Third World Health Assembly in 1950. The final draft was adopted by the Fourth World Health Assembly in 1951 as WHO Regulations No. 2, which came into effect on 10 October 1952.[34]

In the 1951 Regulations the special provisions for the Hajj were incorporated in Annex A, "Sanitary Control of Pilgrim Traffic Approaching or Leaving the Hedjaz During the Season of the Pilgrimage," and Annex B, "Standards of Hygiene on Pilgrim Ships and on Aircraft Carrying Pilgrims."[35] The Hajj regulations not only consolidated previous regulations but also, in the relaxation of many provisions, reflected improvements in sanitary measures both in the Hijaz and worldwide. Improvements in the mode of transportation were also reflected, especially Part II of Annex B governing air travel. Article B 25 stated that the provisions of the Chicago International Civil Aviation Convention of 1944 would govern air transport of Hajjis as well.[36]

The quarantine station at al-Ṭūr was to remain in operation (under the Egyptian government, since it had assumed the responsibilities of the Egyptian Quarantine Board), but after the 1951 Hajj the station at Kamarān Island was closed. The Expert Subcommittee on the Revision of the Pilgrimage Clauses had earlier recommended maintaining Kamarān until a quarantine station was established at Jiddah "to the satisfaction of the Jeddah health authorities and in such a manner as to create confidence in the countries closely concerned with the Pilgrimage."[37] However the Subcommittee on the Mecca Pilgrimage, created in 1951 by the Special Committee, determined that there was insufficient support for the maintenance of the station at Kamarān. Thereupon the Special Committee set up a Working Party on the Kamarān Quarantine Station on 15 May 1951. The Working Party stated that Great Britain undertook operation of the Kamarān station for the 1951 Hajj, and "that the Government of Saudi Arabia undertook to have available at Jeddah, a sanitary station equipped and able to perform its function regarding the Mecca Pilgrimage, for the Pilgrimage of 1952 and thereafter."[38]

Annexes A and B of the 1951 Regulations were clearly transitional in nature. Their inclusion at all was protested by Saudi Arabia, together with Pakistan, Iran, Iraq, Syria, Jordan, and Afghanistan. As a result a compromise was worked out whereby the Fourth World Health Assembly resolution adopting the Regulations stated:

> Considering that the provisions of Annex A are of a transitional nature, applicable only until such time as the health administration for Saudi Arabia is fully equipped to deal with all sanitary problems connected with pilgrimage within its territory. . . .
>
> Requests the Executive Board to keep the situation continuously under review and to recommend to the Health Assembly such modification in the provisions or in the applicability of Annex A as it deems appropriate.[39]

Provisions under Annex B, hygienic standards on Hajj ships and aircraft, were deemed not entirely within the jurisdiction of the WHO. The Executive Board of the WHO was therefore requested to share responsibility with the Intergovernmental Maritime Consultative Organization, when that body was "fully constituted."[40]

The chief hurdle to the assumption by Saudi Arabia of full responsibility for the Hajj was the need for construction of a modern, well-staffed quarantine station. After five years of planning and construction, and with WHO assistance, the new Jiddah Quarantine Center was completed in 1956, replacing smaller facilities on two islands in Jiddah's outer bay. Its formal inauguration was held on 3 April 1957 and was attended by health delegations from all over the world. The new station, a city within a city, is composed of 150 buildings in an area of 228,000 square meters. In addition to the administrative offices and specimen receiving centers, there are steam sterilization rooms, public baths, a laundry, a bacteriological laboratory, and a power station. There are also a health training school and the center's main hospital with a capacity of forty beds.[41] Following the completion of the Jiddah Quarantine Center, the Ninth World Health Assembly, on May 23, 1956 adopted a resolution stating:

> Considering that special measures for the sanitary control of pilgrim traffic approaching or leaving the Hedjaz during the season of the pilgrimage are no longer required and that consequently the relevant provisions of the International Sanitary Regulations and of Annexes A and B thereto may be abrogated. . . .
>
> These Additional Regulations [i.e., abrogating Annexes A and B] shall come into force on the first day of January 1957.[42]

Thus sixty-five years after the first effective international health control was instituted by the International Sanitary Convention of

Venice of 1892, the health administration of the Hajj became the sole responsibility of the Saudi Arabian government.

Since 1957 Saudi Arabia has rigorously enforced the international sanitary regulations as they apply to the Hajj. When an unusually bad cholera outbreak occurred in Bengal in 1959, Saudi Arabia refused to allow Indian and Pakistani Hajjis entry by air. Other modes of travel were not restricted, but air travel could be accomplished in less than the five-day incubation period for the disease. Because 1,900 Indian and Pakistani Hajjis had already made preparations to fly, those two countries appealed to the WHO, giving assurances that all Hajjis would be properly immunized.

Since the Hajj was no longer subject to international sanitary control, however, the WHO could only advise Saudi Arabia to accept these assurances. But the Saudi health authorities were unwilling to take the risk, in view of the long history of cholera being so closely associated with the Hajj. (At the time the Saudis issued the travel restriction, the Nilratan Sarkar Hospital in Calcutta, which specializes in cholera, was admitting a new patient every four minutes.) Moreover to quarantine 1,900 Hajjis for five days after arrival during the height of the Hajj season was more than the Saudi authorities thought they could manage. Thus, although possibly a setback to "more rational and stable" quarantine measures for moving international traffic "with a minimum of interference," the Saudi decision was considered "justified, in the light of the alarming outbreak of cholera in Bengal."[43]

THE DEVELOPMENT OF SAUDI HEALTH INSTITUTIONS FOR THE HAJJ

As was the case with other governmental operations, the first Saudi public health institutions were inherited from the Hashimite regime of King Ḥusayn, which, in turn, had inherited them from the Ottomans. For the first few years after the Saudi conquest of the Hijaz, public health facilities were limited largely to Makkah, Jiddah, and al-Madīnah. Their primary mission was offering health services during the Hajj.

Prior to the formal unification of the Hijaz and Najd into the Kingdom of Saudi Arabia in 1932, the Public Health Department was a part of the Hijaz government under the viceroy, Prince Fayṣal bin ʿAbd al-ʿAzīz. By viceregal Decree of 29 December 1931, the Public Health Department was placed under the Hijazi Ministry of

Interior, also headed by Prince Fayṣal.[44] It consisted of six sections: the Cabinet of the director-general; the Accounting Office; the Health Certificate Office; the Division of Storehouse, for the acquisition, maintenance, and distribution of health supplies; the Division of Pharmacists; and the Institute for Analysis and Bacteriology. The Department ran a dispensary in ʿArafāt and six first aid stations between Makkah and ʿArafāt, including one at Miná and one at Muzdalifah. They were open only during the Hajj.[45]

Also under the Ministry of Interior was the Department of Maritime Health and Quarantine. It was likewise inherited from the two previous regimes and had its origins in the quarantine efforts of the Constantinople Superior Board of Health. The Maritime Health and Quarantine Department was responsible for in-country sanitary and quarantine administration (as distinct from the international control mentioned above) and was the precursor of the present Department of Quarantine under the Ministry of Health. The Maritime Health and Quarantine Department maintained the two quarantine islands in outer Jiddah bay and one at Yanbuʿ. It also maintained small maritime health posts at Ḍabā on the north coast of the Hijaz; Rabigh, north of Jiddah; and al-Layth, al-Qunfudhah, and al-Jīzān (Jāzān), south of Jiddah.[46]

When the Hijazi Ministry of Interior was abolished in June 1934, many of its former functions continued to be administered separately in the Hijaz. Gradually, however, they were absorbed into nationwide governmental institutions. The Public Health Department thus became a semiindependent agency of the state, administered by a director-general under the aegis of the Ministry of Finance.[47]

In 1951 the Public Health Agency was elevated to become the Ministry of Health, with authority over public health and quarantine.[48] Whereas its predecessor institutions had been predominantly concerned with the health aspects of the Hajj, the Health Ministry has expanded its mission to include a comprehensive public health program for the entire kingdom. Nevertheless efforts at improving the health aspects of the Hajj have been and still are a prominent feature of the Ministry's activities.

THE HEALTH ADMINISTRATION OF THE HAJJ

Health services are generally organized in the Saudi Ministry of Health into two main operational directorates-general. The Directorate-General for Preventive Medicine includes the Regional

Directorates of Health. Among the regions is that of Makkah, al-Madīnah, and Jiddah, often called the "Hajj Region" since it includes the main localities concerned with the Hajj. There is also a Directorate-General for Inspection, which makes inspections for the purpose of detecting infectious diseases and possible hazards to public health. During the Hajj season special teams of health inspectors regularly visit Hajj centers and housing accommodations. Inspection includes provision of ventilation to minimize the likelihood of heat illnesses.[49]

In addition to the operational directorates-general, there is also an International Health Department, under the deputy minister, which serves as a liaison with bodies such as the WHO on matters of international concern.

Preventive Medical Services

Preventive measures for the Hajj continue to aim at the control of contagious diseases. As with all Hajj administrative procedures, Saudi health officials are very careful not to impose restrictions designed in any way to restrict any Muslims from making what is considered both a God-given right and a religious duty, provided they are physically and financially able to make the trip. Since health services are provided free of charge to Saudis and visitors alike, no Hajji is irrevocably refused entry solely on the basis of health regulations.

The preventive health regulations applied generally conform to the 1951 International Sanitary Regulations. Among the requirements are vaccination certificates for cholera, required for all over one year of age, and, for those coming from cholera-infected areas, an additional certificate showing that prior to arrival five days have been spent in a cholera-free area. Vaccination certificates for yellow fever are also required for those coming from a country which is in whole or part an endemic zone.[50]

The health authorities are the first to see incoming Hajjis. They carry out disinfection procedures and inspect health certificates for validity and conformity with Saudi and international regulations. Of the "convention diseases," none have been reported during the last few years. Cholera, in particular, has not been reported from the Hajj since 1912. However a cholera outbreak in Egypt in 1947 necessitated use of the old Jiddah quarantine islands to isolate Hajjis from Egypt who had not completed their five-day incubation period on arrival;[51] and in 1968 2,000 Filipinos were quarantined when cholera carriers were discovered among them. They were subsequently allowed to proceed after receiving medication and when further tests proved negative.[52]

Cholera continues to present the most serious threat to the Hajj of all the major communicable diseases. In 1970 Saudi Arabia and nearly all neighboring countries were invaded by a new westward spreading pandemic of cholera, as were a number of countries which normally send many Hajjis. There was some concern that the disease would be spread during the 1971 Hajj, and in October 1970 a WHO team visited Saudi Arabia to study the situation. The team found Saudi health officials "well trained, dedicated, and highly motivated," and its suggestions for improvements were well received. Their report emphasized improved surveillance, education of Hajjis themselves about the causes of the disease (to prevent panic as well as to prevent spread of the disease), and to safeguard against contaminated water supplies, the chief carrier of cholera.[53] Fortunately with rigorous surveillance and application of the sanitary health standards by Saudi Arabia and the other countries involved, no cases of cholera were reported during the Hajj of 1971.

One impediment to surveillance for contagious diseases is the relatively high incidence of improperly issued health certificates. Whether these certificates are issued through poor administrative procedures in countries of origin or through official nonrecognition of cholera outbreaks by certain countries for fear of the adverse political, social, and economic repercussions, or whether they are obtained fraudulently either by the Hajjis or others arranging their travel, there is little the Saudi officials can do if the certificates appear to be in order. Where the documents are not in order, however, as was the case with the two jet planeloads of Sierra Leone Hajjis in the 1972 Hajj, the Saudis may deny their entry. The unfortunate Sierra Leone Hajjis were forced to return after having only time to pray on the airport tarmac. Once home, they vented their wrath by tearing up the office of Middle East Airlines, which they blamed for the mixup.[54]

Curative Medical Services

Although the threat of international epidemics being spread by the Hajj has been considerably reduced in recent years, curative health problems can, almost by definition, never be entirely eradicated. For one thing, in any random group of over one million people the law of averages alone would suggest that some illnesses and even deaths are bound to occur. Moreover, great crowds make accidents by trampling or being run down by vehicles more than likely, especially in areas where thousands are attempting to perform the required rituals at the same time. Particularly bad areas are the Maqām Ibrāhīm in the Haram Mosque, the roads from ʿArafāt during the nafrah or the "rush" to Muzdalifah after sunset prayers on Standing Day, and around the jamrahs in Miná when masses surge forward to throw their stones.

With such a diverse group it is almost impossible to gauge the effect of physical environment on the Hajjis' state of health in more than a general way. Nevertheless two factors do stand out: age and heat.

Numbers of Hajjis are aged and infirm when they make the Hajj, some having saved a lifetime to afford the trip, and many would feel fortunate to die in the Holy City of Islam. Their age plus the rigors of the trip are often sufficient to lower their resistance to a dangerous degree. Moreover in many cases religious fervor may lead to overexertion, which in turn can have serious health consequences. At the other end of the spectrum, infants are also more susceptible to sickness and suffer more from the rigors of the trip than young or middle-aged adults.

The second factor, heat, is the result of the desert climate found throughout most of the Hijaz. In the summer maximum temperatures exceed 100 degrees F. in the shade and have been recorded over 126 degrees F.[55] Although the winter climate is more balmy, constant exposure to the sun can still be debilitating. The ports of Jiddah and Yanbuʿ are quite humid, but inland the mean relative humidity ranges from between 9 to 36 percent.

The high temperature and low air humidity present a constant threat of heat illnesses, particularly in the summer months. Those most adversely affected are infants and the aged. Since the Hajj occurs according to the Muslim lunar calendar, which is eleven days shorter than the solar calendar, the Hajj falls in each solar month in roughly thirty-four year cycles, falling in the summer (April through September) seventeen years and the winter months another seventeen. The last time that the Hajj fell in the summer was in the 1950s. In the June 1959 Hajj 454 died of heat illness, compared to 377 in 1960, 194 in 1961, 34 in 1962, and none in 1965, when the Hajj was in early April.[56]

Now that the Hajj is occurring in the winter months, the danger of heat illnesses has diminished considerably. In the meantime many of the measures which the Saudi government is taking to improve other aspects of Hajj administration—better transportation, housing facilities, water distribution, etc.—will help to lessen the effects of exposure to the sun, necessary in so many of the Hajj rites. Nevertheless in the 1980s when the Hajj will again come in the summer, the problem of heat illness will once more arise.

The curative health services for the Hajj are organized under the regional health director of the Hajj Region. The ongoing services in the region—hospitals, clinics, ambulance services, refuse disposal, etc.—are augmented each year during the Hajj season. Ministry of Health officials generally meet several months before the Hajj to plan the special measures which are then presented in detail in an "Annual Health Program of the Hajj."[57] These measures are in effect from the sixth to the fourteenth day of Dhū al-Ḥijjah, i.e., during the height of the Hajj ceremonies. (The Hajj Health Program also explains the preventive health measures with which all incoming Hajjis must comply.)

Among the special measures, supervised by senior staff members of the Ministry, are field hospitals, health centers, and mobile health units which roam the overland Hajj routes. The Ministry also provides for refuse collection for the tent cities which are created, especially at ʿArafāt.

Three field hospitals are operated from the sixth to the fourteenth of Dhū al-Ḥijjah, two at ʿArafāt and one at Miná. They provide both in-patient and out-patient services. They are fully equipped for general curative medicine and most general surgery. Cases where prolonged treatment or major surgery is required are transported to the general hospitals in Makkah and al-Madīnah. The field hospitals also have clinical laboratories and dental facilities. As of 1964 they had a combined capacity of 485 beds.[58]

On 10 Dhū al-Ḥijjah, when the ceremonies at ʿArafāt have ended, patients from the ʿArafāt hospitals are transferred to Makkah, and the staffs are transferred to Miná. Meanwhile the hospitals at Makkah are maintained at full capacity.

As an illustration of the efforts Saudi health officials make to aid Hajjis in performance of the required religious rites despite their infirmities, special vehicles are provided to transport in-patients who are physically able to travel to the appropriate sites, particularly ʿArafāt on 9 Dhū al-Ḥijjah for the Standing Day prayers. The vehicles can accommodate eight patients lying in their beds plus two male nurses and two attendants. The vehicles transport the Hajjis to the sites and return them to the hospital.[59]

In addition to the hospitals, over twenty health centers are opened each year in the ʿArafāt-Miná-Muzdahifah area, beginning on 6 Dhū al-Ḥijjah. Those in ʿArafāt and Muzdalifah close on the 10th of Dhū al-Ḥijjah, when the Hajjis move on to Miná. The centers at Miná remain open until the evening of 13 Dhū al-Ḥijjah. Each station is staffed by a doctor, a pharmacist, four male nurses, eight assistants, and three clerks. An ambulance and a Land Rover are assigned to each station for transportation. In addition, living quarters are provided for the staff.[60]

The health centers are equipped to render first aid treatment, perform minor incisions, apply dressings, and give injections. Having electric power, they also provide ample potable water and ice. The centers are visited constantly day and night by the health inspectors to assist in any emergency or relay urgent requests for extra staff or supplies.[61]

Additional Services

An additional but very important task of the Ministry of Health is to supervise, in cooperation with the Makkah municipal authorities, the sacrificial slaughtering of animals during the Īd al-Aḍḥá (the 10 of Dhū al-Ḥijjah and the two succeeding days). While it is ritually permissible to give the money value of the animal to charity instead of actually making the sacrifice, most Hajjis prefer to sacrifice the animal, and on the first day at that. In the old days no facilities existed to handle the slaughter. Though much of the meat was dried for the homeward journey (the three days at Miná were often called *"ayyām al-tashrīq"* or "days of flesh-drying"), sanitary conditions were horrendous. With the large increase in Hajjis in recent years, however, sanitary measures became mandatory.[62]

An estimated 800,000 to 1,000,000 sheep, goats, and camels are annually slaughtered in the three-day period. The magnitude of this slaughtering is staggering. A single slaughterhouse area in Miná is designated for the sacrifice and to sacrifice an animal elsewhere than the pavilions provided for that purpose is punishable by fine. In order to prevent the spread of disease from such a large number of slaughtered animals, no one is allowed to keep from the animal he slaughters more than meat which he and those with him can actually cook and eat (an estimated ten to twenty pounds per animal). The animals, covered with lime or other disinfectant, are then pushed by tractors and bulldozers into huge pits prepared beforehand and buried.

Even with these measures the Saudis are hard pressed to cope with the sacrifice. In 1972 the slaughterhouse area was blocked with carcasses and emergency gates had to be opened with bulldozers. Even so it took some time before the carcasses could be buried in the prepared pits.[63] Numerous proposals have been made about how to alleviate the problem, a commonly heard one of which is to build facilities for preserving the meat and giving it to the poor. While this would be in keeping with the spirit of the sacrifice (it is intended as a charitable act of giving the meat to the poor, not a blood sacrifice), it would hardly lessen the burden of administering the butchering. Ultimately regulations will probably have to be made to space out the sacrificing over the three-day period. As for the facilities for preserving the meat, since they would be used only once a year, they would hardly be any less "wasteful" in strict economic terms than the present practice of burying the meat. Since the whole observance is intended as a sacrifice, however, the economics are probably not all that important. In time such facilities will in all probability be built.

In addition to the Saudi health services, many countries send special medical delegations with the Hajjis from their countries. Foreign doctors, either coming from home or resident with their countries' diplomatic and consular missions in Jiddah, have treated their countrymen for years. The 1937 Egyptian Quarantine Board Report mentions foreign medical missions from Egypt, India, Java ("un docteur résident à la Mecque et un pharmacien"), Algeria, Afghanistan, Russia, and Italy (for its colonies).[64] In 1972 twenty-three countries sent medical missions.[65] The missions are charged with looking after the health of their countrymen and are cooperating with Saudi health officials in both preventive and curative health fields. Their utility, however, has probably diminished over the years as Saudi facilities have expanded and improved.

Finally, the Saudi Red Crescent Society (equivalent of the Red Cross) also operates dispensaries and first aid stations on the overland routes to the Hijaz and in the Hajj areas themselves.

Problems and Prospects

In the field of preventive medicine the Saudis have succeeded, since taking full responsibility for sanitary and quarantine measures in 1957, in keeping the Hajj free of communicable diseases. There have been some close calls, notably during the cholera pandemic of 1970, 1971, and 1972–73, and reports of Syrian Hajjis contracting smallpox in 1972, but Saudi diligence in enforcing sanitary regulations for the Hajj is well documented. Because prevention of these diseases is an international problem, Saudi Arabia must share the credit with the many countries from which the Hajjis embarked. On the other hand, should a serious outbreak of quarantinable disease ever occur in the future, the blame must also be shared with those countries and not applied to Saudi Arabia alone.

In the field of curative medicine the record is not quite so bright. In many cases implementation does not measure up to organization. Every year there are complaints of poor or inadequate health treatment. It would be unfair to criticize the Saudi health officials too harshly, however. First of all, although much still needs to be done in improving health services, that should not detract from recognition of the progress that has already been made. Second, it should always be borne in mind that meeting the health needs of the Hajj must be done under such trying geographic, climatic, sociological, and logistical conditions that even the public health services of the most industrialized countries would find the task difficult.

PART THREE

The Impact of the Hajj on Saudi Arabia

6. The Social, Economic, and Political Significance of the Hajj

Before the Hijaz was incorporated into the Kingdom of Saudi Arabia, the Hajj was the dominant fact of social, economic, and political life. The Hijaz is possessed of few natural resources, an inhospitable climate, and is physically isolated from the large population centers of the Middle East—Egypt, Turkey, and the Fertile Cresent. Had it not been the cradle of Islam, the location of its two most holy sites, Makkah and al-Madīnah, and host to the annual Hajj, the Hijaz would in all probability have continued right up to the present day to be an insignificant backwater.

The impact of the Hajj on the Hijaz and Saudi Arabia as a whole has diminished in recent years. The Hijaz has become just a province of Saudi Arabia; great oil wealth has freed the country from economic dependence on Hajj revenues; and modern technological advances imported with vast new oil wealth have ushered Saudi Arabia into a twentieth-century world far broader than the Islamic world with which the Hajj has so long kept it in yearly contact.

At the same time the Hajj continues to be the greatest single recurring event of social and political importance in the kingdom, quite aside from its overwhelming religious significance. It also constitutes the most important commercial season in the Saudi business year, somewhat analogous to the Christmas season in the United States. The Hajj, therefore, while not dominating Saudi Arabia as it once did the Hijaz, still has a major impact on the country.

THE SOCIOLOGICAL IMPACT OF THE HAJJ

The Hajj as a Melting Pot

Important as the economic and political effects of the Hajj on Saudi Arabia may have been, the social impact has been the oldest and perhaps the most fundamental. Over the centuries the Hajj has drawn people to the Hijaz from all over the Muslim world. Many of them stayed, so that now over half the urban population of the Hijaz is of non-Saudi origin. According to a population study made in the early 1960s, 19 percent of the population of Makkah and 35 percent of the population of Jiddah did not have Saudi nationality. Of the remainder, more than half were of non-Saudi origin.[1]

The figures are probably still valid today. Many of the muṭawwif families originally came from the lands whose Hajjis they later served. In Makkah, colonies of Ḥaḍramīs, East Asians, Indians, Egyptians, Levantines, Turks, and North Africans all lived side by side with native Makkawis, and in many instances their descendants eventually became assimilated. A nineteenth-century Egyptian observer, Sadiq Bey, described the Makkah immigrants as "a mixture of Jawah, Indians, Egyptians, Turks, Takruris, Yemenites and Bedouins."[2] Snouck Hurgronje devoted the final chapter of his classic book, *Mekka*, to the Jawah community (Indonesians) there, who he said numbered in the thousands.[3] Writing forty-one years later, in 1929, Eldon Rutter described the sub-Saharan African quarter of Makkah:

> There is a great village of huts constructed of scrub bushes, camel grass, skins of animals, petrol tins beaten flat, and other material, situated in the Misfala quarter of Mecca. This is where the majority of the Africans live.[4]

In brief the Hajj turned Makkah into one of the most cosmopolitan cities in the Muslim world; and what was the case in Makkah was also to a lesser extent true of al-Madīnah and Jiddah. Many of the resident Hajjis considered themselves temporary sojourners, staying a year or perhaps longer for religious reasons or merely to save enough money for the return trip. Many of these, of course, never returned, and others desired to settle in the Hijaz permanently. Especially in Makkah, their descendants came to be considered part of the indigenous population.

In recent years the Saudi government, with the cooperation of the countries of the Hajjis' origin, has sought to end the age-old influx of permanent and semipermanent Hajj residents. Through the system of passport and visa regulations and the requirement to show evidence of a round-trip ticket and means of support while on the Hajj, the Saudis have fairly effectively cut off this form of immigration.[5] Moreover efforts have been made to repatriate indigent and illegally resident Hajjis. The large cardboard villages of African Hajjis outside Makkah and Jiddah that still existed as late as the early 1950s, for example, have all but disappeared.[6] Nevertheless despite the present ban on Hajj immigration, centuries of past immigration have been a major contributor to the sociological makeup of the Hijaz. Unlike more isolated Najd, the Hijaz has been thoroughly cosmopolitan and worldly, albeit in the context of the Muslim world.

The Hajj Service Industry

Much has been said about the Hajj service industry in Chapter 3. It is sufficient to note here that as a result of the Hajj, a considerable number of people in the Hijaz are employed full time, or at least full time during the Hajj, in an industry which would not otherwise exist.

In recent years, as Saudi oil revenues have opened up alternative means of employment, the number and social importance of the guildsmen in the Hajj service industry have declined. A muṭawwif told the writer in 1967 that of 800 recognized muṭawwif families, only about 120 were active, i.e. 120 families were represented in the guild. (The number of muṭawwifīn was actually much larger if one counts the other members of each family.) Nonactive families, he said, received annual government "pensions" ranging from SR 5,000 to SR 10,000 ($1,111 to $2,222 under the pre-August 1972 rate).[7]

What is true for the muṭawwifīn is probably also true for the other guilds. On the other hand the number employed by the guildsmen has probably increased to accommodate the ever-increasing numbers of Hajjis. Streamlined administrative practices can enable a muṭawwif to care for more and more Hajjis, but also demand a larger staff. Thus the total number of those attached to the Hajj service industry may number as high as 15,000 to 20,000. Since many of these are "seasonal workers," however, they may also be employed at other jobs during the rest of the year. One of the muṭawwifīn interviewed by the writer even sold furniture in Jiddah in the "off season."

The Impact of the Contemporary Hajj

The contemporary Hajj has also had a major social impact on Saudi Arabia. It has already been noted that most of the government is involved in one way or another with the Hajj. In addition, the Hajj constitutes the largest single period of commercial activity during the year. Thus the Hajj is a major focus of attention for a large majority of the government and business classes, which together comprise most of the upper and middle classes in the kingdom.

No one, not even Westerners resident in Saudi Arabia, can escape the presence of the Hajj. In Jiddah as Standing Day approaches the streets are full of Hajjis. Prices are higher. The pace is quicker, in anticipation of the final Hajj rites. Then on Standing Day Jiddah becomes a ghost city much as Nallino described it over thirty years ago: "the town is deserted; shops are closed; there are no servants to render help in the hotels."[8] At the end of the Hajj the city is revived, full of returning Hajjis and Jiddawis alike. Al-Riyāḍ is much the same. When the king leaves for Jiddah before the Hajj, most of the government officials also quit the capital, leaving only skeleton staffs in most of the ministry buildings. In other population centers, the scene, though less pronounced, is also much the same. All non-Hajj-related government business and commerce comes to a halt for a week or more. Saudi and foreign residents who do not make the Hajj often take a holiday during the Hajj season. In sum, no one in Saudi Arabia, not even non-Muslim diplomats, businessmen, and oil men, can avoid being caught up in the yearly spectacle of the Hajj.

The Impact of the Hajj on Saudi Religious Attitudes

Far more has been written on the religious significance of the Hajj than on any other aspect.[9] Almost nothing, however, has been written on the religious impact of the Hajj on Saudi society—i.e., as a sociological phenomenon. The following, therefore, are merely a few impressions based on observations made during the writer's three years of residence in Jiddah, 1967–69.

Saudis appear generally to have an ambivalent attitude about the religious aspects of the Hajj, similar to that of peoples in most countries where a popular holy shrine is located. On the one hand they view the Hajj not as the culmination of a life's mission, as do so many Hajjis from distant lands, but as an annual religious event in which they are most likely to participate. No Saudi would ever take the title Ḥājj—one who has made the Hajj—before his name, although in some Muslim countries this is a title of highest respect. Moreover the high degree of commercialization of the Hajj which has developed over the centuries and which still exists despite Saudi efforts to eliminate abuses, gives a decidedly secular aspect to the Hajj in the minds of many Saudis, particularly the Hijazis. This secular cast is reinforced for many Saudi officials by the onus of their yearly administrative responsibilities.[10]

On the other hand, what is for many Muslims an abstract idea (unless they have made the Hajj) is for the Saudi a living reality.

While he may try to take advantage of the Hajj in every way possible for commercial gain, or is forced to work long, thankless hours in helping to administer it, the Saudi nevertheless has a very close and personal perception of this element of his religious life.

Another significant social impact of the Hajj in Saudi Arabia has been its effect on fundamentalist Wahhābī attitudes. Wahhābism, which has been the traditional ideological underpinning of Saudi society, has mellowed considerably from the strict Islamic code of a harsh, primitive eighteenth- and nineteenth-century Najd. It would be difficult to measure the effect of the Hajj on this process in comparison with other modernizing influences, especially since practically no research on Saudi social and religious attitudes exists. In recent years rapid social and economic development in Saudi Arabia made possible by the discovery of oil has probably become more important than the Hajj in affecting religious and social attitudes. But if it is no longer the major factor, the Hajj is certainly an older influence in mellowing Wahhābism. The Wahhābī leaders of Najd were called upon to reconcile their attitudes towards Islam with those of other Muslims when they undertook being hosts to the Hajj in 1924. Since that time their efforts to make the Hajj more accessible to all Muslims, including heterodox Shīʿites, and their contacts with a broader Islamic world brought about by the Hajj, could only have broadened Wahhābī attitudes generally.[11]

THE ECONOMIC IMPACT OF THE HAJJ

The economic impact of the Hajj can be divided into its effect on the public and private sectors of the Saudi economy. Both have changed greatly in the nearly half century since ʿAbd al-ʿAzīz first took over the Hijaz and the administration of the Hajj.

The Hajj and the Saudi Public Sector

When ʿAbd al-ʿAzīz conquered Makkah, and throughout virtually the entire Islamic history of the Hijaz prior to that, the Hajj was the economic backbone of the country. In the years preceding World War II, Hajj receipts not only had to finance the Hijazi economy but the rest of the kingdom as well:

> The income from the *hajj* had now not only to provide for the needs of the Holy Land but also to meet the yearly deficit

> on the rest of the Wahhabi state. The Hijaz now had to provide for itself and for Nejd as well.[12]

Hajj revenues were primarily collected through direct taxes. They were first imposed by ʿAbd al-ʿAzīz in 1927, when each Hajji was charged a fee of seven gold Indian rupees or its equivalent ($16.80).[13] Carl Rathjens wrote of a £1.5 ($7.20) landing and sanitation tax in 1931.[14] This was apparently separate and is still reflected in the "Fee for General Services" (SR 63 or $12.88) charged in 1972.[15] The government also taxed internal transportation. According to Duguet, each round-trip motorcar fare between Makkah and al-Madīnah was taxed £7½ ($36.00) by the government in the late 1920s.[16] By 1931 it had been reduced to £6 ($28.80).[17] The round trip from Jiddah to Makkah was £3 ($14.40), of which £1 was tax.[18] In addition, licensing and other fees charged to the Hajj service industry, customs on goods imported for resale to Hajjis, and other miscellaneous Hajj-related income also augmented the more direct sources of Hajj revenue.

In the 1930s the numbers of non-Saudi Muslims making the Hajj drastically declined—from nearly 100,000 in 1929 to less than 20,000 in 1933, though climbing back up to about 50,000 in 1937.[19] The two major factors in the decline were the Great Depression and the growing international political unrest before World War II. As a result Hajj receipts also declined sharply. Indeed the Hajjis "had to be taxed more heavily to meet the needs of the state."[20] Thus while ʿAbd alʿAzīz was able to reduce the financial exploitation and other abuses formerly experienced by Hajjis, the need for revenues forced him to perpetuate the commercialization of the Hajj by the public as well as the private sector of the economy.

Dependence on Hajj revenues ceased abruptly at the end of World War II. At that time the first sizable revenues from oil, which had been discovered in the previous decade, were paid to the Saudi government; almost overnight Saudi Arabia was transformed from a land of poverty to a land of plenty. Hajj head taxes were abolished altogether by 1952.[21] The Saudis have since sought to emphasize the point that current Hajj fees are solely for services to Hajjis and not for revenue. Saudi officials abroad are urged to make the distinction clear. The 1972 Hajj Instructions, for example, includes the following paragraph:

> All Saudi Embassies in countries from which Hajjis arrive are requested to explain to the Governments of the Islamic countries that the sums charged the Hajjis represent the wages

> of the various persons who serve Hajjis during their visit to the Holy Lands, as well as other expenses including food, rent, transportation, etc., so that they may not think that the sum is being charged by the Government as taxes.[22]

Since Saudi Arabia has become a wealthy oil-producing state, the Hajj has changed from a source of government revenue to a major area of government spending—somewhat like a gigantic continuing public works project. Although there are few statistics on the economics of the Hajj, informed observers are certain that Saudi Arabia spends far more on the Hajj, directly or indirectly, than it receives in the form of fees.

Of the total Hajj fees collected by the government, a large part are returned to the private sector—mainly to the Hajj service industry. These revenues are considered separately below in an analysis of the private sector. According to the 1972 schedule, the fees which were kept by the government were SR 63 ($14.00) for general services; and SR 12.60 ($2.79) for lodging at the Hajj villages at Jiddah or Yanbuʿ seaports, or SR 40 ($8.88) for lodging at Jiddah airport or other airports.[23] Taking the official 1972 Hajj figures—479,339 foreign Hajjis, of whom 238,658 arrived by air and 99,023 arrived by sea[24]—the Saudi government would have received in fees about $5,710,000 in general service fees, $275,000 for seaport Hajj village lodging, and $2,130,000 for airport Hajj village lodging, or a total of $8,105,000.[25] If one estimates that around $400,000 more would accrue to the government as a result of indirect revenues from the Hajj (customs for foods for resale to Hajjis, gasoline and other commodity taxes, etc.), the government received an estimated $8.5 million in 1972.

Against this the Saudi government spent an estimated SR 200 ($44.44) per Hajji[26] for care and welfare of Hajjis, extending security and other services. Not only does this exceed the fees collected per Hajji, but the 600,000 Hajjis resident in Saudi Arabia pay no fees at all yet benefit from the services. Based on the 1972 figures of around one million Hajjis, Saudi expenditures just for Hajj services for that year were roughly $45 million.

Many ancillary activities, such as maintenance of the holy shrines or the traditional water systems supplying Hajjis (such as the ʿAyn al-ʿAzīzīyah which also operates the Jiddah Airport Hajj village), are administered as religious endowments by the Directorate for Waqfs (Religious Endowments). In former times part of the Hajj fees were allocated to these waqfs.[27] Although this is no longer the case, some Hajjis do contribute to Saudi Hajj-related waqfs as an exercise in religious piety. Also foreign waqfs, particularly from Pakistan and India, are said to be presented annually to the Saudi Waqfs Directorate. Although there are no published statistics of such charitable contributions, the writer was told by more than one Saudi observer that the amount is fairly large, though nothing near the magnitude of other Hajj revenues—perhaps as much as one hundred thousand dollars.

An additional indication of the magnitude of Saudi Hajj expenditures is the size of the budget for the Ministry of Hajj and Waqfs. For the Saudi A.H. 1391 (1971–1972) fiscal year, it exceeded SR 88,000,000, or about $20,000,000.[28] Since nearly the entire energies of the Hajj Ministry are devoted to administering the Hajj, and since it is only one of many Saudi governmental agencies involved, the overall figure of roughly $45 million spent each year is probably conservative and could reach as high as $60 million. Now with the revaluation of the Saudi riyal (from 4.5 to the dollar in 1971 to 3.85 to the dollar in 1973), these figures will be even higher (e.g., from $45 million to $52 million) for expenditures based on the same level of spending and number of Hajjis as in past years. In fact if past trends are an indication, both the level of spending per Hajji and the number of Hajjis is likely to increase in future years.

No analysis of government spending on the Hajj would be complete without mentioning the expenditures which, though made primarily for economic and social development, are in fact closely Hajj-related. For example, the national all-weather road system now under construction was designed to a great extent with the Hajj in mind, at a cost of millions of dollars. The enlargements of the Prophet's Mosque in al-Madīnah and the Haram Mosque in Makkah, at a cost of $11 million and $155 million respectively, were also Hajj-related. Without these enlargements it would simply have become impossible in a few years for all the Hajjis to perform the rituals in Makkah or visit the Prophet's Mosque in al-Madīnah, given the yearly increase in numbers. Jiddah port improvements are also Hajj-related, and the new Jiddah airport project, which may exceed $200 million in cost, would be totally unnecessary were it not for the Hajj. Given the desire of the government to conduct the Hajj in as efficient a manner as possible and in an atmosphere as conducive to worship as possible, the costs of many of these projects are perhaps even higher than the strict dictates of economic feasibility would call for.[29]

Saudi Arabian Airlines and the Hajj

Another major Hajj revenue earner in the public sector is Saudi Arabian Airlines, now called Saudia.[30] Wholly owned by the Saudi Arabian government, it is operated as a semiautonomous public corporation under the Directorate of Civil Aviation of the Saudi Ministry of Defense and Aviation.

Saudia was founded in 1945 by order of King ʿAbd al-ʿAzīz and incorporated in 1963. A major reason for establishing the airline, in addition to providing internal and external air communication for the kingdom, was to provide air service "for Moslems on pilgrimage to the Holy Cities of Islam in Saudi Arabia."[31] To do this it has acquired one of the largest fleets of aircraft of any airline in the Middle East.

As the airline has grown, dependence on the Hajj market has lessened, but it is still important. An indicator of the degree of importance which the airline management places on the Hajj is seen in the following paragraph, taken from the Saudi Arabian Airlines Annual Report of 1970:

> . . . SDI maintains international routes that blanket the Middle East and North Africa and serve Turkey, Iran, Yemen, Pakistan and India. Aside from the economic implications this route structure presents, there are religious, social and cultural elements involved as well. In effect, the airline has opened the Holy Cities of Islam to the major Muslim populations of the world, making the Hajj pilgrimage a possibility to millions of Muslims. During the annual period of Hajj, countless races and nationalities of Muslims converge on Saudi Arabia. Forty percent, or some 150,000 come by air [based on 1970 figures]. To the pilgrim, that short time of intensive exposure to Saudi Arabia and the Holy Places is a permanent memory he carries back with him to his country. Consequently, social and cultural ties are strengthened in light of the common bond of Islam, laying the groundwork for greater political and economic relations between Saudi Arabia and the entire Muslim world.[32]

In fact Saudia must compete with many other airlines for the Hajj trade. In order to give it an advantage, as the home-based airline of the Hajj, the Saudi government has required that all airlines competing as Hajj carriers (i.e., excluding regularly scheduled flights—special Hajj flights are obviously all chartered) must conclude an agreement with Saudia each year in advance of the Hajj, taking into consideration:

> (1) Joint transportation on a fifty-fifty basis of all Hajjis coming to the point of destination (Jiddah) excluding Hajjis in transit who will be transported on a competition basis.
>
> (2) If the corporation [i.e., referring to both SDI and the competing airline] selected does not transport its portion, it will receive a commission amounting to 15% of the transport fare [for all passengers included in its portion carried by the other airline].
>
> . . . .
>
> (5) Landing clearance for aircraft carrying Hajjis is conditional on the agreement with the corporation in this connection.[33]

Issuing the regulations is one thing, enforcing them has been another. According to a Saudia official, one of the main problems has been that most other airlines carrying Hajjis are also state-owned, and thus what starts out as a strictly commercial matter often takes on a political coloration. Some competitors, to get better terms, hint that if the Saudis refuse to allow their aircraft to land, it is the Saudis who are denying Muslims the right to make the Hajj. In cases where the Saudia share of its 15 percent commission comes from soft-currency countries or countries with few Hajjis, the matter is seldom contested by Saudia or the Saudi government; on more lucrative routes it is; but in no cases have Hajjis not been allowed to land.[34]

In order to coordinate relations with other airlines participating in the Hajj traffic, Saudia has created a Special Projects Office. This office not only negotiates the above-mentioned agreements with other carriers but also participates in the deliberations of the Supreme Hajj Committee. The efficiency with which the Special Projects Office has been run has been cited as a major reason for the increased share of Hajj revenues which Saudia earned in 1970—almost SR 17,000,000 ($3,778,000), or a 32 percent increase over 1969. This figure represents 11.7 percent of total operating revenues for 1970, which totaled SR 745,448,443 ($22,330,000).[35]

By 1971 annual gross Hajj earnings for Saudia approached SR 26,000,000 ($5,777,000); and more importantly, with little increase in Hajj-related expenses, the net gain almost doubled—from around SR 8,750,000 ($1,944,000) in 1970 to as much as SR 17,500,000 ($3,900,000) in 1971.[36] Net earnings from the Hajj trade are particularly important to Saudia in that they help to offset the many nonprofitable but necessary internal communications routes Saudia maintains to remote areas of the farflung desert kingdom. Thus for Saudia the Hajj is not only still an important portion of its total business but a most lucrative one as well. If Hajjis flying regularly scheduled flights were included in Saudia's Hajj revenues, the figure would be even greater. And if Saudia maintains its share of the market, as the agreements regulations stipulate, each year's increase in Hajjis arriving by air should make the Hajj market an even more important portion of Saudia's overall operation.

The Hajj and the Saudi Private Sector

Within the private sector the Hajj service industry financially benefits most directly from the Hajj. Although there are no firm statistics on overall Hajj service industry income, some simple computations based on the numbers of non-Saudi Hajjis and fees for services will give some idea of its magnitude. In 1972, 479,339 Hajjis each paid SR 74, or a total of SR 35,471,806 (roughly $7,881,000) in fees to the muṭawwifīn, wukalāʾ, and zamāzimah. Assuming three-fourths of them went to al-Madīnah (there are no accurate figures), another SR 10 or total of SR 3,594,930 (roughly $798,000) was paid to the adillāʾ.[37] To the extent that the fees were augmented by gratuities, the total gross income for the four guilds could have run as high as $10 million.

Closely associated with the guilds are those who rent lodgings to Hajjis and the transportation syndicate. There is probably no good way to estimate housing income, since the suggested rates[38] are frequently violated and since Saudi as well as non-Saudi Hajjis must have lodgings while performing the Hajj. The writer was told by a Makkawi who rents rooms that a plain room with bed and chair but no bath goes for as much as SR 1,000 per day—or $222.22 under the pre-August 1972 rate—in the last week of the Hajj. In terms of earnings, however, high prices for a room are offset by the common occurrence of three or four families occupying the same room. The writer's guess, based on interviews with Hajjis after the 1967, 1968, and 1969 Hajj, is that each Hajji spends an average of $50 on lodgings. Based on a figure of 800,000 Hajjis (i.e., 1,000,000 minus 200,000 from Makkah and their guests), that would total $40,000,000, of which around $24,000,000 would have accrued in foreign exchange. As for the transportation syndicate, it earned a gross income of possibly as much as $12,000,000 in 1972, based on the average fares paid by air and land Hajjis.[39]

Although these figures are simply rough estimates, they do indicate that the gross income for the Hajj service industry, including private landlords renting lodgings to Hajjis, was in the neighborhood of $61,000,000 for the 1972 Hajj. If the present trend for a larger number of Hajjis each year continues, together with the new exchange rate, gross revenues in terms of dollars could well reach $85,000,000 in the next few years, even by the most conservative estimates.

Compared to gross earnings, it would be next to impossible to estimate the net earnings of the Hajj service industry. For example, some services, offered only once a year, make the cost of fixed capital expenditures—e.g., buses, tents, and hotel rooms at Miná and ʿArafāt—quite high. It will take further research to come to a reasonable net earnings estimate.

The economic impact of the Hajj on the private sector extends far beyond the Hajj service industry. Saudi merchants, particularly those based in the Hijaz, look on the Hajj season much in the same way as merchants in the United States look on the Christmas season. Prices skyrocket, despite government efforts to eliminate exploitation. Goods offered in the *suqs* (markets) cater to the Hajji.

The two major items of expense for Hajjis are food and an animal to sacrifice at the ʿId al-Aḍḥá. The price for a sheep in 1967, normally around SR 40 ($8.88), jumped to between SR 60 and SR 100 ($13 to $22) during the Hajj; the price of a young camel for the sacrifice similarly doubled from around SR 200 ($44.44) to SR 400 ($88.88).[40] In addition to food and sacrificed animals, Hajjis also purchase large quantities of luxury consumer items which are unavailable or prohibitively taxed in their home countries.

In addition several million dollars of trade is done in carpets, prayer beads, fountain pens, and cheap wrist watches, most of them bought for gifts back home. Many of the prayer beads sold are actually made in Makkah by a plastics factory which opened a few years ago. Most of the items, however, are brought in from all over the world. One rug dealer told the writer that over a million prayer rugs, mostly cheap Belgian-made carpets with bright scenes from Makkah and al-Madīnah, are sold each year, priced from one to ten dollars each. The wrist watches are mainly from Switzerland and Japan; some of the more expensive textiles are from Europe but most come from Asia, particularly Japan; nearly all of the wheat, many of the cosmetics, pharmaceuticals, and canned goods come from the United States.[41]

Mainland Chinese goods, because of their cheap prices, are also being sold in larger quantities at the Hajj. Chinese "Hero" fountain pen sets which resemble "gold plated" Parker and Schaeffer pens and cost about $.89 have been very popular. Chinese umbrellas (for the sun during the Hajj and the rain at home) also sell well, and a large amount of canned goods is brought in especially for the Hajj (the local market requires a higher quality).

The local banks (most of which are foreign-owned) also do a good business in currency exchange since there are no exchange controls in Saudi Arabia. Many Hajjis, however, do not like to conduct business with modern banks, preferring to deal with the traditional money changers found in the suqs (markets). According to a Jiddah representative of the First National City Bank of New York, the money changers thereupon conduct their business with the banks, sometimes dealing in hundreds of thousands of dollars.[42]

Although the growing number of foreign Hajjis each year has resulted in an increasing amount being spent in Saudi Arabia, the structure of the market has been changing in the past few years. As the traditional length of stay has been shortened from several months to a few weeks, purchases of foodstuffs (as well as housing rentals) have decreased on a per capita basis, particularly in comparison with luxury consumer goods.[43] At the same time a growing number of Hajjis come by air, with smaller baggage allowances than those coming by land or sea, and, especially when purchasing presents for those at home, tend to buy smaller items such as pens and watches. If the trend toward proportionately more Hajjis traveling by air continues, the structure of the Hajj market should continue to shift away from food and bulky items.

Quite apart from the change in Hajj buying habits, the relative importance of the Hajj market to the private sector in general is diminishing. As Saudis increasingly flock to the cities—Jiddah and al-Riyāḍ numbered under 30,000 in 1940 and Makkah under 80,000;[44] all exceed 300,000 today—a Saudi-based consumer market has built up which has lessened the dependence of the local, particularly the Hijazi, merchants on the cyclical and unstable Hajj market. In a 1968 survey of major Saudi importers for four base commodities commonly purchased by Hajjis—textiles, canned goods, cereals and fresh produce, and pharmaceuticals—the writer estimated that the goods purchased for the Hajj represented about one-fourth of the total purchased for the entire year. The consensus of the merchants interviewed was that a decade earlier it would have been between one-third and one-half the total volume of trade (depending on how large a part of the Saudi national market the importer had).

On the other hand, with one-fourth the volume of trade sold in a few weeks, Hajj sales are still large enough to shape the commercial year. It is estimated that the average foreign Hajji spends an average SR 1,000 ($240; or $222.22 under the pre-August 1972 exchange rate). Of this, about half, or $111.11 under the old rate, is spent in the market place (including food purchases).[45] Thus the gross revenues earned from foreign Hajjis by Saudi merchants during the 1972 Hajj were roughly $53,000,000. If one estimates that resident Saudi and non-Saudi Hajjis spent about two-thirds of that in the market place, or around $75 each, the gross earnings for Saudi merchants for 1972 would be about $92,000,000. Unlike income earned by the Hajj service industry, this income enters the economy immediately, much of it paid directly to hundreds of small merchants in a relatively small area. Hajj service industry revenues and government spending, on the other hand, must first filter through the bureaucracy.

The Economics of the Hajj: A Balance Sheet

According to estimates by the Saudi Arabian Monetary Agency (SAMA), gross foreign Hajj receipts now exceed $100,000,000.[46] The income generated by the Hajj of course is even greater. Adding government spending which exceeds $45,000,000, government receipts of around $8,500,000, Hajj service industry earnings of about $61,000,000, Saudi merchant earnings of about $92,000,000, and Saudia gross Hajj earnings of around $6,250,000, approximately $212,750,000 in gross income was generated by the 1972 Hajj in less than two months (See table 1).

In overall economic terms this figure is small compared to oil revenues (currently running between $35 and $40 billion per year). The economic impact of the Hajj, therefore, is not primarily in the magnitude of the revenues it generates. Rather it lies in the still large number of people employed in the Hajj service industry and, since a large proportion of Hajj revenues are spent in the market place, in the effect it still has on Saudi commercial patterns

THE POLITICAL IMPACT OF THE HAJJ

Politicization of the Hajj Prior to 1924

Throughout the history of Islam there appear to have been periods of political interest in the Muslim holy places of the Hijaz alternating with periods of neglect. One period of political interest oc-

TABLE I
Estimated Gross Income from the Hajj for Saudi Arabia, 1972

Item	Gross Hajj Income (In $1,000)	Foreign Exchange Component (In $1,000)
Saudi government receipts in fees and indirect taxes from foreign Hajjis	$ 8,500	$ 8,500
Private sector earnings from Saudi government spending on the Hajj	45,000	—
Lodging accrued by the private sector		
(a) 480,000 nonresident Hajjis at $50 @	24,000	24,000
(b) 320,000 Hajjis resident in Saudi Arabia, excluding Makkawis and their guests at $50 @	16,000	—
Government-set Hajj service industry fees for nonresident Hajjis	10,000	10,000
Food and other market purchases		
(a) 480,000 nonresident Hajjis at $111 @	53,000	53,000
(b) 520 resident Hajjis at $75 @	39,000	—
Internal travel (motorcar syndicate receipts)	12,000	12,000
Saudia earnings	6,250	6,250
Totals	$213,750	$113,750

curred in the late nineteenth and early twentieth centuries under the reign of the Ottoman sultan, Abdulhamid II (1876–1909). Abdulhamid II, taken with the idea of pan-Islam and hoping to restore to his position as caliph the honor and allegiance throughout the Muslim world it had once had, took special interest in the affairs of the Hijaz.[47]

About the only positive accomplishment to come out of Abdulhamid's interest was construction of the Hijaz Railway, completed in 1908. Unlike the other railroad lines being constructed in the Ottoman Empire at the time, the Hijaz Railway was funded solely from non-Western sources—the contributions and religious taxes of pious Muslims throughout the Ottoman Empire and the Muslim world.[48] Donations were solicited for the avowed religious purpose of improving access to the Muslim holy places. During the few years the Hijaz Railway was in operation, it did serve as a major Hajj carrier.[49] Nevertheless political and military reasons seem to have been the chief motivation for building it—to strengthen the sultan's authority in western Arabia.[50] In fact so great was the overlap of political and religious motivations in Abdulhamid's pan-Islamic policies that one Western writer has impugned his religious motives altogether:

> With a view to maintaining his dwindling position amongst the Western Great Powers, Sultan Abdul Hamid brilliantly exploited the current misconceptions regarding Islam in order to pursue a Pan-Islamic policy. (He tried, for instance, to strengthen the false notion that the Caliphate was identical with Papal dignity.)[51]

During the reign of King Ḥusayn (1916–1924), guardianship of the holy places and administration of the Hajj became even more politicized. In fact it was largely because of Ḥusayn's pretensions to be king of the Arabs and caliph of all Muslims that he was ultimately deposed. In 1916 he assumed the title, "King of the Arabs," and in 1924, after the Turkish caliphate was abolished, he took the title of Caliph. The latter act served to bring on the final break in Ḥusayn's seriously deteriorating relations with the Najdi sultan, ʿAbd al-ʿAzīz Āl Saʿūd, and ultimately led to ʿAbd al-ʿAzīz's invasion of the Hijaz.[52]

King Ḥusayn tried to use his guardianship of the Hajj to further his political pretensions as a Muslim world leader. Among other things he convoked international conferences on several occasions during the Hajj season. At the most important of these, an Islamic Congress held in Makkah during the 1924 Hajj, the delegates discussed such issues as the Palestine Mandate, which they condemned, and the Balfour Declaration, in addition to calling for Muslim unity.[53] The conferences were of little help to King Ḥusayn in keeping his throne, but the idea of holding Islamic conferences in Makkah (not all of them during the Hajj) has persisted to the present time.

Politics and the Hajj Under the Sa'ūds

Two of the avowed purposes of 'Abd al-'Azīz in conquering the Hijaz were to open the Hajj to all Muslims and to reform its administration—neither of which tasks, he charged, was being done under King Ḥusayn. In short 'Abd al-'Azīz was determined to purge the Hajj of secular politics and administer it as a purely religious event.[54] This was made clear in the Islamic Congress he called during the 1926 Hajj season to discuss the guardianship of the holy places. The delegates were instructed to confine their discussion to the Hijaz and the Hajj and not concern themselves with international questions or even intra-Muslim world politics.[35]

It has been the policy of the Saudi government ever since to prevent the Hajj from being exploited by any state or group for political gain. For example, in 1937 King 'Abd al-'Azīz prohibited the Supreme Arab Committee of Palestine from holding a conference in Makkah during the Hajj. In a letter to the Committee he said that he did not wish to mix religion and politics.[56]

Another interesting example of the Saudi determination to keep the Hajj and the Muslim holy places above secular politics appears in the Saudi declaration of war against Germany and Japan in early March 1945. In the declaration King 'Abd al-'Azīz stipulated that Makkah and al-Madīnah should remain neutral and should be regarded as "a zone of safety and peace for all those who live therein and all those Muslims who came to it."[57]

In more recent times the Saudis have taken pains to prevent intra-Arab politics from being aired at the Hajj when such appeared to be a threat. During the Saudi-Egyptian political confrontation of the 1960s, for example, special measures were taken to prevent Egyptian Hajjis from propagandizing their side. In the 1966 Hajj a large number of Egyptian Hajjis reportedly began singing the praises of President Nasser but were quickly quieted by Saudi police.[58]

The task of preserving the religious atmosphere of the Hajj has generally been made easier by the deep-seated respect throughout the Muslim world, even among nonpracticing Muslims, for the religious significance of the Hajj. When states or leaders do attempt to use the Hajj for their own political ends, it is generally within the bounds of discretion. Saudi Arabia, for its part, accords the same rights and privileges to all Muslims, regardless of the state of political relations between it and their home countries. Each year, for example, a small group of Soviet Hajjis makes the Hajj, even though Saudi Arabia has no diplomatic relations with the Soviet Union or any other communist state. The only exception was the Saudis' refusal to allow entry to anyone with Israeli travel documents. For Israeli Arab Muslims who could obtain other documents, this did not pose an insoluble problem. In 1978, however, 5,000 Israeli Muslims were allowed to make the Hajj for the first time.[59]

Scrupulous adherence to a policy of maintaining the Hajj as a strictly religious event has not, however, freed the Hajj entirely from politics, particularly in cases of political questions with major religious implications. Saudi Arabia has been forced to deal with the political aspects of religious questions arising at the Hajj from the very beginning of the Saudi conquest of the Hijaz.

The earliest political problems of the Hajj facing King ʿAbd al-ʿAzīz centered primarily on the Wahhābīs' interpretation of how the Hajj should be conducted religiously, and their fear that non-Wahhābī Hajjis would follow what Wahhābīs considered heretical practices. To ʿAbd al-ʿAzīz's strict followers, not only were many of the traditional practices which had grown up around the Hajj contrary to the fundamental teachings of Islam, but performing the Hajj by the prescriptions of any madhhab except the Ḥanbalī school was also wrong. Prohibiting practices not strictly in accordance to the *sharīʿah* could not be criticized too greatly by other Muslims, but prohibition of the other orthodox madhāhib was greatly resented. The matter was resolved, however, in a statesmanlike way, by a resolution of the 1926 Islamic Congress allowing for equality of all four madhāhib. The resolution read:

> Since the holy Hijaz is a religious center, Muslims converging every year from all parts and regions, the Congress resolves that in this matter, Muslims can fulfill their religious duties and the right of pilgrimage according to their different madhahib and the various varieties of their beliefs; and that no one should be constrained to omit anything from his madhhab; and that the right to adjudicate whether anything belongs to a given madhhab or not is the duty of the ʿulamaʾ of a given madhahib and of no one else.[60]

A second religious question with political overtones was the status of the Egyptian maḥmal, a procession of ceremonial camels which annually led the Egyptian Hajj caravan and accompanied the kiswah, which was then also made in Egypt.[61] The Wahhabis had repudiated the maḥmal as idolatrous once before, when they occupied the Hijaz in the early nineteenth century, and when it arrived for the 1926 Hajj, an incident occurred in which several persons were killed. Ultimately the maḥmal had to be withdrawn that year before it had visited al-Madīnah.[62]

King ʿAbd al-ʿAzīz referred the question of the maḥmal, together with other questions, to the ʿulamāʾ of Najd for a *fatwá* (Islamic legal opinion). The decision was delivered on 11 February 1927 (8 Shaʿbān 1345). That portion dealing with the maḥmal read:

> As for the entrance of Egyptian Pilgrims with weapons and military force, into the sacred precincts of God, we have told the Imam [ʿAbd al-ʿAzīz] to forbid their entrance with arms and military force as these are manifestations of polytheism and all manner of other abominable acts.
>
> And, as for the maḥmal, we have answered that it should be prohibited from entering the Great Mosque, and that no one should be permitted to caress it or kiss it. Those who accompany it will be forbidden to make music or do any other abominable acts which have been done in the past. As for the absolute prohibition of the entry of the maḥmal into Makkah, if this can be done without causing a disturbance this shall so be established; otherwise, tolerating one or two infractions in order to eliminate the more serious of the two is permissible under sharīʿah law.[63]

On hearing of ʿAbd al-ʿAzīz's conditions, based on the fatwá, for sending the maḥmal, the Egyptian government decided to cancel it the following year. The Egyptians also refrained from sending the kiswah or their traditional alms (waqfs) for the poor of Makkah.[64] Relations deteriorated between the two countries for a few years. They eventually improved, but the centuries-old tradition of the maḥmal was no more.

Another religious problem with a political dimension was Saudi treatment of Shīʿah Hajjis. Wary of Wahhābī antipathy toward heterodox Shīʿism, predominantly Shīʿah Persia officially prohibited its citizens from making the Hajj in 1927.[65] In spite of that, an estimated 5,000 made the trip anyway.[66] They and Shīʿites from other countries found that they were not ill-treated by the Wahhābī guardians of the Hajj. One Shaykh Ahmad Rida, leading a small group of Syrian Shīʿites in 1927, for example, praised the Saʿūd's administration of the Hajj.[67] Little by little the number of Shīʿah Hajjis increased. Still it was not until well after World War II that Iranian Hajjis began to arrive in large numbers, reaching an all-time high of 48,367 in 1971.[68]

After World War II the political impact of the Hajj expanded considerably beyond the questions of orthodoxy or even heresy which had at times strained Saudi Arabia's relations with other Muslim states in the prewar period. Two ideologies which were totally alien to the Saudis' Islamic perception of world order had become for the first time major political factors in Middle East politics: Zionism and Marxist-socialist doctrines. As a result the idea of a dual Zionist-Communist threat emerged, particularly in the last decade, as a major theme in Saudi foreign policy.[69]

Saudi opposition to Zionism is, of course, centered on the state of Israel. While respecting Judaism as one of the three chosen religions (together with Islam and Christianity), the Saudis have never accepted Israel as a Zionist state ruling what they believe to be sacred Arab-Islamic soil. Hence, whereas the request of the Supreme Arab Committee of Palestine to hold a meeting in Makkah during the 1937 Hajj was refused on the grounds that it was political, post-1948 anti-Zionist activities are seen more in the context of meeting a threat to Islam than of purely secular politics.

An interesting addendum to the implications of Zionism on the Hajj concerns the argument put forth by the heads of Arab diplomatic missions in Washington to the United States secretary of state in 1957 as to why Israel should not occupy land on the Gulf of ʿAqabah, and why the Gulf is solely within territorial waters:

> The Gulf of Aquaba [sic.] is unique in its nature as being Tariq El-Haj (the Route of Pilgrimage) and Bab El-Harameen (Door to the Most Holy Sites of Islam). The Moslems, the Prince in his palace and the common man, are, thus, enjoined to defend the Gulf of Aquaba as one would defend the apple of his eye. The issue of the Gulf of Aquaba is one of great concern to the Moslem world.[70]

It is interesting to note that this same argument was used by the delegates of the 1926 Mekkah Islamic Congress in a resolution protesting the British annexation of ʿAqabah town from the Hijaz to Transjordan.[71]

Marxist-socialist doctrines, in the Saudi view, include not only international communist and socialist ideologies but radical Arab nationalist doctrines as well. All are seen as atheist doctrines seeking the destruction of Islamic society and of religion itself. Thus to the Saudis they are at least as great a threat as Zionism to Islam and the Islamic social and political order Saudi Arabia seeks to maintain.

Since Zionism and Communism are seen as threats not only against the Arab political order but against Islam itself, the Saudi regime has in the last few years begun to look on the Hajj as an appropriate forum for speaking out against them. At a speech during his annual banquet for the heads of the Hajj delegations and other honored guests during the 1966 Hajj, King Fayṣal said:

> In our call for Islam, for the pursuit of God's books and His Prophet's Sunnah, we encountered allegations, opposition and muddling. However, as your brother, I am telling you now, frankly, that what we call for is Muslim rapprochement, love, cooperation and mutual assistance in all their needs of life in this world and the hereafter. It is not our intention at all that Muslims commit aggression against anyone. We do not wrong believers and monotheists [i.e., Christians, Muslims, and Jews] no matter what their color, race or doctrine. However, we urge our Muslim brothers to be [as] one hand, observe the Qur'ān and the Sunnah and neglect any system, ideology or positive [i.e., secular] law which contradicts the Qur'ān and the Sunnah.
>
> If this call, brothers, offends or displeases certain circles and some evil powers like imperialism, Communism and Zionism, I am absolutely sure that Muslims will not be feeble, and will not fail to support the right, uphold their religion, unify their ranks, and cooperate in righteousness and piety.[72]

Since the Arab defeat in the June 1967 war, the Zionist threat has emerged as the principal theme of public statements and radio and press commentary during the Hajj. Saudi bitterness at the outcome of the June war was particularly acute because of Israel's occupation of the old city of Jerusalem. In it is located the Aqṣá Mosque, the third most holy site in orthodox Islam after the Harem Mosque in Makkah and the Prophet's Mosque in al-Madīnah. In one impassioned speech at the 1968 annual banquet for distinguished Hajjis (the first Hajj after the June 1967 war), the late King Fayṣal vehemently denounced the desecration of the Muslim holy places, in particular the "Third Holy Mosque," and the allegedly criminal actions directed by Israeli authorities against the Arab population of the occupied territories. He insisted that the Muslim shrines belong not just to Arabs but to all Muslims and called upon them to rise up and defend their faith and their profaned sanctuaries.[73]

During the Saudi radio coverage of Standing Day that year, a Jordanian commentator, Ibrāhīm Zayid al-Kilani, was permitted to broadcast denunciations of Israel and Zionism with vehemence never heard before during Hajj broadcasts.[74]

At the annual Hajj banquet the following year King Fayṣal first called for jihād or holy war to liberate Palestine and the Muslim holy places of Jerusalem.[75] Also during the 1969 Hajj the Palestinian commando group Fataḥ was allowed to distribute literature giving the theological justification for its actions and to solicit contributions. One of the booklets, which came into the writer's possession, contained fatwás by the chief qādī (Islamic judge) of Saudi Arabia and Islamic leaders of Egypt, Iraq, and Iran, declaring it the duty of all Muslims to support the commandos and calling for jihād. The call for jihād has been repeated during subsequent Hajj seasons.[76]

In sum, despite Saudi policy to ban secular politics from the Hajj, an element of politics has been in fact reintroduced in recent years in the form of public statements against Zionism and Communism. To the Saudis, however, the Zionist-Communist threat is not so much a question of secular politics as of the survival of Islamic society.

7. The Hajj Today

A PERIOD OF CHANGE

Like many historical institutions, the Hajj has changed more in the last fifty years than in the rest of its 1,300 years combined. Although there were signs of change during the late Ottoman and Hashimite periods, the major transformation of the secular aspects of the Hajj took place under the Saudis. From a colorful but hazardous medieval religious undertaking, the Hajj has become a gigantic exercise in organized religious tourism.[1]

One of the most visible changes is in transportation. The Hajj camel caravans from Egypt, Damascus, and Yemen, and, in the case of the first two, their gaily decorated maḥmals, have been replaced by modern trucks, buses, and motorcars traveling largely paved roads. Physical security along the route, a sometime thing in the past, is now taken for granted. Yet both overland and sea travel to the Hajj have been surpassed in magnitude by air travel, a thing almost unknown fifty years ago. Modern jets land, discharge Hajj passengers, and take off again from Jiddah airport at a rate of over 300 movements a day. Once in Saudi Arabia, moreover, buses and motorcars carry Hajjis to prearranged destinations for each stage of their sojourn, guided at some points by closed circuit television traffic control.

The length and nature of the Hajj visit have also changed. The average stay, including a visit to al-Madīnah, has been reduced from a period of months and even years to a period of several weeks. Whereas Hajjis formerly made their own travel and living arrangements, albeit with the advice and assistance of their muṭawwif, today each step of the Hajj is prearranged from the time they arrive to the time they depart, and for many from the time they leave home until the time they return.

The impact of the Hajj on Saudi Arabia has also changed greatly in the last fifty years. At the time the Hijaz was conquered by ʿAbd al-ʿAzīz, the Hajj was the mainstay of the Hijazi economy as well as the most important single factor in its politics. Sociologically the Hajj had over the centuries made a melting pot of the Hijaz, bringing together peoples from all over the Muslim world. In brief it was almost impossible to think about the Hijaz without also thinking about the Hajj.

Even in the early years of the Saudi regime, the Hajj retained a central role in the economics of not just the Hijaz but Saudi Arabia as a whole. Until after World War II, when oil revenues transformed Saudi Arabia from one of the poorest to one of the wealthiest states in the world, the preoccupation of the government and business community alike centered around how large the Hajj receipts would be for a given year.

Today Hajj receipts are insignificant as a source of government revenue compared to oil receipts. The Saudi government probably spends more than it earns on the Hajj. At the same time the combination of what the Hajjis spend and what the government spends has continued to make the Hajj the pivotal season in the Saudi commercial year—somewhat analogous to the Christmas season in the United States, only more so. Thus while no longer a significant factor in the Saudi economy as a whole, the Hajj is still the most important single commercial event of the year. Moreover in terms of manpower and the labor force, while the oil industry may have a higher payroll, more people are employed in providing services for the Hajj, whether full or part time, private or government employees, than any other economic activity in the country.

Sociologically the Hijaz is no longer the melting pot that the Hajj once made it. Stricter Saudi immigration regulations and improved Hajj administration have better enabled Saudi officials to insure that Hajjis depart the country after the Hajj is over. However with the ever increasing number of non-Saudi Hajjis making the Hajj (479,000 in 1972, and 688,000 including non-Saudis resident in Saudi Arabia),[2] the Hajj is still helping to make Makkah and the Hijaz generally one of the most cosmopolitan areas in the East.

The most subtle change in the significance of the contemporary Hajj on Saudi Arabia has been its political impact. After taking over the Hijaz, King ʿAbd al-ʿAzīz worked hard to purge the Hajj of secular politics. This policy has been espoused to the present day. However since World War II, there has been a shift in the Saudi interpretation of which politics are purely secular and which are essentially Islamic in nature. Two ideologies have appeared on the Middle Eastern political scene which are alien to the Saudis' essentially Islamic perception of world order: Zionism and Marxist-socialist doctrines.

Saudi opposition to Zionism is, of course, focused on Israel. While respecting Judaism as one of the three chosen religions (together with Islam and Christianity), the Saudis have become even more embittered against Zionism since the June 1967 war, when

Israel seized the old city of Jerusalem including the Aqṣá Mosque, the third holiest site in Islam after Makkah and al-Madīnah.

In the Saudi view Marxist-socialist doctrines include not only international socialist doctrines but radical Arab nationalist doctrines as well. They are all seen as atheist doctrines seeking the destruction of Islamic society and of religion itself. Thus to the Saudis they are at least as great a threat as Zionism to the Islamic social order Saudi Arabia is attempting to preserve.

The Zionist and Communist threats have been major themes in Saudi foreign policy for the last decade. Since the threat is seen as not only against the Arab political order but also against Islam itself, the Saudi regime has in the last few years begun to look on the Hajj as an appropriate forum for speaking out against it. Emphasis in the early and middle 1960s was on the threat of Marxist-socialist doctrines, particularly radical Arab socialist doctrines, but after the June 1967 war there has been a decided emphasis on the Zionist threat. The tone of these attacks has been more measured since the October 1973 war but no less heart felt. Public statements of King Khalid, Prince Fahd, other Saudi and foreign dignitaries at the Hajj, and commentaries by the Saudi news media covering the event have been vehement in attacking Zionism. During the 1969 Hajj King Fayṣal first called for jihād or holy war against Israel. In sum, despite Saudi policy still calling for a ban of all secular politics at the Hajj, an element of politics has in fact been reintroduced. To the Saudis, however, the Zionist and Communist threats are not so much a question of secular politics as of the preservation of Islamic society.

Perhaps the greatest changes in the Hajj in the last fifty years are in its administration. The system the Saudis inherited from the Hashimites was still basically a traditional laissez faire system, largely self-administered by the Hajj service guilds. Far from regulating the guilds for the good of the Hajjis, the Hashimite government, and the Ottoman administration before it, joined the guilds in extracting as much financial advantage as possible from the Hajj. Today strict government regulations, including fixed or regulated prices, seek to safeguard the Hajjis from exploitation by the Hajj service industry. In addition the government now offers many direct administrative services for the aid and comfort of the Hajjis.

Among the first priorities of King ʿAbd al-ʿAzīz after taking over the Hijaz were reform of the administration of the Hajj and elimination of the exploitation of the Hajjis. Reform took the form of setting up administrative procedures to regulate the guilds for the

Hajjis' welfare rather than absorbing them directly into the government administration. This was in fact the only possible alternative at the time. Except for the rudimentary bureaucracy inherited from the Hashimites, King ʿAbd al-ʿAzīz really had no governmental machinery in which to incorporate Hajj administration. Saudi public administration and Hajj administration in large measure developed simultaneously, and in some cases Saudi national administrative institutions were actually preceded by and developed from Hajj administrative institutions. For example, the Ministry of Health had its origins in Hijazi public health institutions, created primarily for the Hajj. The national ministry was not established until 1951, and it was not until 1957 that it acquired full responsibility for sanitation and quarantine during the Hajj. Prior to that time they had been under international supervision. The Ministry of Hajj and Waqfs itself, the ministry with the major responsibility for administering the Hajj, was not established until the early 1960s.

As the ease and safety of making the Hajj increased, a result in part of both Hajj administrative reforms and great strides in transportation technology, the numbers of those making the Hajj also increased, and now exceed one and a half million a year. This in turn has placed new strains on the Hajj administrative machinery, which has required even more reforms. Thus the development of modern Hajj administration has not only contributed to the growth in the size of the Hajj, but that growth has also contributed to the development of modern Hajj administration.

HAJJ ADMINISTRATION: A BALANCE SHEET

One can readily find much to criticize and much that is praiseworthy in the current administration of the Hajj. There are many areas which could stand improvement and for which the gap between administrative procedure and actual operation is still quite wide. One of the greatest gaps is in the curative medical services and sanitation at the Hajj. Among the greatest sanitation problems is the mass slaughtering each year on the first day of the ʿĪd al-Aḍḥá. Another major problem arises from the huge crowds gathering for the various Hajj rites. So great are the crowds at the ṭawāfs and the lapidations at Miná, for example, that there is a constant danger of being crushed or trampled. Similarly the nafrah, during which all Hajjis move simultaneously from ʿArafāt to Muzdalifah, has become so large an undertaking that there is a constant threat that it will degenerate into a gigantic traffic jam, as happened in 1968. Despite strict government regulation, cases of gross exploitation of Hajjis by the Hajj service industry are also heard each year, such as overcharging for lodgings or transportation for latecomers, who have little choice but to pay if they wish to get to ʿArafāt in time for Standing Day.

Many of these and other shortcomings can be attributed to the still evolving state of Saudi public administration, which is often frustratingly cumbersome and slow. A major problem is a shortage of trained manpower. While Saudi Arabia has spent millions of dollars on improving health services, not only for the Hajj but for the entire country, there is still an acute shortage of doctors and medical technicians which will take many years to overcome. As an interim measure the Saudi government has hired several thousand Pakistani doctors and technicians, and since they are all Muslims, they can also serve at the Hajj. Shortages of trained manpower also exist in the other ministries and agencies dealing with the Hajj.

To a great extent, however, administrative problems at the Hajj have less to do with the quality of the bureaucracy than with the extremely adverse conditions under which it must so often work. For example, most of the Hajj rites are performed in the open, where fierce desert heat and large crowds make efforts to provide not only adequate health services but lodging and transportation all the more difficult. Many of the Hajjis are elderly, with low physical resistance, and a high proportion of them are illiterate and ignorant of modern hygiene, making efforts to serve them often very frustrating. The logistics of housing and transporting the Hajjis, moreover, are staggering. Great tent cities must be erected in ʿArafāt and Miná each year; food, water, and sanitation services provided; transportation prearranged; and all the while constant surveillance must be maintained lest Hajjis get lost in the crowds.

There is an additional problem in administering the Hajj. Although only a few of the rites are absolutely mandatory (wājib), tradition has dictated that they all be done, and done in a traditional manner. The Saudis, therefore, have been rather reluctant to alter the Hajj rites in order to improve administrative efficiency. To alter the nafrah, for example, in order to prevent traffic jams, or the lapidations at Miná to avoid the physical crush of people, or to reorganize the slaughtering at the ʿĪd al-Aḍḥá would almost certainly result in opposition from those who believe that it would be going against Muhammad's instructions at the Farewell Hajj.

Despite these problems, there is much that is praiseworthy about current Hajj administration. One has only to recall how the Hajj was administered fifty years ago to realize what great improvements have been made in recent years. The Hajj service industry has been brought under strict government regulation; an internal transportation system has been established which is both safe and cheap; and to correct shortcomings which do arise, a system for hearing complaints has been instituted which appears to work fairly well.

The task of evaluating current Hajj administration is not so much one of finding things to praise or criticize as of choosing an acceptable yardstick by which to measure them. In addressing the problem of finding a suitable yardstick, let us examine some of the more common criticisms voiced by Hajjis and the standards of judgment which they themselves used.

During the three years I spent in Saudi Arabia, 1967 through 1969, I asked many who had made the Hajj for their views about how well it was administered. Most of the criticisms I heard were of a personal nature—i.e., about shortcomings affecting individual Hajjis. In the main the Saudi government was held responsible not only for its direct administrative responsibilities but also for the Hajj service industry. Moreover most of the criticisms leveled at Hajj administration concentrated, as might be expected, on the end result of certain situations witnessed, rather than on an assessment of the factors, many of them quite adverse, which caused that result to come about. For example, few who criticized poor health conditions had considered the extremely adverse conditions under which health officials must work.

Those Hajjis most critical of Hajj administration were generally from the wealthier and better educated classes and appeared in many cases to judge the Hajj by the standards of their class rather than by those of the rank and file of their home countries. I am reminded in particular of the attractive wife of a Muslim diplomat in Jiddah, who articulated her criticisms of the Hajj so well that one tended to overlook the fact that her standard of judgment stemmed more from her British education and high place in society than the overall administrative practices found in her home country, much less in Saudi Arabia.

As for the poor Hajjis with whom I talked, many of whom had spent years saving for the trip, they were so happy to be there that it seldom occurred to them to complain (unless some personal tragedy had befallen them). Moreover for many of them the living standards at the Hajj were probably not much worse, and in some cases perhaps even slightly better, than what they experienced at home.

In short, most of the criticisms of exploitation and inefficiency which Hajjis expressed to me were based on very high standards of judgment. It is my view that if judged instead by the standards of public administration generally found in developing countries—and most Muslim countries fall into that category—the Hajj is administered rather well.

Even by Western standards, moreover, it is not so bad. By way of comparison, let us consider how well the state of Virginia[3] would administer a month-long gathering in Williamsburg of over one million people from more than seventy-five countries, most of whom did not speak English and were probably illiterate in any language. Those not coming overland would all enter (and clog up) the sea and airports of Norfolk; they would all spend several nights in the open at Jamestown and points between there and Williamsburg (about the same distance as between Makkah and ʿArafāt); and after slaughtering 1,000,000 sheep or cows (we will omit camels), they would disperse, many to travel across the state to visit Charlottesville. In order to compensate for the lack of Makkah's desert climate, let us say that the gathering was being conducted in midwinter in a snow storm. Finally, to administer the Hajj and keep the local merchants from exploiting the visitors, only Virginia state officials could be used. For all the administrative expertise we have developed in the West, I am inclined to believe that serious administrative problems would plague the whole affair from start to finish, even if it were done on a yearly basis.

The point to emphasize in my view, therefore, is not the admitted inadequacies of the administration of the Hajj, but the fact that it is administered as well as it is, given the monumental size of the logistical problems involved and the still early stage of development of administrative expertise in Saudi Arabia.

LOOKING TO THE FUTURE

D. van der Meulen, who was for many years the Dutch consul in Jiddah and thus responsible in part for Indonesian Hajjis then under Dutch colonial rule, wrote of the pre-World War II period:

> All our attention was concentrated on the pilgrimage (which was the major source of Saudi Government revenue at the

> time) and most of the local conversation turned on that problem. Would the *hajj* increase in importance in the world of Islam or would obedience to the fifth pillar of the faith decrease? Would the amelioration of conditions in the Holy Land draw more pilgrims to Mecca or would it make this road to salvation lose its value? The better hygiene conditions, a modernized transport system, security, in short a streamlining of the *hajj* in conformity with the rest of the world—would it attract greater numbers of believers?[4]

Van der Meulen's verdict was that it would not; that in making the Hajj a comparatively safe, healthy, and easy undertaking, the Saudis had made it spiritually cheap as well.[5]

The intervening years have proved otherwise. Nearly every year since World War II the number of non-Saudi Hajjis has increased. Moreover the number is expected to continue to increase until it reaches a saturation point early in the next century. In a recent detailed study of the future prospects of the Hijaz, a British consulting firm estimated that by the year 2006, the number making the Hajj will reach three million, the maximum number of Hajjis which can be accommodated on the land available at Miná and ʿArafāt. The study concluded that this figure would have been reached sooner, based on present trends, but as the saturation point nears, the rate of increase is expected to slow down. By 1991 it was estimated that the number of non-Saudi Hajjis would be about 1.2 million and the number of Saudi Hajjis another 920,000.[6]

Even if the rate of increase is not as fast as the study predicts, the chances that the number of Hajjis will continue to grow at a rapid pace over the next several decades appear almost certain. One might well ask why, in a world of increasing secularism, this is so. It seems more logical to assume that as living standards in the Muslim world rise generally, spirituality, together with an interest in making the Hajj, would decrease.

This assumption might be partially true for the elite and rising middle classes, although even among them Islam probably has a stronger hold than outward appearances might indicate. For the poor and elderly, however, religious fervor does not seem to have abated. In the case of the elderly, the motivation to make the Hajj is enhanced by the desire to prepare for the hereafter. Many Muslims even believe that to die on the Hajj guarantees passage into heaven. For the poor, who appear to make up the highest proportion of the Hajjis,[7] God's generosity still holds more promise than a secular society in which they have been able to obtain few material benefits. It is this class, still highly motivated by Islam, which has most benefited from the great reduction in the cost of the Hajj. Just as thirty-five years ago few would have envisioned working-class Americans flocking to Europe on cheap charter package tours, few would have envisioned cheap Hajj package tours catering primarily to the poor of the Muslim world. And yet that appears to be what has happened.

If the Hajj is to increase so dramatically in size, how able will Saudi Arabia be to cope with it? In terms of physical infrastructure the country appears to be in fairly good shape. The planned new Jiddah international airport will not only be capable of carrying more air traffic, but according to present plans a separate Hajj reception center will be built from which Hajjis will go directly to Makkah, thus alleviating traffic congestion in Jiddah itself. In addition al-Ṭāʾif airport could be upgraded to take international traffic without too much difficulty if the need arose. Port and road facilities, given ongoing expansion programs for both, are also considered adequate for the present; and only minor improvements will be needed in the future.[8]

The present Hajj administrative structure—a highly regulated private Hajj service industry augmented by direct government administrative services—also appears adequate for the future. It is occasionally suggested that the Hajj service industry be taken over completely by the Saudi government in order to eliminate exploitation of the Hajjis and increase efficiency. It is difficult to see how another layer of government bureaucracy could provide services more efficiently than private businessmen spurred by competition, particularly since the Saudi government, lacking any expertise of its own, would have to hire as government bureaucrats the same people who are already running it. The human avarice which is behind the exploitation of Hajjis will doubtlessly never be eliminated under any structure and will always require surveillance.

Although as a general rule the more bureaucratic the administrative structure the less the efficiency, the real heart of the problem of Hajj administration is the quality of the administrators. With all the attention being given in Saudi Arabia to training and education, one may hope that many current shortcomings of Hajj administration will be eliminated as the quality of public administration in Saudi Arabia improves generally.

There is one way, however, in which the predicted increase in numbers could seriously affect the Hajj—by making it almost physically impossible for Hajjis to have room to perform the prescribed rites. There are already examples of how large crowds can impede such performance. The heavy traffic during the nafrah which caused the huge traffic jam in 1968 and the overtaxing of facilities for slaughtering animals on the first day of the ʿĪd al-Aḍḥá in 1972 are two dramatic examples. Performing the ṭawāf and the saʿy at the height of the Hajj and stoning the Jamrat al-ʿAqabah are also very difficult, sometimes even resulting in bodily injury, because of crowds. Consider how much more congested the sites will be with three million instead of one and a half million Hajjis.

Administrative considerations have already come to play almost as important a role as theological considerations in how the Hajj rites are performed, despite the hold of tradition. As the number of Hajjis increases, more adjustments will almost certainly have to be made in order for everyone to be able to observe the required rites. Such changes will probably be in the nature of greater regimentation and prohibition of optional observances. For example, private autos to and from ʿArafāt, especially during the nafrah, may have to be banned completely (there is already a partial ban); and Hajjis may have to be assigned a special time to make the sacrifice in order to distribute the slaughtering more evenly throughout the entire ʿĪd al-Aḍḥá period.

Since, as we have mentioned, changing the manner in which the Hajj rites are observed is almost certain to meet with resistance from Muslim traditionalists, such changes will probably come about gradually, and only as the need for them can no longer be ignored. Still, only four rites are mandatory (wājib): iḥrām, ṭawāf, saʿy, and wuqūf (to which the Shāfiʿīs add taḥallul). So long as these are met, the Hajji can in good conscience ask God to accept his Hajj as the fulfillment of his obligation of the Fifth Pillar of Islam.

On balance, the Hajj is a remarkable synthesis of sacred and secular, of old and new. It combines extreme piety and devotion to religious duty with unadorned commercialism, public administration with private enterprise, and even religion with politics. Perhaps the greatest synthesis of all is the shared experience of over one million Hajjis a year from all corners of the Muslim world.

The Hajj is also a synthesis of constancy and change. Balanced with the monumental changes which have taken place in the last fifty years, the Hajj has also been a major constant around which the political history of the Hijaz has ebbed and flowed since the beginning of Islam. The caliphs, Ottomans, Egyptians, and Hashimites have all come and gone, but the Hajj remains, now administered by Saudi Arabia.

With the rapid social, economic, and political changes which are now sweeping the Middle East, it is next to impossible to predict what the future holds in store for the Hijaz and Saudi Arabia as a whole. Whatever the political future, however, the Hajj is certain to remain not only a major religious event, but a major administrative responsibility and challenge as well.

APPENDIX A
Hajj Statistics

According to pious legend, the number of Hajjis at ʿArafāt was always a constant of 700,000—the difference between the actual number there and the ideal being made up by the angels.[1] Within the last generation and quite without angelic assistance the number has far exceeded 700,000 and is now over one million.

Only the most general references, however, have been made to Hajj statistics in the text of this study. The principal reason is that for most of the period under review, they are far too unreliable to form the basis of any meaningful statistical analysis. This appendix, therefore, is more of an analysis of the statistics than a statistical analysis.

Prior to the nineteenth century Hajjis reportedly tried to hide their numbers from European colonial powers in order to prevent them from learning more about Hajj travel.[2] But during the nineteenth century colonial administrators began a more precise count of those under their jurisdiction making the Hajj. Moreover European observers, such as Burkhardt and Burton, who made the Hajj, greatly added to Western perceptions of its magnitude, and toward the latter part of the century the quarantine stations established by or at least operated under the provisions of the international sanitation conventions also began to keep records.

Still, these early figures were little more than rough guesses. Not only was the state of the art of statistics far more primitive, but there were certain built-in obstacles which no longer exist today. One was that, while the quarantine authorities could get a fairly accurate idea of the number of seaborne Hajjis, all of whom they processed, there was no similarly effective means of counting overland Hajjis. A second problem was that little accurate means existed to distinguish between foreign and local Hajjis. Some idea existed of how many came each year, particularly by sea (and also by rail during the few years that the Hijaz Railway was in operation), but there was little way of knowing how many foreign Hajjis were resident in the area. Hajjis tended to stay longer in those days, sometimes a year or more. Others never left. For the latter it would have been very difficult to determine, even if the means were available, at what point one ceased being a foreign Hajji and became a permanent resident of Makkah.

Finally, changes in political boundaries over the years have reduced the comparability of earlier figures with more recent ones. Many Saudi Hajjis, whose numbers are now kept separate from non-Saudi Hajjis, come from areas which prior to the consolidation of Saudi Arabia by King ʿAbd al-ʿAzīz would have been considered foreign.

Since World War II, and particularly in the last ten years, the quality of Hajj statistics has greatly improved. Not only are procedures better, but the streamlining of the entire Hajj has made keeping track of foreign Hajjis easier also.

There have also been signs of improvement in estimating the number of local Hajjis, always a difficult task since neither Saudis nor resident aliens have to register with a muṭawwif or other official to make the Hajj as foreigners have to do. In the 1972 Hajj statistics the number of local Hajjis (562,688) was down from previous years, probably a sign of better counting than of fewer Hajjis. Moreover this figure was further broken down into Saudi Hajjis (353,480) and resident non-Saudis (209,208). If the latter figure is added to the number of non-Saudis entering the country for the Hajj (479,339), the total of non-Saudis making the Hajj in 1972 (688,547) is half again as large as the arrival figures indicate.[3]

Bearing these difficulties and discrepancies in mind, Table 2 is presented as a rough estimate of foreign arrivals for the Hajj between 1807 and 1942.

We can see from the figures that both World War I and King ʿAbd al-ʿAzīz's conquest of the Hijaz cut deeply into Hajj attendance, and that the Great Depression years of the 1930s and World War II resulted in additional setbacks. It is also noteworthy that, although sea travel gained steadily in popularity, overland travel held its own until after World War I. Many of the overland Hajjis, of course, came from Najd, in Saudi Arabia, and would no longer be included in figures of foreign arrivals.

Table 3 cites Hajj arrivals from foreign countries for the years 1943 through 1972. Since the figures are all based on official Saudi statistics, they are not rounded off to the nearest 1,000, as was generally done in Table 2.

A glance at Table 3 reveals steady overall growth after about 1947, with the exception of a brief period in the early 1960s. The number of Hajjis has generally increased from all Muslim states, but nearly every year there is a drastic decrease or increase in the number of Hajjis from one or more particular countries, usually for political reasons, such as wars or crises, or economic reasons, such as a state's policy to limit Hajjis in order to save foreign exchange. For example, the number of Yemeni Hajjis dropped from 28,885 in

TABLE 2
Hajj Arrival Figures for Selected Years, 1807–1942

Year	By Sea	By Land	Total
1807	—	—	83,000
1831	33,000	79,000	112,000
1865	—	—	90,000
1869	24,000	86,000	110,000
1870	41,000	159,000	200,000
1872	—	—	—
1873	40,000 (Jiddah)	—	150,000
1874	—	—	166,000
1877	46,000	154,000	200,000
1880	60,000 (Jiddah)	—	—
1881	38,000 (Jiddah)	—	—
1882	26,000	44,000	70,000
1884	—	—	51,000
1885	53,000	67,000	120,000
1886	27,000	—	—
1887	46,000	94,000	140,000
1890	—	—	132,000
1893	96,000	106,000	202,000
1905	—	76,000	—
1906	—	—	195,000
1907	—	—	250,000
1908	84,000	105,000	200,000
1909	—	—	300,000
1910	—	—	310,000
1911	90,000	27,000	117,000
1912	100,000	200,000	300,000
1913	—	—	140,000
1914	—	50,000 (Jiddah)	—
1917	—	—	60,000
1918	—	20,000 (Jiddah)	—
1919	—	20,000 (Jiddah)	—
1920	58,000	11,000	69,000
1921	60,000[a]	11,000	71,000
1922	58,000	12,000	70,000
1923	66,000	11,000	77,000
1924	92,000	9,000	101,000
1925	3,000	75,000[b]	78,000[b]
1926	57,000	20,000	77,000

TABLE 2—*Continued*

Year	By Sea	By Land	Total
1927	150,000[c]	27,000	150,000
1928	97,000	50,000	147,000
1929	90,000	58,000	148,000
1930	84,000	33,000	116,000
1931	50,000	34,000	84,000
1932	29,000	11,000	40,000
1933	19,500	1,000	20,500
1934	22,000	3,000	25,000
1935	30,000	4,000	34,000
1936	33,000	47,000	80,000
1937	49,000	1,000	50,000
1938	64,000	3,000	67,000
1939	49,000	10,000	59,000
1940	32,000	4,000	36,000
1941 (Jan.)	9,000	1,000	10,000
1941 (Dec.)	24,000	16,000	40,000
1942	25,000	—	—

[a] Of which 57,000 landed at Jiddah.

[b] A high proportion of this total was actually comprised of Najdi Hajjis, many of whom had not been able to make the Hajj in the last years of King Ḥusayn's reign.

[c] Of which about 126,000 landed at Jiddah.

1966 to 2,095 in 1967, mainly because of the Yemeni civil war; it then increased to 31,489 in 1968 and 51,577 in 1969. Likewise the number of Hajjis from the Sudan increased 96 percent in 1972, from 14,865 the previous year to 29,004, largely as a result of a stabilization of internal politics. Turkey and Iran have also had major fluctuations in recent years.

Over the longer run the number of Hajjis from some countries is very large for years, and then recedes as political, economic, and perhaps sociological factors change. For example, up to the 1930s the largest single group of Hajjis came from Indonesia. In 1927 they numbered 52,410 according to one source[4] and according to another source numbered 65,000 the following year.[5] Although still sending between 15,000 and 23,000 per year, Indonesia has dropped off to ninth place in 1972. On the other hand the Hajjis from India and Pakistan combined still constitute a large number as, when

TABLE 3
Foreign Hajj Arrivals, 1943–1972

Year	Total	Year	Total
1943	62,590	1958	206,399[a]
1944	37,857	1959	204,403[a]
1945	37,630	1960	266,100[a]
1946	61,286	1961	285,948[a]
1947	55,244	1962	216,455[a]
1948	75,614	1963	197,141[a]
1949	99,069	1964	260,284[a]
1950	107,652	1965	283,319
1951	100,578	1966	294,118
1952	148,515	1967	316,226
1953	149,841	1968	318,507
1954	164,072	1969	374,784
1955	232,971	1970	406,295
1956	200,722[a]	1971	431,270
1957	215,565[a]	1972	479,339

[a]Total differs in one or more official set of statistics.

British India, they did before World War II. Table 4 shows the top twenty countries for 1972 and the number of Hajjis from each over the last eight years plus 1928 (a big year) and 1933 (a small year due to the Great Depression).

In the early post-World War II period, sea travel had become the most widely used means of transportation to the Hajj. As international air transportation began to come into its own, however, air travel began to challenge sea travel and surpassed it after the closure of the Suez Canal in 1967, which considerably reduced Hajj sea traffic from the Mediterranean. Given the increased efficiency of air travel and the fact that many state-owned airlines stand to gain by the Hajj traffic, air travel would probably have surpassed sea travel at any rate by about 1970.

Overland traffic at first diminished after World War II in favor of sea and air travel, but as new paved roads have begun stringing out across the Middle East, it has made a comeback. Most Iraqi, Jordanian, Syrian, and Kuwaiti Hajjis come by road, and until the last few years most Turkish Hajjis did also. Probably the greatest drawbacks to overland travel are political (Hajjis must cross international borders) and economic (package tours using state-owned airlines

TABLE 4
The Top Twenty States Sending Hajjis in 1972 and their Record in Past Years

Rank	State	1972	1971	1970	1969
1.	Yemen (YAR)	60,358	50,269	54,658	51,577
2.	Nigeria	44,061	35,187	24,185	16,177
3.	Iran	30,299	48,367	15,132	13,642
4.	Egypt	29,171	11,490	10,875	12,413
5.	Sudan	29,004	14,865	20,495	21,649
6.	Syria	27,045	42,339	22,383	12,814
7.	Turkey	23,922	13,269	56,578	51,055
8.	Pakistan	23,344	38,256	28,535	27,402
9.	Indonesia	22,753	14,633	10,615	17,062
10.	Iraq	17,628	19,482	24,902	24,857
11.	Libya	16,861	11,835	13,547	16,565
12.	India	16,657	16,470	16,057	15,154
13.	Jordan	15,933	10,909	6,376	5,179
14.	Morocco	15,463	10,640	10,943	9,449
15.	Afghanistan	10,744	13,663	9,125	8,744
16.	Malaysia	10,650	10,361	8,353	6,591
17.	Yemen (Aden)	9,320	7,103	10,310	7,865
18.	Algeria	8,894	3,936	8,537	7,053
19.	Kuwait	8,370	8,072	6,935	6,684
20.	Tunisia	7,500	4,207	2,016	1,349

[a]In 1928 and 1933 Pakistan was part of India.

save foreign exchange for the home state), rather than the condition of the roads. Table 5 shows the means of transportation used by Hajjis from outside Saudi Arabia since 1956.

The last three tables are presented as a profile of the 1972 Hajj, the last one held before the completion of this study. Table 6 gives a complete breakdown of Hajjis by country for 1972 and the four preceding years. Table 7 gives breakdowns of resident and non-resident Hajjis and Saudi and non-Saudi Hajjis for 1972. Finally, Table 8 gives a breakdown of the number of Hajjis both by sex and mode of transportation.

From it one can see that men outnumber women almost two to one. In comparison with male Hajjis, proportionately more women come from Africa and fewer from Asia among the major Muslim states; and proportionately more women come by sea than over-

.968	1967	1966	1933	1928
31,498	2,095	28,885	2,504	1,242
10,790	8,535	7,623	—	—
22,903	35,334	24,937	586	3,403
7,134	10,005	19,495	1,625	14,099
18,035	20,168	6,454	420	1,104
14,521	19,208	18,458	504	1,109
41,998	39,309	24,984	52	875
25,052	23,951	8,694	[a]	[a]
17,569	16,130	15,291	2,417	49,394
19,475	20,519	18,338	149	528
10,444	18,326	14,788	—	—
15,826	15,865	16,006	7,040[a]	13,781[a]
4,449	7,380	10,434	—	—
8,208	8,266	11,242	1,284	2,825
5,841	5,740	2,190	2,403	2,022
6,226	6,718	6,639	—	—
1,569	4,148	3,381	17	—
4,663	6,609	11,442	—	—
8,783	6,677	5,660	—	—
1,015	630	535	—	—

land or by air. Finally, Table 9 shows the number of Hajjis arriving on specified dates during the 1972 Hajj season. Over half the Hajjis arrived in the last twelve days, a sign of the generally shorter period of stay over previous years.

SOURCES

The tables and figures used in this appendix were gathered from many sources, only the principal ones of which will be mentioned. For the early figures, used in Table 2, the principal source is Carl Rathjens, *Die Pilgerfahrt nach Mekka.* Rathjens's figures are themselves compiled from numerous sources, from which he chose what he believed to be the best or else used the average from sev-

TABLE 5
Mode of Travel by Hajjis from Abroad

Year A.H.	Year A.D.	Sea	Air	Land	Total
1375	1956	124,087	31,141	45,595[a]	200,722
1376	1957	114,317	43,758	57,490	215,565
1377	1958	122,169	32,047	52,183	206,399
1378	1959	114,452	31,724	58,227	204,403
1379	1960	128,883	50,825	86,392	266,100
1380	1961	149,834	51,030	85,084	285,948
1381	1962	92,943	54,580	69,032	216,455
1382	1963	80,840	60,261	56,040	197,141
1383	1964	105,604	85,369	69,311	260,284
1384	1965	128,498	83,478	71,343	283,319
1385	1966	101,406	90,980	101,732	294,118
1386	1967	113,391	107,103	95,732	316,226
1387	1968	83,984	119,194	115,339	318,507
1388	1969	94,248	129,744	150,792	374,784
1389	1970	90,992	144,972	170,331	406,295
1390	1971	84,574	208,663	138,060	431,270
1391	1972	99,023	238,658	141,658	479,339

[a]Some official statistics make this figure 15,494 and the total for 1964, 170,722.

eral sources. Also used was Firmen Duguet, *Le Pèlerinage de la Mecque au point de vue religieux sociale et sanitaire*, especially for estimates of Hajj attendance at the turn of the century. For the 1920s and 1930s I used figures from Eldon Rutter, "The Muslim Pilgrimage"; H.U.W. Stanton and Claude Leon Pickens, "The Mecca Pilgrimage"; and D. van der Meulen, "Importance of the Mecca Pilgrimage." For the years 1928–38 the *Rapports sur le Pelerinage du Hadjaz* of the Counseil Sanitaire Maritime et Quarantenaire d'Egypte (Egyptian Quarantine Board) were very helpful, although they contained only figures for Hajjis traveling by sea. A number of totals were cited in *Umm al-Qurá*, the official Saudi gazette. There are also some official Saudi statistics dating back to 1928, but since they appeared to coincide with figures of Hajjis coming by sea reflected both in the *Rapports* and Rathjens, I generally used the latter's overall figures for the 1930s.

For post-World War II figures I used official Saudi statistics. Most

TABLE 6
Comparative Figures by Country, 1968–1972

Country	1387 (1968)	1388 (1969)	1389 (1970)	1390 (1971)	1391 (1972)
Abu Dhabi	2,029	441	672	815	721
Afghanistan	5,841	8,744	9,125	13,663	10,744
Ajman	32	38	32	61	47
Algeria	4,663	7,053	8,537	3,936	8,894
Bahrain	2,573	1,974	1,940	2,418	2,287
Britain	759	573	696	786	834
Cambodia	80	80	80	1	4
Cameroon	631	1,263	1,244	808	916
Central African Republic		129	262	151	229
Ceylon	462	450	472	152	40
Chad	2,236	3,065	4,271	2,034	4,806
Dahomey	164	214	356	468	475
Dubai	151	193	207	355	180
Egypt	7,134	12,413	10,875	11,490	29,171
Ethiopia	2,329	1,840	2,349	2,955	2,317
France	302	346	341	372	514
Fujayrah	2	—	10	27	[a]
Gambia	276	285	379	263	389
Ghana	248	295	518	402	443
Greece	85	183	147	223	235
Guinea	2,573	1,616	1,786	2,630	2,168
India	15,836	19,854	16,057	16,470	16,657
Indonesia	17,569	17,062	10,615	14,633	22,753
Iran	22,903	13,642	15,132	48,367	30,299
Iraq	19,475	24,857	24,902	19,482	17,628
Ivory Coast	614	597	683	567	997
Jordan	4,449	5,139	6,376	10,909	15,933
Kenya	355	326	333	467	500
Kuwait	8,783	6,684	6,935	8,072	8,370
Lebanon	3,563	3,901	4,570	6,712	6,404
Liberia	33	48	126	85	60
Libya	10,444	16,565	13,547	11,835	16,861
Malagasy	91	32	20	31	37
Malaysia	6,236	6,591	8,353	10,361	10,650
Mali	916	1,010	998	1,123	1,226
Mauritania	437	4,048	316	724	792
Mauritius	4	45	59	111	131
Morocco	8,208	9,449	10,043	10,640	15,463
Nationalist China (Taiwan)	6	8	8	11	11

TABLE 6—*Continued* Country	1387 (1968)	1388 (1969)	1389 (1970)	1390 (1971)	1391 (1972)
Nepal	52	79	94	—	1
Niger	2,383	2,058	2,810	1,827	3,206
Nigeria	10,790	16,177	24,185	35,187	44,061
Oman	2,186	1,617	1,826	1,569	2,262
Pakistan	25,052	27,402	28,535	38,256	23,344
Palestine	780	536	496	838	901
Philippines	4,072	2,823	1,765	150	221
Portugal	29	41	51	79	56
Qatar	2,017	1,690	1,131	1,392	1,216
Ras al-Khaymah	11	24	37	87	40
Senegal	2,011	2,067	2,097	2,422	2,569
Sharjah	18	29	42	62	44
Sierra Leone	84	188	284	353	391
Singapore	158	255	391	404	370
Somalia	2,199	1,517	1,457	190	1,502
South Africa	1,580	1,333	1,426	1,951	2,285
South Vietnam	34	164	1	71	27
Spain	[b]	[b]	[b]	[b]	106
Sudan	18,035	21,649	20,495	14,865	29,004
Syria	14,521	12,814	22,383	42,339	27,045
Tanzania	579	392	309	331	544
Thailand	—	2,399	4,263	4,981	2,448
Togo	62	50	94	111	140
Tunisia	1,015	1,349	2,016	4,207	7,500
Turkey	41,998	51,055	56,578	13,269	23,922
Uganda	348	400	408	950	760
Umm al-Qaywayn	—	3	2	—	[a]
Upper Volta	659	1,184	630	540	869
Yemen (Aden)	1,569	7,865	10,310	7,103	9,320
Yemen (YAR)	31,489	51,577	54,658	50,269	60,358
Yugoslavia	1,317	1,554	1,517	2,211	2,734
Zaire (Congo Kinshasa)	18	23	7	7	20
Other Asian countries	393	418	428	256	116
Other African countries	72	74	137	126	97
Other European countries	77	42	38	27	37
Other countries	64	2	970	41	1,477
American countries	—	92	52	84	137
Totals	318,507	374,784	406,295	431,270	479,339

[a]Totals for Umm al-Qaywayn and Fujayrah are listed jointly: 23.
[b]Totals for Spain in past years not avilable.

TABLE 7
Total Number of Hajjis in 1972

From	Saudi	Non-Saudi	Total
Makkah	128,347	50,031	178,378
Saudi Arabia (excluding Makkah)	225,113	159,177	384,290
Abroad			479,339
Total	353,460	209,208	1,042,007

of these appeared in the annual *Pilgrims Statistics*, published after each Hajj by the General Directorate of Passports and Nationality of the Saudi Ministry of Interior. Some figures also appeared in various issues of the Saudi Arabian Monetary Agency's *Annual Report*. Also after each Hajj most of the official figures are published in the Saudi press. Not all of these figures agree, especially for the years 1956–64, and in such cases I used the figures which most closely agreed with other published statistical information.

TABLE 8
Attendance at the 1972 Hajj by Sex and Mode of Transportation

Region	Sea	Air	Land	Total
Arab States				
Male	16,122	64,479	85,283	165,879
Female	9,125	46,879	37,789	93,793
Total	25,247	111,351	123,072	259,672
Other Asian States				
Male	35,387	46,531	12,224	94,142
Female	23,781	20,388	3,296	47,465
Total	59,168	66,919	15,520	141,607
Other African States				
Male	7,996	35,542	56	43,594
Female	6,586	21,736	14	28,336
Total	14,582	57,278	70	71,930
European States				
Male	8	2,341	1,440	3,789
Female	2	600	125	727
Total	10	2,941	1,565	4,516
American States				
Male	2	98	8	108
Female	—	29	—	29
Total	2	127	8	137
Other States				
Male	14	27	992	963
Female	—	13	501	514
Total	14	40	1,423	1,477
Total				
Male	59,529	149,013	99,933	308,475
Female	39,494	89,045	41,725	170,864
Grand Total	99,023	238,658	141,658	479,339

TABLE 9
Chronology of Pilgrimage Arrivals

A.H.	A.D.	Total (Cumulative)
4/11/1391	12/31/71	31,129
15/11/1391	1/1/72	54,617
21/11/1391	1/7/72	118,363
25/11/1391	1/11/72	190,708
26/11/1391	1/12/72	220,447
28/11/1391	1/14/72	264,702
29/11/1391	1/15/72	292,794
30/11/1391	1/16/72	317,938
2/12/1391	1/18/72	364,781
5/12/1391	1/21/72	440,550
7/12/1391	1/23/72	447,929
8/12/1391 [a]	1/24/72 [a]	479,339

[a] Last day Hajjis permitted to arrive.

APPENDIX B
Glossary

The following Arabic transliteration system has been used.

ء	ʾ	غ	gh
ا	ā	ف	f
ب	b	ق	q
ت	t	ل	l
ث	th	م	m
ج	j	ن	n
ح	ḥ	ه	h
خ	kh	و	w
د	d	ي	y
ذ	dh	ى	á
ر	r	ـَوْ	aw
ز	z	ـَيْ	ay
س	s	ـِي	ī
ش	sh	ـُو	ū
ص	ṣ	ـَة	ah (in pause) at (in construct)
ض	ḍ		
ط	ṭ		
ظ	ẓ		
ع	ʿ		

Adillāʾ	Plural of dalīl.
ʿArafāt	An arid, gravelly plain near Makkah where one must be standing on the afternoon of 9 Dhū al-Ḥijjah, Standing Day, in order for the Hajj to be valid.
Dalīl	(pl. adillāʾ) (lit. guide) A member of a guild in al-Madīnah who looks after visitors to that city, particularly during the Hajj season.
Dhū al-Ḥijjah	The twelfth month of the Muslim lunar calendar. The high point of the Hajj is 9 Dhū al-Ḥijjah, Standing Day.
Ghusl	The ritual ablution that forms a part of the iḥrām ceremonies. All of the body may be washed; or if that is not possible, a limited ablution may be performed

	(wudū'); or if no water is available, a "dry ablution" may be performed (tayammum).
Ifāḍah	(lit. pouring forth) The mass exodus from 'Arafāt to Muzdalifah after sunset on Standing Day, also called the nafrah. Tawāf al-ifāḍah: The circumambulation of the Ka'bah performed on 10 Dhū al-Ḥijjah.
Ḥajj	The Great Pilgrimage to Makkah. It may be performed alone (ifrād) or together with the 'Umrah, the Lesser Pilgrimage, (qirān).
Ḥājj	(Ḥājji in Farsi) (pl. Ḥujjaj) One who makes the Hajj. The anglicized spelling, Hajji/Hajjis, is used throughout this study.
Hijrah	Muhammad's departure from Makkah to al-Madīnah on 16 July 622. The Muslim calendar begins on that date and is called Hijrīyah or A.H. to distinguish it from the Christian A.D.
'Īd al-Aḍḥá	The Feast of the Sacrifice, observed usually by butchering a blemishless animal, not only at the Hajj but throughout the Muslim world, on 10, 11, and 12 Dhū al-Ḥijjah.
Iḥrām	The ritual of purification performed before entering Makkah to perform the Hajj or the 'Umrah. It also refers to the special garments worn by one in the state of iḥrām—two seamless, usually white pieces of toweling or sheeting. The upper part is called *izār* and the lower part is called *ridā'*.
Jamrah	The term used to designate three pillars in Miná at which stones are thrown during the Hajj ceremonies. Representing "shaytāns" or satans, they are the Jamrat al-'Aqabah, al-Jamrah al-Wusṭá, and al-Jamrah al-'Ulá.
Ka'bah	(lit. cube) The stone structure in the center of the Haram Mosque in Makkah toward which all Muslims face while praying. It is covered by a black brocade and gold cloth called the kiswah.
Kiswah	The black brocade and gold cloth covering the Ka'bah. Made in a factory in Makkah, it is replaced each year.
Madhhab	(pl. madhāhib) A school of orthodox Islamic jurisprudence. There are four: Ḥanafī, Mālikī, Shāfi'ī, and Ḥanbalī.
Maḥmal	Ceremoniously decorated camel litters which formerly accompanied Hajj caravans from Egypt and Syria.

Al-Marwah	An elevated spot in Makkah. The sa'y rite consists of seven one-way trips between al-Ṣafā and al-Marwah.
Miná	A small town between Makkah and 'Arafāt in which are located the three jamrahs and which is the site for the observance of the 'Īd al-Aḍḥá for those making the Hajj.
Muḥrim	One who is in the state of iḥrām.
Mutamatti'	One who is in the tamattu' stage of iḥrām.
Muṭawwif	(pl. muṭawwufīn) A Hajj guide who looks after the secular as well as the spiritual needs of Hajjis under his charge. Muṭawwifīn are members of a guild headed by a shaykh al-muṭawwifīn. An alternate term for muṭawwif is shaykh al-Ḥajj.
Muzawwir	(pl. muzawwirīn) One who looks after the spiritual needs of the visitors to al-Madīnah, especially in guiding them through the Prophet's Mosque. All adillā' are muzawwirīn, but not all muzawwirīn are adillā'.
Muzdalifah	A small town between Miná and 'Arafāt.
Nafrah	(lit. rushing) The mass exodus from 'Arafāt to Muzdalifah after sunset on Standing Day. Also called the ifāḍah.
Al-Ṣafá	An elevated spot in Makkah. The sa'y rite consists of seven one-way trips between al-Ṣafá and al-Marwah, another elevated spot nearby.
Sa'y	(lit. running) One of the rites for the Hajj and/or the 'Umrah, consisting of seven one-way trips between al-Ṣafá and al-Marwah.
Taḥallul	The ritual haircut which marks partial desacralization from the state of iḥrām.
Tā'ifah	(pl. tawā'if) Term to connote members of the Hajj service industry who specialize in Hajjis from a specific geographical area. The head of a tā'ifah is given the title shaykh al-mashā'ikh (shaykh of shaykhs).
Talbīyah	A special ritual prayer repeated throughout the Hajj.
Tamattu'	A type of iḥrām which allows the Hajji to put off Hajj restrictions temporarily after performing the ṭawāf and sa'y and then return to iḥrām for the rest of the Hajj rites.
Ṭawāf	The sevenfold circumambulation of the Ka'bah. There are generally three ṭawāfs during the Hajj: the ṭawāf al-

	qudūm, (arrival ṭawāf), the ṭawāf al-ifāḍah, and the ṭawāf al wadāʿ (farewell ṭawāf).
ʿUmrah	The lesser Pilgrimage, which can be performed conjointly with the Hajj or separately any other time during the year. It consists of the ṭawāf and saʿy.
Wājib	Obligatory in Islamic law.
Wukalāʾ	Plural of wakīl.
Wakīl	(pl. wukalāʾ) (lit. agent or deputy) One who looks after the needs of Hajjis from their arrival in Saudi Arabia until the time of their departure from the country after the Hajj. Wukalāʾ, who are members of a guild, work in the name of a muṭawwif (or muṭawwifīn).
Wuqūf	(lit. standing) The vigil at ʿArafāt which begins at noon and ends after sunset on 9 Dhū al-Ḥijjah.
Yawm al-Tarwīyah	The day the Kaʿbah is ceremoniously washed, 8 Dhū al-Ḥijjah.
Yawm al-Wuqūf	Standing Day. The high point of the Hajj, falling on 9 Dhū al-Ḥijjah.
Zamāzimah	Plural of zamzamī.
Zamzamī	(pl. zamāzimah) One who provides water from the holy Zamzam well to any who want it, at any time but particularly during the Hajj. Zamāzimah are organized into a guild.

APPENDIX C
Maps

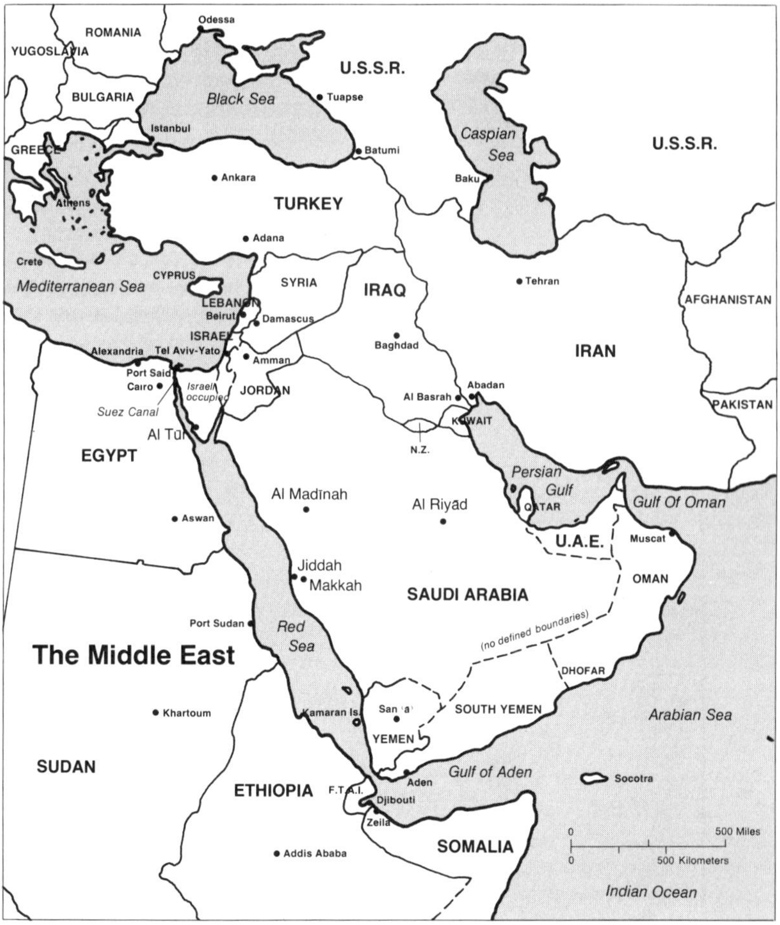

Map 1: The Middle East

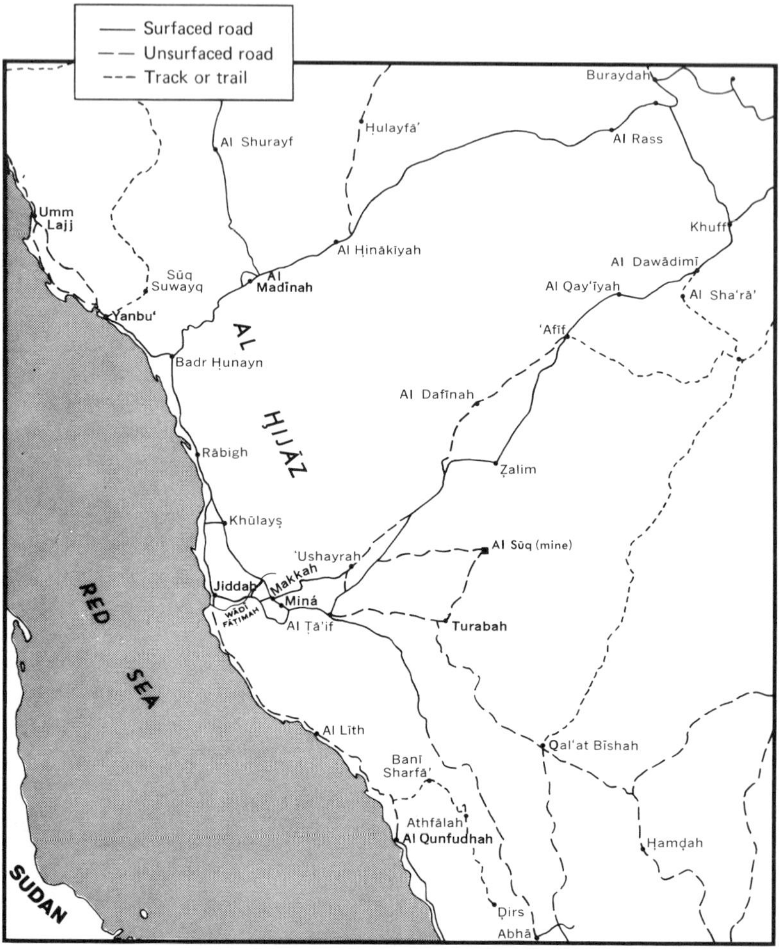

Map 2: The Hijaz

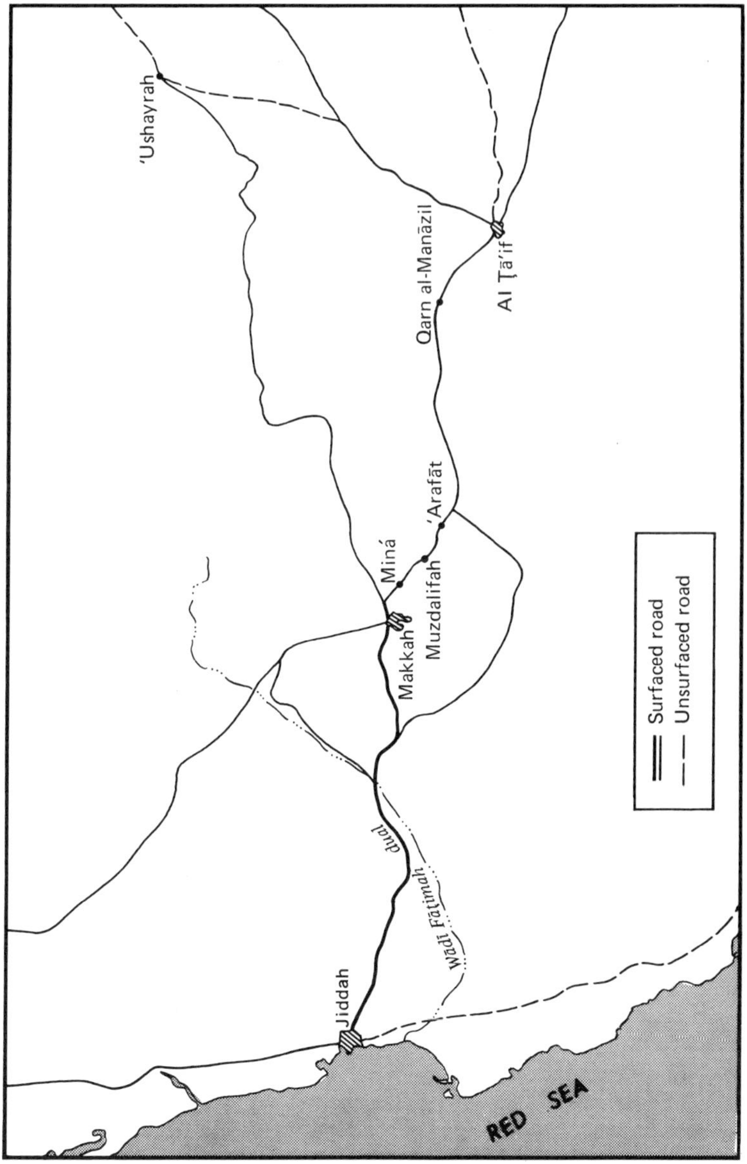

Map 3: Makkah and Environs

Bibliography

NOTE

The sources cited below give as much of an indication of what is not available on the contemporary Hajj as they do of what is available. Sources on the religious aspects of the Hajj are relatively plentiful, as are those on the health aspects. The latter case is undoubtedly related to the fact that Hajj health administration was under international supervision until 1957.

Sources for the administration of the Hajj and for the Hajj service industry, on the other hand, are uneven and range from excellent to virtually nonexistent. For example, the various works of C. Snouck Hurgronje present a detailed analysis of the Hajj service industry in the 1880s, and Eldon Rutter's *The Holy Cities of Arabia* gives a good description of how it was conducted forty years later. There has been nothing written on Hajj administration or the Hajj service industry in recent times, however, and the writer had to rely almost exclusively on personal interviews and texts of Saudi regulatory acts and official pronouncements. The latter were located either in the official Saudi gazette, *Umm al-Qurá*, as cited in the study, in other official Saudi publications cited below, or in the private papers of the writer, Ambassador Hermann Fr. Eilts, or Dr. Herbert J. Liebesny. Since nearly all of the interviews—with Saudi officials, Saudi businessmen, members of the Hajj service industry, and Hajjis—were in confidence, their names have been withheld.

Of the periodicals mentioned, *Umm al-Qurá* was used mainly for texts, citations of official acts, and, in some cases, statistics. The Saudi daily newspapers, *al-Nadwah*, *al-ʿUkāz*, *al-Bilād*, and *al-Madīnah*, were used extensively for news reports of the Hajj and also for official statistics and texts of important speeches and documents, beginning in 1967 when the writer first began to follow the Saudi press. Another very valuable periodical was *Oriente Moderno*, particularly for the period 1920–40.

OFFICIAL DOCUMENTS

Unpublished documents

Saudi Arabia. Ministry of Foreign Affairs. "Circular Note to all Diplomatic and Consular Missions." Note No. 5/1/35/11341/2 [concerning Hajj air carriers]. Dated 2 Ramadan A.H. 1386 or 15 December 1966.

———. ———."Circular Note to all Diplomatic and Consular Missions." Note No. 11/3/7871/2 [concerning cooperation between the Saudi

Ministry of Health and Special Hajj medical teams.] Dated 24 Jumada I A.H. 1392 or 7 May 1972.
U.S. Department of State. American Embassy, Jiddah. "The Economic and Social Significance of the Hajj Today," by G. Lane. Airgram No. A–410, 10 June 1964, to Department of State, Washington, D.C.
———. ———. ———. "The Hajj," by D. E. Long. Airgram No. A–396, 3 May 1967, to Department of State, Washington, D.C.
———. ———. ———. "The Hajj," by D. E. Long. Airgram No. A–391, 18 April 1968, to Department of State, Washington, D. C.
———. ———. ———. "The Hajj," by D. E. Long. Airgram No. A–92, 18 March 1969, to Department of State, Washington, D.C.
———. ———. ———. "The Hijaz Today and in 1991," by T. M. Deford. Airgram No. A–104, 19 September 1972, to Department of State, Washington, D.C.
———. ———. American Legation, Jiddah. "The Organization of the Government of Saudi Arabia," by Roger P. Davies, Third Secretary. 16 February 1948.

Published Documents

Conférence sanitaire internationale (1859). Protocoles. Paris: Imprimerie imperiale, 1859.
Conférence sanitaire internationale (1866). Procès-verbaux, 2 vols. Constantinople: Imprimerie central, 1866.
Conférence sanitaire internationale (1874). Procès-verbaux. Venice, 1874.
Conférence sanitaire internationale de Rome, 1885. Protocoles et Procès-verbaux. Rome: Imprimerie du Ministere des Affaires étrangères, 1885.
Conférence sanitaire internationale de Venise (1892). Protocoles et Procès-verbaux. Rome: Imprimerie nationale, 1892.
Conférence sanitaire internationale de Dresde (1893). Protocoles et Procès-verbaux. Dresden: Imprimerie B.G. Teubmeir, 1894.
Conférence sanitaire internationale de Venise (1897). Procès-verbaux. Rome: Forzani et cie., 1897.
Conférence sanitaire internationale de Paris (1903). Procès-verbaux. Paris: Imprimerie nationale, 1904.
Conseil Sanitaire Maritime et Quarantenaire d'Egypt. *Rapport sur le Pèlerinage du Hedjaz de l'année de l'Hégire 1356* (A.D. 1938). Alexandria: Societe de Publications Egyptiennes, 1938. Also for the Hijrah years 1345–55 (1927–37).
Conventions Sanitaires Internationales de Venise 1892–Dresde 1893–Paris 1894–Venise 1897. Textes juxtaposés. Brussels: Hayez, Imprimeur de la Chambre des représentatives, 1897.
Great Britain. Admiralty. *Western Arabia and the Red Sea.* Geographical Handbook Series, BR–527. London: June 1946.
———. Parliament. House of Commons. "Agreement Between the United Kingdom and the Netherlands Regarding the Sanitary Control over

Mecca Pilgrims at Kamaran Island, Paris, June 19, 1926, Treaty Series No. 26 (1926)." Cmd. 2741. London: His Majesty's Stationery Office, 1926.

———. ———. ———. Exchange of Notes between His Majesty's Government in the United Kingdom and the Government of India and the Netherlands Government amending the agreement of June 19, 1926 regarding the Sanitary Control over Mecca Pilgrims at Kamaran Island, London, June 13, 1939." Treaty Series No. 42 (1939), Cmd. 6069. London: His Majesty's Stationery Office, 1939.

———. ———. ———. "Additional Regulations amending the International Sanitary Regulations adopted by the World Health Assembly on the 25th of May 1951." Miscellaneous No. 3 (1957), Cmd. 30. London: Her Majesty's Stationery Office, 1957.

Saudi Arabia. Ministry of Hajj and Waqfs. *What a Muslim is Required to Know About His Religion.* Makkah (?) A.H. 1386 (1966–1967).

———. ———. "Statement of Hajj Instructions." Separate editions in Arabic, English, and other languages. A.H. 1386–1390 (1966–1971).

———. Ministry of Health. "Ministry of Health." Jiddah (?), Sah'bān 1375 (March 1956).

———. ———. *Jeddah Quarantine Station.* Jiddah (?): Asfahan and Company, 21 Sha'bān A.H. 1375 (3 April 1956).

———. Ministry of Information. *Saudi Arabia: Land of Achievement.* Book VIII, 3rd ed. al-Riyāḍ: Ministry of Information, 1969–1970.

———. ———. *The Kingdom of Saudi Arabia: Facts and Figures* (Series) *Health for All.* al-Riyāḍ: Ministry of Information, October 1971.

———. ———. *The Kingdom of Saudi Arabia: Facts and Figures* (Series) *In the Service of Islam.* al-Riyāḍ: Ministry of Information, February 1972.

———. ———. *The Kingdom of Saudi Arabia: Facts and Figures* (Series) *Progress and Development.* al-Riyāḍ: Ministry of Information, April 1972.

———. Ministry of Interior. General Directorate of Passports and Nationality. *Pilgrims Statistics for 1391 A.H.–1972 A.D.* al-Riyāḍ: Ministry of Interior, 1972. Also for the years A.H. 1386–90 (1967–71).

———. Monetary Agency. *Annual Report 1389–1390 A.H.* (1969–70). Jiddah: Saudi Arabian Monetary Agency, 12 August 1971.

Turkey. Dairei Umuru Sihhiye. "Le Lazaret de Camaran et la quarantaine des pèlerins pendent cinq années d'exercise. Rapport du docteur Duca, directeur du Service, au Conseil supérieur de santé, publié par l'Administration sanitaire ottomane." Constantinople: Typ et lithographie du journal, "La Turquie," 1887.

———. ———. "Mouvement générale du pèlerinage du Hedjaz par les ports de la mer Rouge. A.H. 1318 (1900–01)." Constantinople: Bureau du controle statistique: 1906–07.

———. ———. "Rapport de la commission des lazarets." Projets pour la reorganisation des lazarets de l'Empire ottoman; actes du conseil superieur de sante, 1889–94. Constantinople, 1894.

———. ———. "Dispositions applicables aux pèlerins et aux navires à pèlerins pendant le Pelerinage du Hedjaz." Constantinople, 1914.

U.S. Congress. House. Committee on Foreign Affairs. Subcommittee on National Security Policy and Scientific Developments. *The Politics of Global Health*, by Freeman H. Quimby. Science, Technology and American Diplomacy Series. Washington, D.C.: Government Printing Office, May 1971.

———. Department of Health, Education and Welfare. Public Health Service. Health Service and Mental Health Administration. "International Trip Report on Visit to Saudi Arabia." Memorandum from Dr. Eugene J. Gangarosa, Deputy Chief, Bacterial Diseases Division, Center for Disease Control to Dr. David J. Spencer, Director, Center for Disease Control, 4 December 1970.

———. Department of State. *American Foreign Policy: Current Documents, 1957.* Department of State Publication 7101, released February 1961. Washington, D.C.: Government Printing Office, 1961.

———. Department of the Treasury. U.S. Public Health Service. *International Sanitary Convention of Paris of June 22, 1926.* Washington, D.C.: Government Printing Office, 1928.

World Health Organization. "International Sanitary Regulations: Proceedings of the Special Committee and of the Fourth World Health Assembly on WHO Regulations No. 2." *Official Records of the World Health Organization* No. 37. Geneva: World Health Organization, April 1952.

———. "Proposed Programme and Budget Estimates for the Financial Year 1 January–31 December 1956: With the Proposed Programme and Estimated Expenditure for Technical Assistance for Economic Development of Underdeveloped Countries." *Official Records of the World Health Organization* No. 28. Geneva: World Health Organization, December 1954.

———. Regional Office for the Eastern Mediterranean. "Report on a Visit to Saudi Arabia, 1–9 March 1967," by Dr. R. Oseasohn, Epidemiologist, WHO Cholera Team. EM/Chol/7 EMRO 0136/R, June 1967.

Young, George. *Corps de Droit Ottoman.* Vol. III, *Droit Exterieur.* Oxford: Clarendon Press, 1905.

BOOKS AND ARTICLES

Al-Alem, Mustafa. "A Guide to Hajj Rituals." *Muslim World League Monthly Magazine* 3, 10 (Dhū al-Ḥijjah A.H. 1385–March-April 1966): 52–58.

Alexander, Grant. "The Story of the Kaba." *The Muslim World* 43 (January 1953): 43–53.

Ali, Jawad. *Taʾrīkh al-ʿArab qabl al-Islam.* Baghdad: Jamil, 1951.

Arabian American Oil Company. *Aramco Handbook.* Three editions,

Dhahran. Saudi Arabia: Arabian-American Oil Company, 1952, 1960, 1968.
Arberry, A. J., ed. *Religion in the Middle East.* Cambridge: The University Press, 1969.
Assad, Muhammad [Leopole Weiss]. *The Road to Mecca.* New York: Simon and Shuster, 1956.
d'Avril, A. *L'Arabie contemporaine avec la description du pèlerinage de la Mecque.* Paris: Challamel, 1868.
Baer, Gabriel. *Population and Society in the Arab East.* Translated by Hanna Szoke. New York: Praeger, 1964.
Begam, Shah Jahran. *The Story of a Pilgrimage to Hijaz.* Calcutta: Thacker, Spink and Co., 1909.
Bell, R. "The Origin of the Id al-Adha." *The Muslim World* 13 (February 1933): 117–20.
———. "Muhammad's Pilgrimage Proclamation." *Journal of the Royal Central Asian Society* 24 (April 1937): 223–44.
Bernard, E. *Le Conseil Sanitaire et Quarantinaire d'Egypte.* Alexandria: Societe de Publications Egyptiennes, 1897.
Blackwood, P. "The Pilgrimage in 1934." *The Muslim World* 25 (August 1935): 287–92.
Bousquet, G.-H. *Les grandes pratiques rituelles de l'Islam.* Paris: Presses universitaires de France, 1949.
———, and Schacht, J., eds. *Selected Works of C. Snouck Hurgronje.* Leiden: E. J. Brill, 1957.
Burkhardt, John Lewis. *Travels in Arabia.* London: Henry Colburn, 1829.
Burton, Richard F. *Personal Narrative of a Pilgrimage to al-Madinah and Meccah.* 2 vols. London: George Bell and Sons, 1898. (one of many editions.)
Cherif, Ahmed. *Le Pèlerinage de la Mecque. Essai d'histoire, de psychologie et d'hygiène sur le voyage sacré de l'Islam.* Beirut: Imprimerie Angelil, 1930.
Clemens, C. "Der ursprungliche Sinn des *hagg.*" *Der Islam* 10 (1920): 161– 77.
Clemow, F. G. "The Constantinople Board of Health." *Lancet* 1 (1923): 1074–80.
Cobbold, Lady Evelyn. *Pilgrimage to Mecca.* London: John Murray, 1934.
Cordier, G. "Un Voyage a la Mecque." *Revue du monde musulman* 14 (1911): 510–13.
Coulson, N. J. *A History of Islamic Law. Islamic Studies No. 2.* Edinburgh: The University Press, 1964.
Courtellemont, G. *Mon Voyage à la Mecque.* Paris: A Cadet, 1896.
Cragg, Kenneth. "Pilgrimage Prayers." *The Muslim World* 45 (August 1955): 269–80.
Davis, Helen Miller. *Constitutions, Electoral Laws, Treaties of States in the Near and Middle East.* Durham, North Carolina: Duke University Press, 1947.

De Gaury, Gerald. *Faisal, King of Saudi Arabia.* London: Arthur Baker, 1966.

Dhorme, E. "Les Religions arabes preislamiques." *Revue de l'histoire des religions* 133 (1948): 143–68.

Doughty, C. M. *Travels in Arabia Deserta.* Cambridge: Cambridge University Press, 1888.

Duguet, Firmin. *Le Pèlerinage de la Mecque au point de vue religieux, sociale et sanitaire.* Paris: Editions Rieder, 1932.

The Encyclopedia of Islam. 1st ed., 4 vols. and Supplement; Leiden: E. J. Brill and London: Luzac and Company, 1931–42; New Edition, 3 vols. and continuing, Leiden: E. J. Brill and London: Luzac and Company, 1960 and continuing.

Fleugel, Gustav, *Corani Textus Arabicus.* Leipzig: Ernst Bredt, 1893.

Freeman-Grenville, G.S.P. *The Muslim and Christian Calendars: Being tables for the conversion of Muslim and Christian dates from the Hijra to the year A.D. 2000.* London, New York and Toronto: Oxford University Press, 1963.

Gaudefroy-Demombynes, Maurice. "Notes sur la Mekke et Medine." *Revue de l'histoire des religions* 77 (1918): 316–44.

———. *Le Pelèrinage à la Mekke.* Etude D'Histoire Religieuse. Annales du Musee Guimet. Ministere de L'Instruction Publique et des Beaux Arts. Paris: Paul Geuthner, 1923.

———. *Muslim Institutions.* Translated by John P. Macgregor. London: George Allen and Unwin, 1950.

al-Ghazali. *Iḥyāʾ ʿulūm al-dīn*. Cairo: al-Ahlīyah, A.H. 1289.

Gibb, H. A. R. *Mohammedanism.* London and New York: Oxford University Press, 1953.

Goodman, Neville M. *International Health Organizations and Their Work.* London: J. and A. Churchill Ltd., 1952.

Gouilly, Alphonse. "Le Pèlerinage à la Mecque." *Revue juridique et politique* 18, 1 (January-March 1964): 99–106.

Grunebaum, Gustav E. Von. *Muhammadan Festivals.* New York: Henry Schuman, 1951.

Harrington, C. W. "The Saudi Arabian Council of Ministers." *The Middle East Journal* 12, 1 (winter 1958): 1–19.

Hood, R. "Defeat of Pestilence foreshadows end of quarantine." *World Health* 12, 1 (January-February 1959): 18–22.

Howarth, David. *The Desert King: Ibn Saud and His Arabia.* New York: McGraw-Hill, 1964.

Izzedine, Cassim. *Le Choléra et l'Hygiène à la Mecque.* Paris: 1909.

Juynboll, T. W. *Handbuch des Islamischen Rechtes.* Leiden: E. J. Brill, 1910.

al-Kalbi, Hisham ibn. *The Book of Idols.* Translated by Nabih Amin Faris. Princeton: Princeton University Press, 1952.

Kamal, Ahmad. *The Sacred Journey: Being Pilgrimage to Makkah.* New York: Duell, Sloan and Pearce, 1961.

Keane, T. F. *Six Months in Meccah.* London: Tinsley Brothers, 1881.

———. *My Journey to Medinah.* London: Tinsley Brothers, 1881.
Khan, Hadji, and Sparroy, Wilfred. *With the Pilgrims to Mecca: The Great Pilgrimage of A.H. 1319; A.D. 1902.* London: John Lane, 1905.
Kirimly, H. "The Oldest Tour in the World: Mecca Pilgrimage." *World Health* 20 (August-September 1967): 10–13.
Lammons, Henri. "Le Pèlerinage de la Mecque en 1902: Journal d'un pelerin Egyptien." *Bulletin des missions Belges* (Bruxelles), 1904.
Landau, Jacob M. *The Hejaz Railway and the Muslim Pilgrimage: A Case of Ottoman Political Propaganda.* Detroit: Wayne State University Press, 1971.
Lane, Edward William. *An Account of the Manners and Customs on the Modern Egyptians.* 2 vols. 3rd ed. London: Charles Knight and Co., 1842.
———. *An Arabic-English Lexicon.* 8 vols. London: Williams and Norgate, 1863–93.
Lawrence, T. E. *Seven Pillars of Wisdom.* Garden City: Doubleday, 1935.
Long, David Edwin. *The Persian Gulf: An Introduction to Its Peoples, Politics, and Economics.* Rev. ed. Boulder, Colorado: Westview Press, 1978.
———. *Saudi Arabia.* The Washington Papers, vol 4, no. 39. Beverly Hills and London: Sage Publications, 1976.
Loutfi, Z. E. *La Politique sanitaire internationale.* Paris: Rosseau, 1906.
Maltzan, H. Von. *Meine Wallfahrt nach Mekka.* Leipzig: F. A. Brockhaus, 1865.
Mamidullah, M. "The Pilgrimage to Mecca." *Islamic Review* 57, 9 (September 1969): 17–33.
Meulen, D. van der. "The Mecca Pilgrimage and Its Importance to the Netherlands East Indies." *The Muslim World* 31 (January 1941): 48–60.
———. *The Wells of Ibn Sa'ud.* New York: Frederick A. Praeger, 1957.
Nallino, Carlo Alfonso. *L'Arabia Saudiana (1938).* Vol. 1. *Raccolta di Scritti Editi e Inediti.* Edited by Maria Nallino. Rome: Istituto per l'Oriente, 1939.
Neibuhr, Carsten. *Travels Through Arabia.* 2 vols. Edinburgh: G. Mudie, 1792.
Philby, H. St. John B. *Arabia of the Wahhabis.* London: Constable, 1928.
———. *The Background of Islam: Being a Sketch of Arabian History in Pre-Islamic Times.* Alexandria: Whitehead Morris, 1947.
———. *Forty Years in the Wilderness.* London: Robert Hale, 1959.
———. "Mecca and Madina." *Journal of the Royal Central Asian Society* 20 (October 1933): 504–18.
———. *A Pilgrim in Arabia.* London: Robert Hale, 1946. "Pilgrim Journey." Unattributed pamphlet. (1952).
Rathjens, Carl. *Die Pilgerfahrt nach Mekka: Von der Weihrauchstrasse zur Olwirtschaft.* Hamburg: Robert Molich Verlag, 1948.
Rihani, Ameen [Amin al-Rihani]. *Ibn Sa'oud of Arabia.* London: Constable and Co., 1928.

———. *Ta'rīkh Najd al-Hadīth wa-mulhagātihī*. Beirut: Sadir, 1928.
Robinson, Arthur F. "The Mahmal of the Moslem Pilgrimage." *The Journal of the Royal Asiatic Society* 18 (January 1931): 117–27.
Roman, Jean. *Le Pèlerinage aux lieux saints de l'Islam.* Algiers: Editions Baconnier, 1954.
Royal Institute of International Affairs. *Survey of International Affairs, 1925.* Vol 1. *The Islamic World Since the Peace Settlement.* By Arnold J. Toynbee. Oxford: Oxford University Press and London: Humphrey Milford, 1927.
———. *Survey of International Affairs, 1938*, by Arnold J. Toynbee. Oxford: Oxford University Press and London: Humphrey Milford, 1929.
Rutter, Eldon. "The Muslim Pilgrimage." *Geographical Journal* 74, 3 (September 1929): 271–73.
———. *The Holy Cities of Arabia.* 2 vols. London: P. G. Putnam's Sons, 1928.
Rutter, Owen. *Triumphant Pilgrimage: An English Muslim's Journey from Sarawak to Mecca.* Philadelphia: J. B. Lippincott Co., 1937.
Siraj ab-Din, A. B. "Pilgrimage to Mecca." *Studies in Comparative Religion* 1, 4 (1967): 171–80.
Shorter Encyclopaedia of Islam. Leiden: E. J. Brill, 1953.
Smith, W. Robertson. *The Religion of the Semites.* Meridian edition. New York: Meridian Books, 1956.
Snouck Hurgronje, C. *Het Makkaansche Feest.* Leiden: E. J. Brill, 1880.
———. "La Légende qoranique d'Abraham et lapolitique religieuse due Prophete Mohammad." *Revue africaine* 95 (1951): 273–88.
———. *Mekka: Die Stadt und ihre Herren.* 2 vols. The Hague: Martinus Nijhoff, 1888.
———. *Mekka In the Latter Part of the 19th Century.* Translated by J. H. Monahan. Leiden: E. J. Brill, and London: Luzac and Company, 1931.
———. *Selected Works.* (See Bousquet, G.-H., and Schacht, J.)
Somogyi, J. "Ibn al-Jauzi's Handbook on the Makkan Pilgrimage." *Journal of the Royal Asiatic Society* 25 (1938): 541–46.
Soubhy, Saleh. *Pèlerinage à la Mecque et à Médine.* Cairo: Imprimerie nationale, 1894.
Sprenger, Alois. *Das Leben und die Lehre des Mohammed.* 2nd ed. Berlin: Verlaqbuchandlung, 1869.
Stegar, Winifred. *Always Bells.* London: Angus and Robertson, 1969.
Stanton, H. U. W. and Pickens, Claude Leon. "The Muslim Pilgrimage." *The Muslim World* 24 (July 1934): 229–35.
"To Mecca." *World Health* 15, 3 (May-June 1962): 36–39.
Trimingham, J. S. *Islam in West Africa.* London: Oxford University Press, 1959.
Van der Meulen, D. (See Meulen, D. van der.)
Von Grunebaum, Gustav. (See Grunebaum, Gustav Von.)
Wahba, Hafiz. *Arabian Days.* London: Arthur Baker, 1964.
———. *Khamsūn Am(an) fīJazīrat al-ʿArab.* Cairo, 1960.

Watt, W. Montgomery. *Muhammad at Mecca.* Oxford: Clarendon Press, 1953.
———. *Muhammad at Medina.* Oxford: Clarendon Press, 1956.
Wavell, A. J. B. *A Modern Pilgrim in Mecca.* Constable and Co., 1918.
Weir, Hans. *A Dictionary of Modern Written Arabic.* Edited by J. Milton Cowan. Wiesbaden: Otto Harrassowitz, 1966).
Wellhausen, J. *Reste Arabischen Heidentums.* 2nd ed. Berlin: Walter de Gruyter, 1927.
Winder, R. Bayly. *Saudi Arabia in the Nineteenth Century.* New York: St. Martin's Press, 1965.
Zadeh, H. Kazem. *Relation d'un Pelerinage à la Mecque in 1910–1911.* Paris: Ernest Leroux, 1912.
Zwemer, S. M. "Al Haramain: Mecca and Medina." *The Muslim World* 37 (January 1947): 7–15.

PERIODICALS

Al-Bilād (Jiddah) 1967–72.
al-Ḥajj (Makkah) 1948–49.
al-Madīnah (Jiddah) 1967–72.
al-Muqattam (Cairo) 1920–30, *passim.*
Muslim World League Monthly Magazine. Arabic and English (Makkah) 1966–69.
Near East and India 1928–32, *passim.*
Oriente Moderno 1920–70.
al-Nadwah (Makkah) 1967–72.
al-Qiblah (Makkah) 1922–24, *passim.*
al-ʿUkāẓ (Jiddah) 1967–72.
Umm al-Qurá (Makkah) 1922–72.

UNPUBLISHED PAPERS AND MANUSCRIPTS

Eilts, Hermann Frederick. "Amin Rihani's Abortive 'Peace Mission' in al-Hijaz." Mimeograph, 1972.
Kirimly, H. "Medical Aspects of Mecca Pilgrimage." Dissertation for post-graduate diploma in tropical public health, University of London, June 1966.
Ochsenwald, William L. "The Hijaz Railroad: A Study in Ottoman Political Capacity and Autonomy." Ph.D. dissertation, University of Chicago, 1971.
———. "Opposition to Political Centralization in South Jordan and the Hijaz, 1900–1914." Paper delivered at the fifth annual meeting of the Middle East Studies Association of North America, Denver, Colorado, 1971.

Partin, Harry. "The Muslim Pilgrimage: Journey to the Center." Ph.D. dissertation: University of Chicago, 1967.

PRIVATE PAPERS AND NOTES

The writer borrowed extensively from the private papers and notes of Ambassador Hermann Fr. Eilts and Dr. Herbert J. Liebesny. In addition information from interviews and nonpublished official Saudi sources came from the writer's own private papers, collected in Jiddah, Saudi Arabia, 1967–69, and subsequently in Washington, D.C.

Notes

CHAPTER I

1. In Islamic law, acts fall into five categories: *wājib* or obligatory; *mandūb*, the performance of which brings reward but is not obligatory; *mubāḥ*, about which the law is indifferent; *makrūḥ*, discouraged but commission of which does not entail punishment; and *haram*, which are prohibited outright. See N. J. Coulson, *Islamic Surveys No. 2: A History of Islamic Law* (Edinburgh: Edinburgh University Press, 1964), pp. 83–84.
2. The others are profession of faith, prayer, alms-giving, and fasting during the Muslim lunar month of Ramaḍan. *Jihād* or holy war is sometimes considered a sixth pillar.
3. Translations of the Qur'ān in this study are based on Gustavus Fleugel, *Corani Textus Arabicus* (Leipzig: Ernst Bredt, 1893).
4. The anglicized form, Hajji (plural: Hajjis), will be used throughout this study to connote a Hajj pilgrim. The literary Arabic term is Ḥājj (plural: Ḥujjaj).
5. The Muslim calendar has twelve lunar months and is eleven days shorter than the solar calendar, accounting for Muslim holy days falling at different times during the Western calendar year. The date is generally rendered "A.H.": or "Hijriyah" to differentiate it from the Christian A.D. The Muslim calendar begins with the year one on A.D. 16 July 622, the year Muhammad departed Makkah (the departure is called the Hijrah) for al-Madīnah, where he was to live for the next nine years. All non-Christian calendar dates in this study can be assumed to be Hijriyah dates.
6. Hisham ibn al-Kalbi, *The Book of Idols*, translated by Nabih Amin Faris (Princeton, New Jersey: Princeton University Press, 1952), pp. 23–28.
7. *Ibid.*, p. 477.
8. Harry B. Partin, "The Muslim Pilgrimage: Journey to the Center" (unpublished Ph.D. dissertation: University of Chicago, 1967), p. 55.
9. A. J. Wensinck, "Hadjdj," *The Encyclopaedia of Islam*, New edition (Leyden: E. J. Brill, and London: Luzac and Co., 1971), III, p. 31.
10. *Ibid.*, p. 32.
11. *Ibid.*
12. *Ibid.*, p. 200.
13. Maurice Gaudefroy-Demombynes, *Le Pélerinage à la Mekke* (Paris: Paul Geuthner, 1923), p. 267.
14. Wensinck, "Hadjdj," p. 33.
15. For a discussion of the Jewish influence on Muhammad, see C. Snouck Hurgronje, *Het Mekkaansche Feest* (Leiden: E. J. Brill, 1880), pp. 186–

190; W. Montgomery Watt, *Muhammad at Medina* (Oxford: Clarendon Press, 1956); and Partin, "The Muslim Pilgrimage," pp. 106–108.

16. See Partin, "The Muslim Pilgrimage," pp. 104–105; and Alois Sprenger, *Das Leben und die Lehre des Mohammed*, 2nd edition (Berlin: Verlagsbuchhandlung, 1869), II, pp. 27 and 77, and Gustav Von Grunebaum, *Muhammadan Festivals* (New York: Henry Schuman, 1951) p. 18.
17. Von Grunebaum, *loc. cit.*
18. Sūrah 2:121.
19. Al-Tabarī, *Ta'rikh al-rusūl wal-mulūk*, edited by M. de Goeje (Leiden: E. J. Brill, 1878–1901), I, p. 257 ff., quoted in Partin, "The Muslim Pilgrimage," p. 131.
20. Partin, "The Muslim Pilgrimage," p. 132.
21. Grunebaum, *Muhammadan Festivals*, p. 19.
22. *Ibid.*
23. *Ibid.*
24. Ahmad Kamal, *The Sacred Journey: Being Pilgrimage to Makkah* (New York: Duell, Sloan and Pierce, 1961), pp. 56–60.
25. Partin, "The Muslim Pilgrimage," p. 153.
26. Ali Beg, *Rihlah* (3 Vols.; London: 1814), I, p. 426, quoted in Partin, "The Muslim Pilgrimage," p. 135.
27. Kamal, *The Sacred Journey*, p. 86.
28. Partin, "The Muslim Pilgrimage," p. 132.
29. Kamal, *The Sacred Journey*, p. 68.
30. Sūrah, 9:1, 3a, 17, and 18.
31. Partin, "The Muslim Pilgrimage," p. 119.
32. Kamal, *The Sacred Journey*, p. 83.

CHAPTER 2

1. The four schools are Ḥanafī; named after its reputed founder, Abū Ḥanīfah (d. A.D. 767); Mālikī, named after Mālik ibn Anas (d. A.D. 795); Shāfiʿī named after al-Shāfiʿī (d. A.D. 820) and Ḥanbalī, named after Aḥmad ibn Ḥanbal (d. A.D. 855). Since a religious revival in central Arabia in the mid-eighteenth century led by Muhammad ʿAbd al-Waḥḥāb (his followers were hence called Waḥḥābīs), the inhabitants of what became Saudi Arabia have subscribed to the Ḥanbalī madhhab, the most conservative of the four.
2. The Hanafī school considers the saʿy wājib, but not a pillar. The Shāfiʿī school adds a fifth pillar, the *taḥallul.* It is the ritual haircut (at least three hairs must be cut) performed as partial desacralization from the sanctified state of ihrām. See Mustafa al-Alem, "A Guide to Hajj Rituals," *Muslim World League Monthly Magazine* (in Arabic and English) (Makkah: The Muslim World League) III, No. 10, Dhū al-Ḥijjah A.H. 1385 (March-April, 1966), p. 58.

3. Sūrah, 3:91.
4. T. W. Juynboll, *Handbuch des islamischen Rechtes* (Leiden: E. J. Brill, 1910), p. 142.
5. Grunebaum, *Muhammadan Festivals*, pp. 15–16.
6. Harry B. Partin, "The Muslim Pilgrimage," p. 5.
7. Maurice Gaudefroy-Demombynes, *Le Pèlerinage à la Mekke*, p. 156.
8. Muslim prayers are said in cycles of genuflections called rak'ahs. One rak'ah consists of bending the torso from an upright position, followed by two prostrations. A set number of rak'ahs are prescribed for each ritual prayer.
9. Al-Ghazālī, *Ihyā' 'ulūm al-dīn* (Cairo: al-Ahlīyah, A.H. 1289–A.D. 1872–73), Vol. I, 177, quoted in Partin, *loc. cit.*
10. Partin, "The Muslim Pilgrimage."
11. Ahmad Kamal, *The Sacred Journey*, p. 20. Most of the Hajjis the writer noted debarking at Jiddah airport for the Hajj in 1967, 1968, and 1969 were already in iḥrām.
12. The Malakī and Shāfi'ī schools prefer to perform the Hajj as ifrād, but the Ḥanafī school prefers qirān. See al-Alem, "A Guide to Hajj Rituals," p. 53.
13. *Ibid.* The Hanafī school extends the period to the end of Dhū al-Ḥijjah, enabling the Hajji to perform the 'Umrah after the Hajj.
14. *Ibid.*, p. 19.
15. *Ibid.*, p. 25.
16. *Ibid.*, p. 21.
17. Grunebaum, *Muhammadan Festivals*, p. 27.
18. This is the most common version, although there are others. It is rendered in English:

    Here am I awaiting your command, O God, here am I!
    Thou hast no peer (lit. associate), here am I!
    Yea, praise and grace are Thine, and Dominion!
    Thou hast no peer, here am I!

    The words *talbīyah* and *labbayka* both come from the Arabic root form l-b-y, meaning to obey an invitation, comply with a request or carry out an order. See Hans Wehr, *A Dictionary of Modern Written Arabic*, edited by J. Milton Cowan, (Wiesbaden: Otto Harrassowitz, 1966), p. 857.
19. The writer taped the Standing Day ceremonies live from 'Arafāt on Saudi Radio in 1968. In the background one can hear the constant chanting of the talbīyah.
20. The Ḥanafī school allows a marriage contract to be executed during ihram but, of course, no sexual contact. See al-Alam, "A Guide to Hajj Rituals," p. 57.
21. Eldon Rutter, *The Holy Cities of Arabia* (London: G. P. Putnam's Sons, 1928), I, p. 219.
22. See pp. 67–68.

23. Rutter, *Holy Cities*, I, p. 221.
24. John Lewis Burckhardt, *Travels in Arabia* (London: Henry Colburn, 1828), p. 137.
25. See pp. 68, 109.
26. For practices concerning this and other corners, see Partin, "The Muslim Pilgrimage," p. 25; and Gaudefroy-Demombynes, *Le Pèlerinage à la Mekke*, pp. 211 ff.
27. Kamal, *The Sacred Journey*, p. 45.
28. *Ibid.*, p. 51.
29. Saudi Arabia, Ministry of Hajj and Waqfs, *What a Muslim is Required to Know About His Religion* (Makkah: A.H. 1386–1966/1967) p. 74.
30. Grunebaum, *Muhammadan Festivals*, p. 31.
31. ʿArafāt is not within the sacred precincts (Ḥaram) of Makkah, and although it is prohibited for non-Muslims to visit ʿArafāt as well as Makkah, the former can be seen clearly from the "Christian bypass," the new asphalt road around Makkah built for the use of non-Muslims.
32. See p. 00.
33. Kamal, *The Sacred Journey*, p. 69.
34. See pp. 000–000.
35. Kamal, *The Sacred Journey*, p. 88.
36. Partin, "The Muslim Pilgrimage," p. 34.
37. Von Grunebaum, *Muhammadan Festivals*, p. 33.
38. Partin, "The Muslim Pilgrimage."
39. It is also known as al-ʿĪd al-Kabīr (the Great Feast) in contradistinction to al-ʿĪd al-Saghīr (the Little Feast) at the end of Ramaḍan.
40. See pp. 85–86.
41. Partin, "The Muslim Pilgrimage," p. 37.
42. Sūrah 2:199 reads: ". . . if anyone hastens to leave [the ʿId al-Aḍḥá] in two days, there is no blame on him. . . ."
43. Richard F. Burton, *Personal Narrative of a Pilgrimage to al-Madinah and Meccah* (London: George Ball and Sons, 1898), I, p. 307.
44. al-Alem, "A Guide to Hajj Rituals," p. 57.

CHAPTER 3

1. Rutter, *Holy Cities*, II, p. 148.
2. C. Snouck Hurgronje, *Mekka In the Latter Part of the 19th Century*, translated by J. H. Monahan (Leyden: E. J. Brill and London: Luzac and Company, 1931), pp. 23–24.
3. The term literally means those who guide others on the tawaf, the sevenfold circumambulation of the Kaʿbah.
4. Wakīl literally means "deputy" or "agent" in Arabic. They are in effect "deputy muṭawwifīn" or the "agents" of the muṭawwifīn in Jiddah.
5. Dalīl literally means "guide" in Arabic. The one who actually conducts the visitor to the holy sites in al-Madīnah is called a *muzawwir.*

6. Rutter, *Holy Cities*, I, pp. 113–114.
7. Snouck Hurgronje, *Mekka*, p. 25. Sabī literally means youth.
8. Rutter, *Holy Cities*, *loc. cit.* Bukharan is a term applied in Saudi Arabia to any one from what is now Soviet Central Asia.
9. Snouck Hurgronje, *Mekka*, p. 31.
10. *Ibid.*, p. 38.
11. Although the number appears to have changed at various times, there appear to have been three traditional ṭawāʾif: one for southeast Asian Hajjis, one for Indian subcontinental Hajjis, and one for the Near East and Africa.
12. Snouck Hurgronje, *Mekka*, p. 29.
13. *Muʿallim* in Arabic means "master of a trade."
14. The above description is based on Snouck Hurgronje, *Mekka*, p. 29.
15. Carlo Alfonso Nallino, *L'Arabia Saudiana* (1938), Vol. I: *Raccolta di Scritti Editi e Inediti*, ed. by Maria Nallino (Rome: Istituto per l'Oriente, 1939), p. 143.
16. For an analysis of Hajj statistics, see Appendix A.
17. See Snouck Hurgronje, *Mekka*, pp. 24–25, and Ahmad Kamal, *The Sacred Journey*, p. 27.
18. Richard F. Burton, *Personal Narrative*, I, p. 305; See also Rutter, *Holy Cities*, II, pp. 129, 186.
19. Burton, *Personal Narrative*, I, p. 374.
20. *Ibid.*
21. Personal interview with Mahmoud E. Seiny, Islamic Center, Washington, D.C., June 1972.
22. According to Duguet, in 1927 only 91,000 out of a total of 219,000 Hajjis visited al-Madīnah. See Firmin Duguet, *Le Pèlerinage de la Mecque au point de vue religieux, social et sanitaire* (Paris: Les Editions Reider, 1932), p. 248.
23. Those coming by sea from the north who wished to visit al-Madīnah before the Hajj would land at Yanbuʿ, the port city of al-Madīnah. Burton, for instance, chose this route. Those traveling north who wished to visit al-Madīnah after the Hajj could also proceed from al-Madīnah to Yanbuʿ and thence onward by sea.
24. See Jacob Landau, *The Hejaz Railway and the Muslim Pilgrimage: A Case of Ottoman Political Propaganda* (Detroit, Michigan: The Wayne State University Press, 1971); and William L. Ochsenwald, "The Hijaz Railroad: A Study in Ottoman Political Capacity and Autonomy" (Ph.D. dissertation: University of Chicago, 1971).
25. Rutter, *Holy Cities*, I, p. 147.
26. Snouck Hurgronje, *Mekka*, pp. 62–63.
27. *Ibid.*, p. 22.
28. *Ibid.*
29. G. H. Bousquet and J. Schacht, eds., *Selected Works of C. Snouck Hurgronje* (Leiden: E. J. Brill, 1957), p. 175.
30. Snouck Hurgronje, *Mekka*, p. 5.
31. Rutter, *Holy Cities*, I, p. 80.

32. Kamal, *The Sacred Journey*, p. 28.
33. *Ibid.*, p. 9.
34. Rutter, *Holy Cities*, I, p. 174.
35. *Ibid.*, II, p. 139.
36. *Ibid.*
37. Snouck Hurgronje, *Mekka*, p. 121.
38. *Ibid.*, p. 78. *Wālī*, used here, is the Arabic word from which is derived the Turkish form, *vali.*
39. *Ibid.*
40. *Ibid.*
41. Rutter, *Holy Cities*, I, pp. 80–81.
42. *Al-Muqattam* (Cairo), 26 November 1926, quoted in *Oriente Moderno* 11–12 (November-December 1926): 619.
43. *Ibid.*
44. Nallino, *L'Arabia Saudiana*, p. 60.
45. H.U.W. Stanton and Claude Leon Pickens, "The Muslim Pilgrimage," *The Muslim World*, 24, 3 (July 1934): 229–230.
46. "Pilgrim Tariff for the Season 1367 A.H.–1948 A.C.," a supplement to *al-Ḥajj: An Islamic Monthly Review* (in Arabic with the supplement in several languages) No. 10 (Jiddah: The General Administration for Pilgrim Affairs, 7 Dhū al-Qa'dah, A.H. 1367) p. 47 (or p. 1 of the English text).
47. *Ibid.*, p. 43 (or p. 5 of the English text).
48. *al-Ḥajj* (1368–1949), p. 92.
49. *al-Ḥajj*, A.H. 1367 (1948), p. 44. The Java ("Jawah" was the local name for all Indonesians) and Malay Hajjis had for a long time been provided with lodging at a set fee. In 1948 the fee was 20 pounds sterling. Of that amount £7 was for housing, lights, and "matting" (bedding) at Makkah; £9 for "entertainment," a tent at 'Arafāt, and a place to sleep at Miná; £2 for "arrival entertainment," and £2 for the muṭawwif to make these special arrangements.
50. Saudi Arabia, Royal Decree No. 14/1/140 dated 25 Dhū al-Ḥijjah A.H. 1356 (26 February 1938).
51. Saudi Arabia, Royal Decree No. 14518, dated 21 Shawwal A.H. 1365 (18 September 1946).
52. Saudi Arabia, Royal Decree No. 9267, dated 3 Dhū al-Qa'dah A.H. 1367 (7 September 1948).
53. Saudi Arabia, Council of Ministers, Ministerial Decree No. 54, dated 27 Dhū al-Ḥijjah A.H. 1383 (10 May 1964).
54. The text of the decree together with the citation of the previous decrees it superceded is found in *Umm al-Qurá* No. 2087, 13 Jumādá I A.H. 1385 (9 September 1956).
55. Saudi Ministerial Decree No. 7–3 of 26 Jumādá II A.H. 1385 (22 October 1965) officially designates three ṭawā'if: the Jawah Ṭā'ifah, the Indian Ṭā'ifah and the Arab Ṭa'ifah. For their areas of responsibility, see pp. 00 ff. For the text of the decree, see *Umm al-Qurá* No. 2095, 1 Rabi' II A.H. 1376 (6 November 1956).

56. The Saudi Riyal (SR) was stabilized at $.222 or 4.5 to the dollar in 1960. In December 1971 it was revalued at $.24 or 4.15 to the dollar and in February 1973 it was revalued at $.266 or at 3.85 to the dollar, both as a result of dollar devaluations. For the purposes of comparability, the 1960 rate will be used in this study unless otherwise noted.
57. For example, compare the tariffs listed in a statement of general Hajj information found in *Umm al-Qurá*, No. 2147, 5 Shaʿbān A.H. 1386 (19 November 1966), and the Hajj Instructions for 1972, found in Saudi Arabia, Council of Ministers, "Statement by the Ministry of Hajj and Waqfs of the Kingdom of Saudi Arabia regarding instructions for the Hajj season 1391 A.H. corresponding to 1971–1972 A.D." Ministerial Decree No. 191 dated 5 Rabīʿ II A.H. 1391 (31 May 1971) (in Arabic) (Jiddah: Ministry of Hajj and Waqfs, No. 1301/W/M, 5 Rabīʿ II A.H. 1391 [31 May 1971]), Statement No. 1, Fees for General Services.
58. Instructions for collection are set forth in Article II, Paragraph 5 of Ministerial Decree No. 313, dated 6 Rajab A.H. 1385 (31 October 1965), as amended by Ministerial Decree No. 274, dated 24 Shaʿbān A.H. 1386 (8 December 1966). The text of the former is found in *Umm al-Qurá*, No. 2147, 5 Shaʿbān A.H. 1386 (19 November 1966). According to the longstanding practice, children up to five years of age pay no fees, and from five to ten years pay half fees. Residents of Saudi Arabia and the Persian Gulf principalities are exempted. Presumably they need no muṭawwif, although they can choose one if they wish.
59. Ministerial Decree 191 (1971), Duties of the Various Ṭawāʾif which render services to the Hajjis, Article V, General Instructions, paragraph 1.
60. Rutter, *Holy Cities*, I, p. 147.
61. Ministerial Decree No. 191 (1971).
62. *Ibid.*, Article I, Services Rendered by the Muṭawwif to the Hajjis, paragraph 1–a.
63. *Ibid.*, Article I, Paragraph 1–c.
64. *Ibid.*, Article I, Paragraph 2.
65. *Ibid.*, Article I, Paragraph 3.
66. *Ibid.*, Article I, Paragraph 4.
67. Procedures for processing this information are found in Ministerial Decree No. 313 (1965), and Ministerial Decree 274 (1966).
68. *Ibid.*
69. Ministerial Decree 191 (1971), Article III, "Services Rendered by the Dalīl to the Hajjis," Paragraph 1–c.
70. *Ibid.*, Article IV, "Services Rendered by the Zamzamī to the Hajjis," Paragraph 1–a.
71. Rutter, *Holy Cities*, I, p. 114.
72. The regulations governing the composition and operation of the boards are found in Ministerial Decree 313 (1965), Article II, Paragraph 2.
73. See Ministerial Decree 274 (1966). See also "Pilgrimage Instructions, 1387 A.H. (1967)," (English version), (Jiddah, Saudi Arabia: Ministry of Hajj and Waqfs, 1966), p. 37. The Arabic "Hajj Instructions" for that year do not mention the decree.

74. Text in *al-'Ukāẓ* (Jiddah) 17 April 1967.
75. *Ibid.*
76. *Ibid.*.
77. *Ibid.*.
78. Ministerial Decree 191 (1971), Article V, "General Instructions," Paragraph 6, based on Royal Decree M/12 (1965), Articles VIII and XII.
79. External Hajj travel will be generally considered beyond the scope of this study, except in specific instances where it bears on the administration of the Hajj or on the impact of the Hajj on Saudi Arabia.
80. See Burton, *Personal Narrative* I, p. 233 (note 2), and II, pp. 143–144; and William L. Ochsenwald, "Opposition to Political Centralization in South Jordan and the Hijaz, 1900–1914" (paper delivered at the fifth annual meeting of the Middle East Studies Association of North America, Denver, Colorado, 11–13 November 1971), pp. 5–7.
81. Snouck Hurgronje, *Mekka*, p. 30.
82. Burton, *Personal Narrative*, I, p. 230.
83. See p. 00.
84. Duguet, *Le Pèlerinage de la Mecque*, p. 61.
85. The shuqdhūf was a large covered sedan platform atop a camel, designed for carrying passengers, particularly Hajjis.
86. *al-Ḥajj* (1949), p. 91.
87. *Oriente Moderno* 2, 5 (October 1922): 329.
88. *Oriente Moderno* 4, 7 (July 1924), quoting *al-Muqattam*, 17 June 1924.
89. Royal Institute of International Affairs, *Survey of International Affairs*, 1928, Vol. I, *The Islamic World Since the Peace Settlement* (Oxford: Oxford University Press, and London: Humphrey Milford, 1929), pp. 295–296.
90. Duguet, *Le Pèlerinage de la Mecque*, p. 255.
91. *Ibid.* Carl Rathjens estimated that there were 400 autos in the 1927 Hajj, 2,000 in 1931, and 6,000 in 1944. See Carl Rathjens, *Die Pilgerfahrt nach Mekka*, (Hamburg: Robert Molich Verlag, 1948), p. 106.
92. *Near East and India* 38 (31 July 1930) p. 117. In fact, because of the competition, the round-trip between Makkah and al-Madīnah, which normally cost 15 pounds sterling (including 7½ pounds sterling for government taxes) had fallen in 1929 to 9 pounds sterling, that is, only 1½ pounds sterling for the owners of the companies. See Duguet, *Le Pèlerinage de la Mecque*, p. 255.
93. Conseil Sanitaire Maritime et Quarantinaire d'Egypt, *Rapport sur le Pèlerinage du Hedjaz de l'année de l'Hegire*, 1355 (A.D. 1937) (Alexandrie: Société de Publications Egyptiennes, 1937), p. 22.
94. Egyptian Quarantine Board, *Rapport* (1938), p. 24.
95. The above account is taken with his kind permission from the personal notes of Ambassador Hermann Fr. Eilts, who served in Saudi Arabia in the late 1940s and again as United States Ambassador, 1965–1970.
96. *al-Ḥajj* (1948), p. 47.
97. Saudi Arabian Airlines, founded in 1945, does transport Hajjis on its regu-

larly scheduled domestic flights, but its main focus as a Hajj carrier is on external transport.

98. Many of the buses have no roof, in deference to many Hajjis, particularly from Iran, who would have no covering over their heads. The companies no longer use trucks.

99. Ministerial Decree 191 (1971), Statement No. 3 Fares Charged by the Operating Companies. In the original Arabic text, "fare" is rendered "ujrat al-irkāb," sedan is rendered "al-ṣayyārah al-saghīrah" (small auto), Makkah is rendered Makkah al-Mukarramah (Makkah the Ennobled), and al-Madīnah is rendered al-Madīnah al-Munawwarah (al-Madīnah the Radiant).

100. Saudi Arabia, Ministry of Hajj and Waqfs, "Hajj Instructions, 1385 A.H. (1967)," A Statement by the Ministry of Hajj and Waqfs in Saudi Arabia (in Arabic), Duties of the Ṭawā'if Toward Hajjis, Article V, General Instructions, Paragraph 9.

CHAPTER 4

1. In 1927 Najd was elevated from a sultanate to a kingdom, and ʿAbd al-ʿAzīz took the title, king of the Hijaz and Najd and its Dependencies.
2. See Helen Miller Davis, *Constitutions, Electoral Laws, Treaties of States in the Near and Middle East* (Durham, North Carolina: Duke University Press, 1947), p. 249 ff.; and Nallino, *L'Arabia Saudiana*, p. 13ff.
3. *Oriente Moderno* 12, 2 (February 1932): 92.
4. Saudi Arabia, Royal Decree 2716 dated 17 Jumāda I A.H. 1351 (18 September 1932), published in *Umm al-Qurá*, No. 406, 22 Jumādá A.H. 1351 (23 September 1932). Also see Davis, *Constitutions. . .* , pp. 259–260.
5. See C. W. Harrington, "The Saudi Arabian Council of Ministers," *The Middle East Journal* 21, 1 (winter 1958): 1–19.
6. *Umm al-Qurá*, No. 315, 28 Rajab A.H. 1349 (19 December 1930).
7. United States, American Legation Jidda, "The Organization of the Government of Saudi Arabia," by Roger P. Davies, Third Secretary. Report No. 3, 16 February 1948, p. 7.
8. Great Britain, Admiralty, *Western Arabia and the Red Sea* Geographical Handbook Series BR–527 (London: June 1946), p. 319.
9. Presumably representing the ṭawā'if.
10. Davis, *Constitutions. . .* , p. 250.
11. Nallino, *L'Arabia Saudiana*, p. 60.
12. *Ibid.*
13. *Ibid.*
14. Under King Fayṣal, and King Saʿūd before him, the office of amir of Makkah, with jurisdiction over Makkah, Jiddah, al-Ṭā'if, and surrounding areas, has always been held by a royal prince.
15. Information about the Supreme Hajj Committee is based primarily on

notes the writer made while living in Jiddah, 1967–1970, including personal interviews and gleanings from the Saudi (Arabic) press, and also from subsequent personal communications with officials in Saudi Arabia.

16. Saudi Arabia, Royal Decree No. 43, dated 8 Shawwal A.H. 1381 (14 March 1962).
17. Saudi Arabia, Council of Ministers, "Statement by the Ministry of Hajj and Waqfs of the Kingdom of Saudi Arabia regarding instructions for the Hajj season 1391 A.H., corresponding to 1971–1972 A.D.," Ministerial Decree 191 dated 5 Rabīʿ II A.H. 1391 (31 May 1971) (in Arabic) (Jiddah: Ministry of Hajj and Waqfs, No. 1301/W/M, 5 Rabīʿ II A.H. 1391 (31 May A.D. 1971), Important Directives to Hajjis.
18. See Chapter 5 for a more detailed analysis of international health controls over Hajj travel.
19. *Oriente Moderno* 9, 2 (February 1929): 112–113.
20. Duguet, *Le Pèlerinage de la Mecque*, p. 61.
21. The International Sanitary Convention of 1926. Article 57 reads:

    The governments taking into account their peculiar situations, may conclude special agreements amongst themselves in order to make the sanitary measures prescribed by this convention more efficacious and less cumbersome. The text of such agreements shall be communicated to the International Office of Public Hygiene.

    For a discussion of the 1926 Convention, see pp. 74–75.
22. *La Syrie*, 6 February 1929, quoted in *Oriente Moderno* 9, 3 (March 1929): 112–113.
23. Duguet, *Le Pèlerinage de la Mecque*, p. 61.
24. See pp. 47 ff.
25. The muṭawwifīn with large operations generally hire agents to go abroad each year, or, in other cases, who are chosen from among the residents of the countries they represent—e.g., local travel agents. See pp. 45–46.
26. Until the late 1960s Hajjis were also required to pay a "*sanbūq* fee" of SR 3 ($.66). Until the construction of modern pier facilities, lighters or sanbūqs were used to deliver goods and people ashore. The fee was to help fund the pensions for *sanbūqīs*, or those who had formerly operated the service. See Hajj Instructions (1967), Table No. 1, General Services Fees.
27. Ministerial Order 191 (1971), "Statement No. 1, Fees for General Services."
28. For an account of West African Hajjis, see J. S. Trimingham, *Islam in West Africa* (Oxford: Oxford University Press, 1959).
29. Example based on personal observation, Khartoum, Sudan, 1963–65.
30. Personal communication with officials in Saudi Arabia, April 1967.
31. Ministerial Order 191 (1971), Statement No. 6, The Routes for Overland Hajjis to Follow at Their Own Responsibility.
32. *Ibid.*

33. *Ibid.*, Statement No. 5, Dates of Arrival and Departure. Occasionally, in emergencies, the airport is kept open beyond this date.
34. See p. 98.
35. A similar crisis occurred in 1952 when the United States Air Force airlifted 3,763 Hajjis who had been stranded in Beirut. See *Pilgrim Journey* (unattributed pamphlet, 1952).
36. Arabian American Oil Company, *Aramco Handbook*, by Roy Lebkicher, George Rentz, Max Steineke, et al. (Dhahran, Saudi Arabia: Arabian American Oil Company, 1960), p. 280.
37. Information developed from personal interviews, personal observations, and numerous articles in the Saudi press (*al-ʿUkāẓ, al-Bilād, al-Nadwah*, and *al-Madīnah*), January-March 1968.
38. Saudi Arabia, Royal Decree No. 5/11/4/8697 dated 3 Ramaḍan A.H. 1370 (8 June 1951). The Ministry should not be confused with the old Hijazi Ministry of Interior, which was abolished in 1934. See p. 53.
39. Ministerial Order No. 191 (1971), "Important Directives to Hajjis."
40. Personal interviews with Hajjis who were caught in the traffic jam, Jiddah, Saudi Arabia, March-April 1968.
41. Interview with a senior Saudi traffic police official, 13 June 1968.
42. *Al-Bilād* (Jiddah), 25 February 1967.
43. Personal interview, Jiddah, Saudi Arabia, 28 March 1968.
44. In 1972 there were five official Hajj delegations and fifty-six other missions. Saudi Arabia, Ministry of Interior, General Directorate of Passports and Nationality, *Pilgrims Statistics for 1391 A.H.–1972 A.D.* (al-Riyāḍ: 1972), pp. 37–38.
45. See p. 42.
46. See p. 75.
47. Snouck Hurgronje, *Mekka*, p. 21.
48. Saudi Arabia, Ministry of Information, *Saudi Arabia: Land of Achievement*, Book VIII, 3rd ed. (al-Riyāḍ, 1969–70), p. 17.
49. Saudi Arabia, Ministry of Information, *The Kingdom of Saudi Arabia: Facts and Figures* (Series), *In the Service of Islam* (al-Riyāḍ: February 1972), p. 15.
50. *Ibid.*, pp. 17–18.
51. *Ibid.*
52. *Umm al-Qurá*, No. 2422, 6 Rabīʿ II A.H. 1392 (20 May 1972).
53. *Oriente Moderno* 7, 5 (May 1927): 213.
54. *Oriente Moderno* 8, 3 (March 1928): 125.

CHAPTER 5

1. Neville M. Goodman, *International Health Organizations and Their Work* (London: J. and A. Churchill, Ltd., 1952), p. 6.
2. Great Britain, Parliament, House of Commons, "Additional Regulations amending the International Sanitary Regulations adopted by the World Health Assembly on the 25th of May 1951." Miscellaneous No.

3 (1957) Cmnd. 30 (London: Her Majesty's Stationery Office, 1957), p. 6.

3. The station and subsequent stations for years were known as "Lazarettos," probably derived from "Lazarus," whose name came to mean, in medieval Latin, "leprous" or "infected." Goodman, *International Health Organizations*, p. 31. The term Lazarett is still used in German to mean military hospital.
4. *Ibid.*, p. 31–32.
5. Duguet, *Le Pèlerinage de la Mecque*, p. 119.
6. See F. G. Clemow, "The Constantinople Board of Health," *Lancet*, No. 2 (1933): 1074–1180; Z. I. Loutfi, *La Politique sanitaire internationale* (Paris: Rousseau, 1906), Goodman, *International Health Organizations*, pp. 237–238; and Great Britain, Admiralty, *Western Arabia and the Red Sea* Geographical Handbook Series, BR–527 (London, June 1946), pp. 464–465.
7. See p. 73.
8. See Goodman, *International Health Organizations*, pp. 235–237, and *Western Arabia*, pp. 465–472.
9. Goodman, *International Health Organizations*, pp. 39–40.
10. Ruth D. Masters, *International Organizations in the Field of Public Health* (Washington, D.C., 1947), p. 2, quoted in U.S. Congress, House Subcommittee for National Security Policy and Scientific Developments of the Committee on Foreign Affairs, *The Politics of Global Health*, by Freeman H. Quimby, Science, Technology and American Diplomacy Series (Washington, D.C.: Government Printing Office, May 1971), p. 5.
11. *Ibid.*, quoting H. van Zile Hyde, "The International Health Program," an address before the Army Medical Service Graduate School, Walter Reed Army Medical Center (Washington, D.C., 9 March 1954), p. 4.
12. George Young, *Corps de Droit Ottoman* (Oxford: Clarendon Press, 1905) III: 131–134.
13. Goodman, *International Health Organizations*, p. 64.
14. The United States, which was invited, did not attend and Egypt, technically under Turkish sovereignty, sent an observer. *Ibid.*, p. 51.
15. *Ibid.*
16. *Ibid.*, pp. 52–54.
17. *Textes juxtaposés des Conventions sanitaires internationales de Venise 1892-Dresde 1893-Paris 1894-Venise 1897* (Brussels: Hayex, Imprimeur de la Chambre des representatives, 1897), p. 8.
18. *Ibid.*, p. 17.
19. *Ibid.*, p. 14.
20. *Ibid.*, p. 15.
21. Goodman, *International Health Organizations*, p. 64.
22. *Ibid.*, p. 66.
23. United States Treasury Department, United States Public Health Service, *International Sanitary Convention of Paris of June 22, 1926*

(Washington, D.C.: United States Government Printing Office, 1928), pp. 35–50.

24. Kamarān Island was taken from the Turks by Britain in 1915 and administered by the Aden government, which at the time was under the British government of India. In 1926 the British and the Dutch, through their colonial governments in India and the Dutch East Indies, agreed jointly to maintain the quarantine stations there. The agreement was amended in 1939. See Great Britain, Parliament, House of Commons, "Agreement Between the United Kingdom and the Netherlands Regarding the Sanitary Control over Mecca Pilgrims at Kamaran Island, Paris: June 19, 1926," Treaty Series No. 26 (1926); and Great Britain, House of Commons, "Exchange of Notes Between His Majesty's Government in the United Kingdom and the Government of India and the Netherlands Government amending the Agreement of June 19, 1926 regarding the Sanitary Control over Mecca Pilgrims at Kamaran Island, London, June 13, 1939," Treaty Series No. 92 (1939) Cmnd. 6096 (London: His Majesty's Stationery Office, 1939).
25. International Sanitary Convention of 1926, p. 47.
26. *Ibid.*, p. 48.
27. *Ibid.*, p. 35.
28. The Paris Office was created at the Twelfth International Sanitary Conference in Rome in 1907 on the initiative of Camille Barrère, French diplomat and president of the International Conferences of 1903, 1907, and 1926. It existed separately from the later Health Organization of the League of Nations, often in competition with it, until both were incorporated into the World Health Organization after World War II. See Goodman, *International Health Organizations*, p. 80ff.; and *Western Arabia and the Red Sea*, p. 467.
29. *International Sanitary Convention of 1926*, Article 151, p. 48.
30. See Conseil Sanitaire Maritime et Quarantenaire d'Egypt, *Rapport sur le Pèlerinage du Hedjaz de l'année de l'Hégire 1348* (1930) (Alexandria: Société de Publications Egyptiennes, 1930), pp. 37ff.
31. World Health Organization, "International Sanitary Regulations: Proceedings of the Special Committee and of the Fourth World Health Assembly on WHO Regulations No. 2," *Official Records*, No. 37 (Geneva: World Health Organization, April 1952), pp. 1–2.
32. Saudi Arabia, Ministry of Health, *Jeddah Quarantine Station*, Introduction by Dr. Rachad Pharaon, Minister of Health (Jeddah: Asfahan and Company, 21 Shaʿbān A.H. 1375 (3 April 1956), pages unnumbered.
33. *Ibid.*
34. See WHO, *Official Records*, No. 37 (1952), p. 2.
35. *Ibid.*, pp. 360–365.
36. *Ibid.*
37. WHO, *Official Records*, No. 8, p. 33, quoted in WHO *Official Records*, No. 37, (1952), p. 252.
38. WHO, *Official Records*, No. 37 (1952), p. 288.

39. Resolution WHA 4.75, 14 and 15 May 1951, *Ibid.*, p. 316.
40. *Ibid.*
41. H. B. Kirimly, "Medical Aspects of the Mecca Pilgrimage" Dissertation for Postgraduate Diploma in Tropical Public Health, University of London, 1966), p. 21.
42. "Amendments to the 1951 International Sanitary Regulations" (1957), pp. 6–7
43. R. Hood, "Defeat of pestilence foreshadows end of quarantine," *World Health* 12, 1 (January-February 1959): 18–19.
44. *Oriente Moderno* 12, 1 (January 1932): 92.
45. Nallino, *L'Arabia Saudiana*, pp. 39–40.
46. *Ibid.*, p. 41.
47. Under King ʿAbd al-ʿAzīz's very powerful finance minister and confidant, Shaykh ʿAbdallah al-Sulaymān (al-Ḥamdan), the Ministry of Finance at one time administered as agencies of state many present-day Saudi Ministries. See *Western Arabia*, p. 321; and David Howarth, *The Desert King: Ibn Saud and His Arabia* (New York: McGraw-Hill, 1964), pp. 198 and 288–289.
48. Saudi Arabia, Royal Decree No. 5/11/4/8697 of 3 Rajab A.H. 1370 (8 June 1951).
49. Kirimly, "Medical Aspects of the Mecca Pilgrimage," p. 55.
50. Saudi Arabian Ministry of Health, "Vaccination Certificate Requirements for Passengers Arriving in Saudi Arabia During the Pilgrimage Season—November 7, 1972 through February 3, 1973" (al-Riyāḍ).
51. *Jiddah Quarantine Station.*
52. Personal interview with a Jiddah private surgeon, 28 March 1968.
53. Eugene J. Gangarosa, "International Trip Report on Visit to Saudi Arabia," (Memorandum to Dr. David J. Sencer, Director, Center for Disease Control, Public Health Service, United States Department of Health, Education and Welfare, 17 December 1970).
54. Personal communication from an official in Saudi Arabia, February 1972.
55. Kirimly, "Medical Aspects of the Mecca Pilgrimage," p. 40.
56. *Ibid.*, p. 41.
57. *Ibid.*, p. 56.
58. *Ibid.*, p. 63.
59. *Ibid.*, p. 65.
60. *Ibid.*
61. *Ibid.*, p. 66.
62. It is interesting to note that the sanitary conditions of the sacrifice were one of the subjects discussed at the Islamic conference convened by ʿAbd al-ʿAzīz during the 1926 Hajj. See *Oriente Moderno* 6, 7 (July 1926): 353–354.
63. Personal correspondence with an official in Saudi Arabia, 16 July 1972.
64. Egyptian Quarantine Board, *Rapport* (1937), pp. 32–33.
65. Saudi Arabia, Ministry of Interior, General Directorate of Passports and Nationality, *Pilgrims Statistics for 1391 A.H.–1972 A.D.* (al-Riyāḍ, 1972), pp. 37–38.

CHAPTER 6

1. Saudi population study quoted in United States, Department of State, American Embassy, Jidda, "The Economic and Social Significance of the Hajj Today," by G. Lane. Airgram A–410, to Department of State, Washington, D.C., 10 June 1964, p. 6.
2. Sadiq Bey, *Kawkab al-Hajj*, p. 20, quoted in Hurgronje, p. 215.
3. *Ibid.* The original work was *Mekka: Die Stadt und ihre Herren*, 2 vols. (The Hague: Martinus Nijhoff, 1888).
4. Eldon Rutter, "The Muslim Pilgrimage," *The Geographical Journal* 74, 3 (September 1929): 273.
5. Personal interviews with Saudi immigration officials, March-April 1967.
6. For an account of West African Hajjis, see J. S. Trimingham, *Islam in West Africa* (Oxford: Oxford University Press, 1959).
7. Personal interview, Jiddah, Saudi Arabia, April 1967.
8. Nallino, *L'Arabia Saudiana*, p. 141.
9. A classic work on the Hajj as a religious rite is Maurice Gaudefroy-Demombynes, *Le Pèlerinage à la Mekke*.
10. Information based on personal interviews with Saudi officials, 1967–69.
11. Consider, for example, King ʿAbd al-ʿAzīz asking for a *fatwá*, or Islamic legal opinion, from the Saudi religious leaders in 1927 concerning a number of Hajj administrative matters (see pp. 108–109) and the Hajj administrative machinery today in which the religious leaders play almost no role at all.
12. D. van der Meulen, *The Wells of Ibn Saʿud* (New York: Frederick A. Praeger, 1957), p. 157.
13. Winifred Stegar, *Always Bells* (London: Angus and Robertson, 1969), p. 91.
14. Carl Rathjens, *Die Pilgerfahrt nach Mekka* (Hamburg: Robert Molich Verlag, 1948), p. 118.
15. Saudi Arabia, Council of Ministers, "Statement by the Ministry of Hajj and Waqfs of the Kingdom of Saudi Arabia regarding instructions for the Hajj season 1391 A.H. corresponding to 1971–1972 A.D." Ministerial Decree No. 191 dated 5 Rabi II-A.H. 1391 (31 May 1971) (in Arabic) (Jiddah: Ministry of Hajj and Waqfs, No. 1301/W/M, 5 Rabi II A.H. 1391 [31 May 1971]), Statement No. 1, Fees for General Services.
16. Duguet, *Le Pèlerinage de la Mecque*, p. 255. For a period up to 1929 cut-throat competition by the transportation companies had reduced the fare to £9 ($43.20), leaving only a £1.5 margin and many companies went bankrupt. See p. 48.
17. Rathjens, *De Pilgerfahrt nach Mekka*, p. 112.
18. *Ibid.*
19. Statistics for this period are conflicting. For a more complete analysis, See Appendix A.
20. Van der Meulen, *The Wells of Ibn Saud*, p. 121.
21. The year 1952 was given to the writer by a Saudi official in 1967. Notice

of the abolition of the Hajj head tax also appeared in *al-Ahrām* of 24 May 1952, quoted in *Oriente Moderno*, 32, 5–6 (May-June 1952): 126. According to a recent official Saudi publication the Hajj taxes were abolished in 1944. See Saudi Arabia, Ministry of Information, *The Kingdom of Saudi Arabia: Facts and Figures* (Series). *In the Service of Islam* (al-Riyāḍ, February 1972), p. 27. However in the "explanation" of the 1948 Hajj fees, 200 riyals (about $87.25) was charged for "Government Dues," out of a total of 401½ riyals (£36/5 or $175.20). The following year "Government Dues" were cited as part of an overall £28 fee, but no breakdown was given. For the same two years quarantine/landing fees were listed at £5 ($28.00). See "Pilgrimage Tariff for Season 1367 A.H.–1948 A.D., a supplement to *al-Ḥajj: An Islamic Monthly Review* (in Arabic with the Supplement in several languages) No. 10 (Jiddah: The General Administration for Hajj Affairs, 7 Dhū al-Qaʿdah, A.H. 1367) p. 43 (or p. 5 of the English text); and *al-Ḥajj*, Rajab A.H. 1368 (1949), p. 90.

22. Ministerial Decree No. 191 (1971), Statement No. 2, Fees to Those Rendering Special Services, Paragraph 7.
23. Some of the fees such as for Hajj village lodgings are included in the ticket and others are actually collected by the wukalāʾ. See pp. 00ff., and Ministerial Order 191 (1971), Statement No. 1, Fees for General Services.
24. Saudi Arabia, Ministry of Interior, General Directorate of Passports and Nationality, *Pilgrims Statistics for 1391 A.H.–1972 A.D.* (al-Riyāḍ, 1972), p. 2. An additional 141,658 Hajjis arrived overland.
25. The writer arrived at this figure by simple arithmetic—multiplying the number of Hajjis times the required fees. A more accurate figure, of course, would have to take into account the number of children, who pay half price but are not listed separately in the statistics, and Gulf Arabs, who are listed but are not required to pay the fees.
26. Saudi Arabia, Ministry of Information, *The Kingdom of Saudi Arabia: Facts and Figures* (Series) *In the Service of Islam* (al-Riyāḍ: February 1972), p. 28.
27. See the Pilgrim Tariff for Season 1367 A.H.–1948 A.D., *al-Ḥajj* (1948), p. 42 (p. 6 in English text).
28. Saudi Arabia, Ministry of Information, *In the Service of Islam*, p. 29.
29. For reference to the road system, see pp. 62–63; the mosque enlargements are mentioned on pp. 67–68; and the airport project on p. 62.
30. The official name was changed to Saudia in 1972. The official abbreviation is SDI.
31. Saudi Arabian Airlines, "The Story of Saudi Arabian Airlines" (pamphlet, 1970, pages unnumbered).
32. Saudi Arabian Airlines, "Annual Report for 1970," (Jiddah: Saudi Arabian Airlines, 1971), p. 5.
33. Saudi Arabia, Ministry of Foreign Affairs, "Circulate Note to All Diplomatic and Consular Missions," Note No. 5/1/35/11341/2 of 2 Ramaḍan A.H. 1386 (15 December 1966).

34. Information based on personal interviews with Saudi Arabian Airlines officials, 1967–72.
35. Saudi Arabian Airlines, "Annual Report for 1970," p. 20.
36. Personal correspondence, Saudi Arabian Airlines officials, March-June 1972.
37. For a list of fees, see Ministerial Order 191 (1971). The number of Hajjis is reported in Saudi Arabia, *Pilgrims Statistics for 1391–1972*, and listed in Appendix A. Many of these fees are now actually collected by the Saudi government, which then reimburses the Hajj service industry.
38. SR 150 for the entire stay. See p. 40.
39. The round-trip bus fare from Jiddah to Makkah was SR 32 ($7.11) and from Makkah to ʿArafāt was SR 22.50 ($5.00). The bus fare from Makkah to al-Madīnah and return to Jiddah was SR 101.25 ($22.50). The figure above was based on the assumption that all air and sea Hajjis (337,681) paid the first two fares and that three-fourths of them (252,261) paid the third fare. The figure was then adjusted slightly upward to account for those who chose to go by sedan at a higher fare. For fares, see p. 00, and for 1972 Hajjis, see *Pilgrims Statistics for 1391–1972*, p. 15.
40. Information based on personal interviews with Jiddah merchants, March-April 1967.
41. The information stated here and in the following paragraph was gathered by the writer who interviewed Saudi businessmen and officials about the Hajj for the years 1967, 1968, and 1969.
42. Personal interview, April 1969.
43. The trend was exemplified in the attitudes of two Jiddah merchants after the 1968 Hajj. A pharmaceutical dealer told the writer it was an excellent Hajj, while a flour dealer wailed that business was off twenty-five percent.
44. Great Britain, Admiralty, *Western Arabia and the Red Sea*, Geographical Handbook Series, BR–527 (London: June 1946), pp. 453, 557, 570.
45. Information obtained from personal interviews with Jiddah merchants and Saudi officials from the Saudi Arabian Monetary Agency and the Central Planning Organization, 1967–69.
46. Saudi Arabia, Saudi Arabian Monetary Agency, *Annual Report 1389–90 A.H.* (Jiddah: 12 August 1971), p. 35. According to SAMA figures, Hajj receipts for 1968, 1969, and 1970, respectively were $72, $94, and $104 million.
47. J. Deny "ʿAbd al-Ḥamid II" in *The Encyclopaedia of Islam*, New ed., Vol. I, pp. 63–65. See also T. E. Lawrence, *Seven Pillars of Wisdom* (Garden City: Doubleday, 1935), pp. 68–100.
48. Jacob M. Landau, *The Hejaz Railway and the Muslim Pilgrimage* (Detroit, Michigan: The Wayne State University, 1971), p. 12.
49. For an interesting account of a trip on the Hijaz Railway by an Englishman who made the trip, see A. J. B. Wavell, *A Modern Pilgrim in Mecca* (London: Constable and Co., 1918).

50. Landau, *The Hejaz Railway*, p. 13.
51. D. van der Meulen, "The Mecca Pilgrimage and Its Importance to the Netherlands East Indies," *The Muslim World* 31,1 (January 1941): 51.
52. The rivalry between King Husayn and ʿAbd al-ʿAzīz Āl Saʿūd, leading ultimately to the downfall of the Hashimite Kingdom of the Hijaz has been the subject of a number of studies. See, for example, Royal Institute of International Affairs, *Survey of International Affairs*, 1925, Vol. I, *The Islamic World Since the Peace Settlement* by Arnold J. Toynbee (Oxford: Oxford University Press and London: Humphrey Milford, 1927), pp. 271–323; Shaykh Hafiz Wahba, *Khamsūn Am(an) fī Jazīrat al-ʿArab* (Cairo: 1960); Shaykh Hafiz Wahba, *Arabian Days* (London: Arthur Baker, 1964); Ameen Rihani: [Amīn al-Rihānī], *Ibn Saʿoud of Arabia* (London: Constable and Co., 1928); Amīn al-Rihānī, *Taʾrīkh Najd al-Hadīth wa-Mulḥaqātihī* (Beirut: Sadir, 1928); Nallino, *L'Arabia Saudiana*; and the numerous works on Saudi Arabia of H. St. John B. Philby, e.g., *Arabia of the Wahhabis* (London: Constable, 1928); and *Forty Years in the Wilderness* (London: Robert Hale, 1959). An interesting facet of the Ḥusayn-ʿAbd al-ʿAzīz rivalry has recently been set down in Herman Fr. Eilts, "Amin Rihani's Abortive Peace Mission in al-Hijaz, 1924–1925," (mimeo., 1972).
53. *Oriente Moderno* 4, 10 (October 1924): 600, quoting *Alif-Ba* (Damascus) 1 August 1924 and *al-Qiblah* (Makkah) 17 July 1924. For previous conferences, see *al-Muqattam* (Cairo) 23 August 1922, quoted in *Oriente Moderno* 2 (15 October 1922): 219–292; and *al-Qiblah* No. 708, 23 Dhū al-Ḥijjah A.H. 1341 (6 August 1923).
54. On the last day of the 1924 Hajj, ʿAbd al-ʿAzīz met in al-Riyāḍ with Wahhabi religious and tribal leaders. Furious at ʿAbd al-ʿAzīz's ban of Najdis making the 1924 Hajj because of Najdi-Hijazi bloodshed the previous year, the conferees claimed peaceful coexistence with Ḥusayn had failed and demanded military action to insure their Hajj rights. ʿAbd al-ʿAzīz acceded to the demands, sent messages through his son Fayṣal to the Islamic countries denouncing Ḥusayn's assumption of the caliphate and his administration of the holy places, and soon after his forces invaded al-Ṭāʾif. See Eilts, "Amin Rihani's Abortive Peace Mission," pp. 13–14. Fayṣal's message appeared in *al-Akhbār* (Cairo) 24 June 1924.
55. See *Oriente Moderno* 11, 6 (June 1926): 309–317 and (7 July 1924): 353–362.
56. *Oriente Moderno* 17, 3 (March 1937): 129.
57. The text of the declaration was taken from the private papers of Dr. Herbert J. Liebesny with his kind permission.
58. Personal interview with an eyewitness at the 1966 Hajj, March 1967.
59. Since 1967 West Bank and Gaza Arabs have regularly been given exit permits by Israel to make the Hajj (presumably with Jordanian or Gaza travel documents), with the exception of residents of East Jerusalem, who are considered "Israeli Muslims." The Saudi approval of Israeli

Hajjis in 1978 belies the long-held Israeli contention, "There are no prospects of a legal formula being found which would enable them [Israeli Muslims] to make the pilgrimage." See *Lamerhav*, 14 February 1968.

60. *Oriente Moderno* 6, 7 (July 1926): 356.
61. Formerly there were also maḥmals from Damascus as well as India and Darfur (Sudan). See Arthur E. Robinson, "The Mahmal of the Moslem Pilgrimage," *The Journal of the Royal Asiatic Society* (January 1931): 117--127.
62. *Oriente Moderno* 6, 7 (July 1926): 362–364.
63. The Arabic text of the fatwá is found in Hafiz Wahba, *Jazīrat al-ʿArab fil-Qarn al-ʿIshrīn* (Cairo: 1935), pp. 319–321. Italian translations are found in Nallino, *L'Arabia Saudiana*, pp. 119–121; and *Oriente Moderno* 7, 6 (June 1927): 276–277.
64. *al-Siyāsah* (Cairo) 13 May 1927, quoted in *Oriente Moderno* 7, 5 (May 1927): 213. As a result of the Egyptian decision King ʿAbd al-ʿAzīz had the kiswah made in India the following year. It is now made in a factory in Makkah. See p. 68.
65. *al-Maqattam*, 3 March 1927, quoted in *Oriente Moderno* 7, 3 (March 1927): 111.
66. *Alif Bā'* (Damascus) 1 April 1927, quoted in *Oriente Moderno* 7, 9 (September 1927): 412.
67. *al-Muqattam* 13 August 1927, quoted in *Oriente Moderno* 7, 9 (September 1927): 412.
68. *Pilgrim Statistics for 1391–1972*, p. 31.
69. King Fayṣal dwelt on this theme many times in public and private statements, not only at the Hajj but on other occasions as well. A typical example of his elaborating on the Zionist-Communist threat was a speech he delivered at the presentation of the *Eighth Annual Report* of the Saudi Arabian Monetary Agency. For the text of the speech, see *News from Saudi Arabia*, 23 September 1969, pp. 5–6. Another example is a Saudi communiqué distributed to the Arab League states calling for holy war against Israel, quoted in *al-Siyāsah* (Kuwait) 28 October 1969.
70. United States, Department of State, *American Foreign Policy: Current Documents–1957*, Department of State Publication 7101 (Washington, D.C., Government Printing Office, February 1961), p. 976.
71. *Oriente Moderno* 6, 7 (July 1926): 360.
72. Text in *al-ʿUkāẓ* (Jiddah) 7 Dhū al-Ḥijjah A.H. 1385 (29 March 1966).
73. For the text of the speech, see *al-ʿUkāẓ* (Jiddah) 4 Dhū al-Ḥijjah A.H. 1387 (5 March 1968).
74. Portions of the broadcast were heard by the writer, who was in Jiddah at the time.
75. For the text of the speech, see *al-ʿUkāẓ* (Jiddah) 6 Dhū al-Ḥijjah A.H. 1388 (24 February 1969).
76. See, for example, the text of the 1972 Hajj banquet speech, found in *Pilgrims Statistics for 1391–1972* (pages of the text unnumbered).

CHAPTER 7

1. As an example of the tourist aspect of the modern Hajj, Pakistan International Airlines offers all-inclusive tours from America. Their brochure announcing the A.H. 1392–A.D. 1973 Hajj tours reads in part, "We are pleased to present five itineraries to suit the growing indigenous Muslim community in America. You may select any itinerary which suits you best. Land arrangements have been made in cooperation with Mutawifs Abdul Aziz Khogir and Sayed Aqil Attas and Sons. . . . Please contact your IATA approved travel agent or the nearest Pakistan International Airlines Sales Office as soon as possible. . . ."
2. See Appendix A, Table 6.
3. I chose Virginia only because it has roughly the same population as Saudi Arabia and access to the sea—some other state would probably serve as well.
4. Meulen, *The Wells of Ibn Saʿud*, p. 121.
5. *Ibid.*, p. 126.
6. Robert Matthew, Johnson Marshall and Partners (RMJM), "Regional Framework, Western Region Plan" (mimeo. 1972), quoted in United States, Department of State, American Embassy, Jiddah, "The Hijaz Today and in 1991," by T. M. Deford. Airgram No. A–104 to Department of State, Washington, D.C., 19 September 1972, pp. 14–15.
7. I have seen no studies of the sociological composition of the Hajj; but it is generally assumed by members of the Hajj service industry that most of the Hajjis are from among the poorer classes.
8. United States, Department of State, "The Hijaz Today and in 1991," p. 16.

APPENDIX A

1. Grunebaum, *Muhammadan Festivals*, p. 32.
2. Rathjens, *Die Pilgerfahrt nach Mekka*, p. 103.
3. Saudi Arabia Ministry of Interior, General Directorate of Passports and Nationality, *Pilgrims Statistics for 1391 A.H.–1972 A.D.* (al-Riyāḍ: 1972), p. 20.
4. H. U. W. Stanton and Claude Leon Pickens, "The Mecca Pilgrimage," *The Moslem World* 24, 2 (June 1934) 2:231.
5. Rathjens, *Die Pilgerfahrt nach Mekka*, p. 105. Stanton uses the figure 49, 349, which appears in Table 4.

Index